Our Native Fishes

Other Books by John R. Quinn

Nature's World Records
Piranhas
The Summer Woodlands
The Winter Woods
The Marine Mammals of the Gulf of Maine (illustrated)

Our Native Fishes

The Aquarium Hobbyist's Guide to Observing, Collecting, and Keeping Them

North American Freshwater and Marine Fishes

John R. Quinn

Former Editor, *Tropical Fish Hobbyist*

Illustrations by the Author

Photographs by Luci Quinn

The Countryman Press
Woodstock, Vermont

Text and illustrations © 1990 by John R. Quinn

Published by The Countryman Press, Inc.
P.O. Box 175
Woodstock, Vermont 05091

Library of Congress Cataloging-in-Publication Data
Quinn, John R.
    Our native fishes : the aquarium hobbyist's guide to observing, collecting, and keeping them : North American freshwater and marine fishes / John R. Quinn ; illustrations and photographs by the author.
        p.   cm.
    Includes bibliographical references (p.   ) and index.
    ISBN 0-88150-181-6 : $14.95
    1. Aquarium fishes.   2. Fishes—North America.   3. Aquariums.
I. Title.
SF457.Q56   1990
639.3′4′097—dc20   90-15080
                                                       CIP

1 2 3 4 5 6 7 8 9 10
Printed in the United States of America
Typesetting by NK Graphics

Cover and interior design by Virginia L. Scott
Cover illustration by John R. Quinn

To the Lord, God . . . Who Created Them All

"O Lord, how manifold are thy works! In wisdom thou hast made them all: the earth is full of thy riches."

Psalm 104: 24

Contents

Preface

My very first, bonafide, genuine "fish collecting" trip took place when I was a callow youth of eight years. At that time, more years ago than I care to count or admit to here, my hometown of Ridgefield Park in overcrowded northern New Jersey was surrounded on three sides by extensive tidal marshes, the respective drainages of the Hackensack River and Overpeck Creek. These "fields of sun and grass" were home to a myriad array of wildlife and had an irresistible lure of of adventure and mystery. My Grandpa Dempsey, in resigned response to my endless pestering and over the motherly concerns of his daughter, finally yielded that year, and the two of us walked down the long hill of his street on the east side of town to the dead end, where the works of man came to an end and "the meadows" began. These were the real thing, not the artificial "Meadowlands" of today, with their Giants Stadium and Meadowlands Racetrack.

We didn't venture far out into the towering reeds that day, for, like most of the town's adults, my grandfather wasn't overly fond of the place. But we did skirt one of the many mosquito control ditches that had been carved into the meadows many years before. Looking into the canal's depths, I saw the shadowy form of a small fish flit by as quick as a thought. Pointing excitedly, I asked him what kind it was. Grandpa peered intently into the greenish flow, patted me on the head, and answered, "Probably a red herring."

I'm embarrassed to say that it wasn't until I was well into adulthood that I was able to identify that particular species with certainty, but I did manage to corner one of those ersatz "red herrings" that day, catch it in an empty can, and triumphantly take it home for a closer look and the beginning of a lifelong adventure.

The fish turned out to be a mummichog, or just plain "killie" to all of the local fishermen. It was a male, in full color, and as it circled frantically, disturbed by the curved glass in the antique fishbowl my mother gave me, I thought it was the most exotic and beautiful living thing I had ever seen— and it was mine.

Catching that fish, taking it home, and placing it in an aquarium of sorts conferred a sense of ownership in my young mind, even though up until that fateful moment of capture, the mummichog had been a free-living creature with all of the rights, privileges, and terrors that go along with that state.

On that fateful day, I became a fisherman in general and a collector in particular, for I was very much infused with the idea of catching and keeping—

permanently, of course—any and all fish I came across in my youthful pere-grinations through the natural world. The inquisitive nature inherent to the naturalist traveled firmly hand-in-hand with the acquisitive philosophy typified by philatelists, antique buffs, and other pack rats of humanity. Except that my collecting instincts revolved around living fish.

This "catch 'em and keep 'em" approach to nature study has remained with me ever since, although, for a number of reasons, it has been tempered con-siderably. Circumstances extant in the world environment today, of which no thinking person can be unaware, dictate—indeed, demand—a modified ap-proach to any activity that takes from the living environment without replace-ment, or is similarly destructive without a valid purpose. Environmental sins are coming home to roost for superabundant, stress-plagued humanity and must be dealt with if we are to survive as a species in any state resembling the "good life."

Over the years, many fellow anglers and outdoorsmen and women in general, finding something unusual or unknown either at the end of their line or in their bait seine or minnow trap, have asked me, "What is it, and can I take it home and keep it in my living room fish tank?" The answer is a qualified "yes." Thus the ultimate goal of this book is a dual yet simple one: To encourage and enhance the combination of two of the more popular pastimes currently pursued in the United States today—fishing and fishkeeping. Although seem-ingly miles apart in overall approach and philosophy, the aquarium hobby and sport fishing are, like it or not, in reality kissing cousins. They both involve removing a fish from its natural environment and putting it someplace else, whether that "someplace else" be a fish tank or a frying pan. But there, of course, the similarity ends, for the fish destined to spend part or all of the rest of its life in an aquarium receives far different treatment than its luckless colleague headed for the dinner table. The nature and intent of that treatment comprises the meat and potatoes of this book.

The fishes are by far the most numerous and diverse of the world's vertebrate animals. Somewhere in the vicinity of 32,000 species are recognized, far out-numbering the reptiles and amphibians (9,000 known species combined); birds (8,900); and mammals (about 6,000).

In no other group of living vertebrates is more diversity exhibited, especially in size. Although there is a world of difference between the three-inch Etruscan shrew and the 100-foot blue whale, there is an even greater disparity between the miniscule, quarter-inch Philippine goby (one of the world's smallest known fishes) and the King Kong–sized whale shark, which reaches reported lengths of 60 feet and weighs in at around 50 tons.

Fishes have evolved beautifully over the eons to exploit an environment that covers 71 percent of the earth's surface in the oceans alone, and they have done so in a galaxy of shapes, sizes, and colors. Colorful trout thrive in mile-high mountain streams, while blind fish live and die on the floor of the Marianas Trench, seven miles below sea level. No wonder we find the idea and image of fishes moving at will through every dimension of the world fascinating.

Although people have been catching fish for a long time—the principal motivation being gustatory—the notion of keeping a fish as a pet is of comparatively recent origin—or is it? The aquarium hobby, as we know it today with all its sophisticated gadgetry and multi-hued livestock, is a rather recent phenomenon, tracing its origins back to the mid-1800s. Its advent was one of the consequences of the Industrial Revolution in which greater numbers of people, relieved of the burden of endless and brutal toil just to make ends meet, suddenly found themselves with leisure time to pursue more genteel activities quite unrelated to the act of making a living. One of these pursuits was the clean, odorless, and generally trouble-free pastime of fishkeeping.

Although state-of-the-art all-glass aquariums and sophisticated filtration and lighting setups often create the impression that the aquarium hobby is strictly a product of the late twentieth century and its high-tech wizardry, a check of the literature on the subject will reveal that the idea of keeping live fish is nothing new.

It began with the ancient Sumerians, some 4,000 years ago. Archaeological digs have uncovered the remains of outdoor pools that appear to have been constructed solely for keeping fishes.

The moray eel was regarded as a status symbol in ancient Rome. A dedicated aquarist named Giaius Hirrius so loved his morays that he declined to sell any of them, even to Julius Caesar. He did, though, agree to lend the emperor a few fish, so that in what was perhaps the world's first fish show, a reported 6,000 live morays were placed on exhibition at a sumptuous feast.

With the advent of the Dark Ages, nobody much admired fish except at the end of a fishing line or spear, and it wasn't until the middle years of the last century that people began to think of a fish's natural habitat as being anything other than a frying pan, or that they could actually be pets or objects of scholarly scrutiny and scientific study.

And so we come to this enlightened day and age. Our pet fish, those purchased at pet shops and shamelessly pampered in fish tanks, are often served more expensive fare than we eat. Marriages have disintegrated over proliferating aquariums crowding a homestead. A one-inch tropical angelfish can cost more than five pounds of flounder fillets. And some people actually write books instructing other people how to keep fishes for purely ornamental purposes.

Popular fishkeeping and all of the related industries that supply and support it have assumed mammoth proportions today. It is a multi-million dollar business empire that, according to industry surveys, serves more than twenty-five million fishkeeping households in the United States alone, and is second only to photography as a popular pastime. An estimated 350 million tropical and ornamental fish are being housed in everything from one-gallon desktop aquariums to expansive outdoor ponds. Given the rapid growth of the more sophisticated marine side of the hobby, a further rise in the pet fish population over the next decade seems assured.

The true definition of an aquarium hobbyist can be somewhat nebulous and difficult to arrive at, but it could be applied to all who successfully maintain a moderately large (ten gallons or more) aquarium or aquariums in the home for more than a year and care enough about the subject to educate themselves through the reading of hobby-oriented books and magazines.

Those impressive aquarium hobby statistics must inevitably raise one fundamental question: How much longer can the freshwater and marine habitats worldwide continue to supply the animals upon which the aquarium hobby depends? Although the majority of bread-and-butter tropical fishes—platies, swordtails, angelfish, tetras—are raised in vast numbers on commercial fish farms, a great number of other, equally popular species that do not lend themselves to aquaculture must still be collected in the wild to satisfy the growing demand.

Given the deteriorating state of freshwater and marine habitats virtually everywhere, the extent of the problem—one recognized by the industry itself—can be quickly perceived. An infinite volume of a given living resource cannot be removed from a finite habitat forever, at least not without allowing it a chance to replenish itself. And this is under the dubious assumption that the habitat will remain healthy and undamaged by human activities so that it can continue to produce and nurture that coveted product. Of all the many solutions offered for the ominous environmental mess our beleagured earth finds itself in today, one of the most valid, and vital, is education. And therein the reason for this book: I want to encourage the reader to get out and get involved in the exploration of the natural aquatic environment, instruct him or her in how to do it and thus gain the most enjoyment and knowledge out of the experience, and, perhaps most important of all, come to realize fully just what's out there to be lost forever should we fail to protect the living water world left to us in the waning years of the twentieth century.

It is my hope that the reader of this book will, whenever possible, consider the fishes and other aquatic animals he or she secures and places in a properly set up aquarium as temporary guests, to be tended, nurtured, studied and enjoyed, and then released to resume their lives in the waters from which they came. Ideally, this is the way the native fish aspect of the aquarium hobby should be pursued unless you're a skilled breeder of fish interested in maintaining a captive-bred population of a species.

Wild fishes can never be considered pets in the traditional sense of the word, thus their capture and housing in aquariums are best practiced with an eye toward a form of environmental recycling.

Dr. Michael Fox, the popular veterinarian/author and proponent of animal rights, says of environmental education: "The child must be taken beyond the world of domestic pets and farm animals that reflect infantilism, dependence, conformity, obedience, and utilitarianism. These humanized animals dilute the experience of other species. They could even lead to misconceptions of animals and nature in general. Contact with natural ecosystems and the diversity therein will deepen the child's experience with otherness and concept of self."

Wise words, indeed, and this book is the culmination of my own fascination and interaction with the water world spanning more than four decades.

My friends and I spent a great deal of time (sometimes a bit too much time, according to our ever-tolerant parents) exploring in the best Huck Finn tradition the mysteries of our even-then rapidly vanishing Eden, and keeping in primitive aquariums the numerous small water creatures we caught. We made a lot of mistakes, and many of our charges subsequently languished in their captivity. But it was that early hands-on contact with the natural world and the myriad life it contains that laid the foundation for my love affair with nature, my desire to communicate my continuing sense of wonder at it all, and my commitment to its preservation for others.

Mankind is not an alien in his own environment unless he chooses to be, and he need only approach and interact with the water world with an enquiring mind, a reverence for life, and an environmental conscience, and it will willingly yield up its kaleidoscopic bounty of beauty and adventure. As slick and dazzling as it may be, no "nature special" or "true-life adventure" series on television can, or ever should, take the place of interaction with the world, on a one-to-one basis.

Today, in an era of burgeoning human numbers and the alarming decline of the environment, it's natural to express concern for the animals remaining in it and to suggest that passive appreciation of them via the electronic media is the best and only way open to the masses. For the most part, I agree, but for those of us who feel that powerful need to maintain a strong touch with nature, the panacea of TV is woefully deficient, nor will it ever truly foster that so-desperately needed desire on the part of the young to work to preserve what they know to be fast disappearing from the face of the earth. Correctly and conscientiously pursued, the intelligent and limited collecting of native fishes and their successful maintenance in home aquariums is not another exploitation of a natural world that has seen all too much of the wrong kind of contact by humankind, but rather a self-sustaining and, above all, educating involvement that will foster a deeper appreciation for the life beneath the surface. And in the process, foster a greater commitment to preserve it among those who will run this beleaguered planet's affairs after we have become history.

Like the proverbial "one that got away," that lengthens with each telling of the tale, a list of "people to thank" for a book on fishing (or a form of it) has about the same propensity for growing from minnow to monster. In my near-lifetime of fishing and fishkeeping, scores of people of like persuasion—and some who couldn't bring themselves to touch a live fish—have guided, influenced, cautioned, praised, derided and—most of all—encouraged me. They include spouse and siblings, parents and progeny, fishing buddies and game wardens, landlubbers and seafarers, publishers and petshop owners, commercial fishermen and oceanarium staffers, and the countless "ordinary" folks you're likely to encounter near, on or under the water. This is the human side of fish collecting, but to name each soul who ever discussed a fish with me over the past forty-plus years would present the reader with a chore akin to wading through one of those endless "family newsletters" received during the holidays. Instead, permit me to mention just a few, namely: the late Dr. Henry W. Fowler, whose patient, almost poetic replies to a fledgling aquarist's endless questions I still have and cherish; the late Jim Clark, a New Hampshire conservation officer who possessed a knowledge and love of nature and the nongame "little critters" of the natural world beyond that of most "fish cops"; my brother Steve, whose boundless enthusiasm for the natural world while we were growing up helped fuel my own lifelong love of the outdoors; Dr. Herbert R. Axelrod, who has probably had more influence on the art of catching a fish and keeping it alive and healthy in a container than any other living person; colleagues and cohorts Bruce Gebhardt, Bob Rosen, John Bondhus, Ray Hunziker, Dr. Warren E. Burgess, Jerry G. Walls, Neal Pronek; and my nephew, Greg Askew, who is always willing to wade into the muck and mire and shows all the signs of terminal fishkeeping.

And the last, and the first—my wife, Luci: "let me count the ways . . ."

Introduction

Between 27,000 and 32,000 species of freshwater and marine fishes world-wide are recognized today, depending on whether you're a taxonomic "lumper" or "splitter." Two-thirds of these species are marine; one-third freshwater. Of that impressive and ever-growing figure, perhaps half are fishes that can, or could conceivably, be kept with varying degrees of success in an aquarium. That's between 13,500 and 16,000 species of the world's fishes that we might, with greater or lesser stretches of the imagination, call "aquarium fish." Of this last rough estimate, some 3,200 marine and about 800 freshwater, potential "aquarium fish" occur within the range of this book—North America, from the East Coast to the West Coast and from northern Canada to the Mexican border.

Given the large number of species in North America, this book is not a field guide in the accepted sense of the word, covering all the freshwater and marine fish species found within its scope, but rather a book on how to recognize, collect, and keep at home representative species among those fish families that can, to one degree or another, be considered aquarium fish.

I have described fishes that almost everyone readily recognizes as aquarium fish, such as the beautiful tropical butterfly fish and angelfish, as well as those not normally considered prime fish tank inhabitants, such as the voracious pickerel and bluefish, and the summer flounder, or fluke. All of these, and many other marine and freshwater species, have been maintained in aquariums with varying degrees of success, a goodly number by me over the years.

With careful attention to the needs of the particular fish, from the moment of capture to its ultimate destination in the home aquarium, there is no reason why most of our temperate and subtropical native fishes cannot be kept in the home, especially on a temporary, "catch, observe, and release" basis.

Overly specialized living requirements and the question of ultimate size are about the only major obstacles to keeping any wild fish in an aquarium. Thus, you'll find skates, dogfish, and largemouth bass within these pages for they can be kept when small, but you'll look in vain for a flying fish, ocean sunfish, or whale shark, which are far too large or specialized to be confined in any home aquarium, no matter what its size.

As a specific example of economy of space, the cyprinid genus *Notropis* contains some 120 species, all of them called something-or-other "shiners." Although there surely exist differences in morphology, habitat, behavior, and aquarium requirements among the many members of this crowded assemblage, they are not great enough to warrant discussing every last one of them in print. That would make a book in itself. Thus, I have chosen four, the common, weed, emerald, and spottail shiners, as they are different enough to serve as representatives for the entire genus. The freshwater darters are another example. Out of some 124 species in three genera (*Ammocrypta, Percina, Etheostoma*), I have chosen nine as divergent enough yet typical of the group as a whole.

On the marine side, the searobins, with twenty-four species in the genus *Prionotus,* are spoken for by the northern searobin (*P. carolinus*). All *Prionotus* searobins are similar in general form, occupy the same habitat, are collected by the same methods, and will present the aquarist with essentially the same set of pros and cons in the aquarium. The northern species is a widely distributed and familiar sport and food fish that adequately fills the bill in a discussion of the group.

I have also omitted discussing, with an eye toward collecting, those species currently classed as endangered or threatened, although some are listed and briefly described to enable the collector to identify and release them if accidentally caught, and to report the sighting to the appropriate state or provincial fish and wildlife agency.

Fish that could be dangerous to the inexperienced aquarist—stingrays, scorpionfish, and the like—are also omitted, although these and other groups are quite popular in the tropical fish hobby today. Unless you know what you're doing, though, avoid handling or keeping any fish known to be highly venomous, overly aggressive, or otherwise dangerous to anyone tempted to dunk a naive or surreptitious hand in your tank.

In the sections on collecting in the individual species accounts, I have avoided giving specific locations. The ranges of marine fishes are often broad. This may not be the case with many freshwater species of more restricted or fragmented range and habitat, and overcollecting at a single location could have an adverse and lasting effect on resident populations. Thus, the habitat of a fish is described under the assumption that the interested reader will research the subject further, then locate specific collecting points.

This omission is much less an effort to jealously guard one's own personal "fishing holes" than a desire to avoid stressing a possibly sensitive environment.

The reader with a burning interest in keeping the pirate perch in an aquarium will use the habitat and range information in this book as a starting point from which to read further, and then get out in the fresh air and sunshine (or rain!) and explore the world of the pirate perch in order to find, catch, and finally keep one. That effort and adventure, after all, is where much of the joy is in keeping native fishes.

My observations on the collecting and maintaining of the species are, for the most part, based on personal experience. The exceptions are many of the western fishes, in which cases I have relied heavily upon the published material of others working with those species.

Since both aquarists and fish are living creatures that behave differently and respond in various ways to the many and varied stimuli that confront them, another reader's experience with a given species may well be at variance with my own.

Tom Baugh, author of *A Net Full of Natives,* reported feeding behavior in the eastern mudminnow (*Umbra pygmaea*) that was quite different from that of my own report on the species published in 1971. The cause, I later realized, was in the nature of the tankmates kept with the fish in my own setup.

I learned something from Baugh's experience, and so to any reader who may have had a contradictory experience from my own with a fish, or who has a better way of doing things in the native fishes hobby I extend the invitation to tell me about it. If there is ever another edition of this book, such new information will be added.

Trap, Net, and Bucket

COLLECTING METHODS

"God never made a more calm, quiet, innocent recreation than angling."

Izaak Walton

The venerable Mr. Webster defines fishing as "the occupation or pastime of catching fish." That's about as no-nonsense and straightforward a definition as you can get. And although people have also been known to "fish for compliments," and "go on fishing expeditions" for elusive facts or evidence, for the most part to go fishing means to gear up with hook, line, and sinker and

Basic equipment for a one-day collecting excursion. Clockwise, from left: dip net with sturdy, triangle frame; insulated cooler for transporting specimens; five-gallon collecting bucket; wire-framed collecting net for moving fish; ten-foot minnow seine; sneakers (a good idea in most waters today); mask and snorkel (for preliminary exploration).

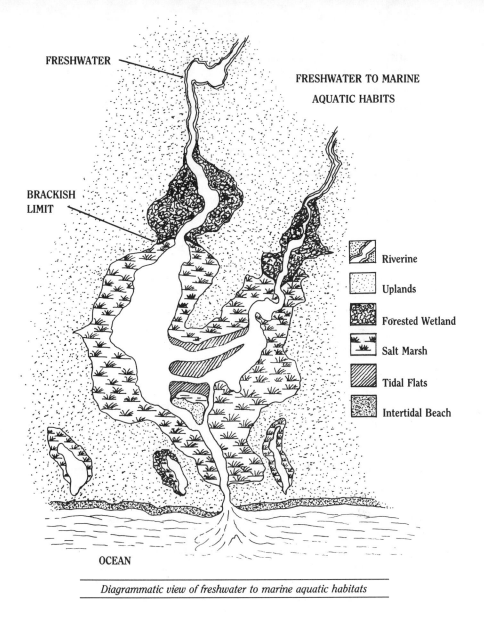

FRESHWATER

FRESHWATER TO MARINE
AQUATIC HABITS

BRACKISH
LIMIT

Riverine

Uplands

Forested Wetland

Salt Marsh

Tidal Flats

Intertidal Beach

OCEAN

Diagrammatic view of freshwater to marine aquatic habitats

trust luck and the weather in the ancient contest between mankind and those members of the order Pisces, more popularly known as the fishes.

People have been fishing for food for many a millennium and have perfected the techniques of capture over the centuries with one goal in mind: to eat it. Until very recently in our history, little thought was given to the fish as a living thing after it was caught, for there was no need to. The fishes' habits, habitats, and food preferences were studied and noted solely for the purpose of enticing them to take a hook, enter a net, or make themselves available to the commercial seine or trawl fisherman.

But with the advent of the aquarium hobby and the growing popularity of large public aquariums, the picture began to change. It was discovered that people would pay good money for fish they could keep alive as pets, or an admission fee so they could admire them in the super-sized tanks of oceanariums. So a small but increasing number of former commercial food fishermen took to the seas and the tropical rivers in the 1930s and 1940s in search of a smaller but colorful quarry. These live-catch anglers became known as collectors.

Fish collecting is regarded as the soft approach to catching fish. Every step of the process is designed to cause the quarry the least amount of stress or injury that might make it difficult for the fish to acclimate to its new life of confinement in an aquarium. Fishes can be collected in almost as many ways as there are kinds of fish, from the traditional though least desirable hook, line, and sinker to a peculiar device called the slurpgun.

Whatever the method employed, the collector/angler must approach the task with considerable sensitivity to the fish's reaction to capture and handling and consequently apply the lightest possible touch at all stages of the operation.

The Hook

The hook is an ancient fish-catching tool, and its design and use are certainly not intended to go easy on the captive. Thus, it is not recommended here as a collecting tool, but discussed because sooner or later the aquarist/fisherman will catch a fish on hook and line that he or she may wish to keep in the aquarium.

The principal complaint against the hook as a live-collecting tool is the physical trauma it causes the fish. This is inevitable, but the abrasions and injuries sustained by a fish during its struggles in a net may often equal or even exceed those of a hook-landed fish. It's all in the handling.

It is often recommended that a hook's barb be either filed or crimped down if the object is either catch-and-release or retention for aquariums. Although this reduces the mount of tissue damage inflicted, it also, in my own experience, reduces the hook's own retaining capabilities by about 75 percent. In other words, depending on the species involved and how vigorously it fights, about three specimens will shake the hook and escape for every one landed. This isn't a bad average when both fish and time are abundant and strikes are frequent, but it may take some time to stock an aquarium with a barbless hook in fish-poor waters.

A barbless hook does facilitate its removal from a fish, but that's about it. If the backside of a barbed hook is pressed carefully against the entry hole opposite the barb, the barb will pass easily through and can be quickly removed from the fish's mouth. Whatever pain the fish experienced in being hooked will have already been inflicted, barb or no barb. The watchwords, then, are speed and gentleness in hook removal.

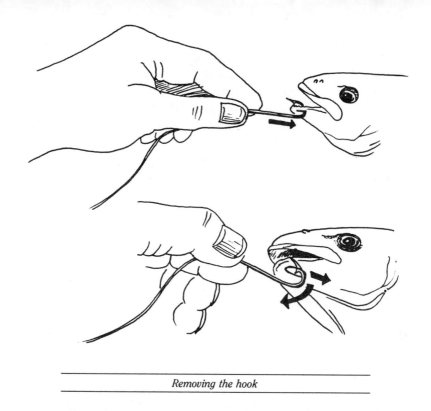

Removing the hook

The size of the hook is important, and it's not always "the smaller the better." Select the size that can just be managed by the target species. Too small and it will be swallowed; too large and the bait will be picked off. Fish with the line taut in order to pick up the first touch of the fish. Do not allow the bait to lie unattended as this will give the fish time to swallow it with the result a useless, gut-hooked specimen. Strike firmly but not violently at the first touch to avoid tearing the fish's mouth.

When landing a fish, do not allow it to flop about on the ground or dock. This will cause abrasions and remove the animal's protective mucus, making it highly vulnerable to disease and infection. Any specimen that comes in violent contact with a dry surface on capture should be released to recover in the wild, no matter how desirable a keeper it may be. A roughly handled specimen is far more likely to fall prey to disease in the alien aquarium environment and, in the process, quickly infect any fishes already there.

Remove a specimen from the hook with wet hands only. This cannot be stressed strongly enough. Use dry hands or a towel only if the fish is destined for the dinner table. The ideal method is to lower the fish, hook and all, into the collecting bucket and carefully remove the hook there.

Hook and line fishing is not a desirable method of live collecting. Most aquarium specimens taken this way are caught incidentally during a sport fishing trip.

The Seine

"The grace of a surfcaster, the skill of a fly fisherman, the stamina necessary to fight a tuna or a mako, the patience of a bait fisherman in a pond—these are all part of what most of us call sportsmanship, but there is no way to go into poetic rhapsodies about dragging a seine up on a beach." So wrote Merv Roberts in *The Tidemarsh Guide to Fishes*. He's right, of course. But the object of using a seine, or any net, is not sportsmanship but rather harvesting. In collecting fish for aquariums, the seine fits the bill as no other smaller nets can.

The seine is an ancient yet highly effective implement and is the most popular

Using a large seine—a 50-footer—in a coastal estuary. Before dragging, the area should be visually reconnoitered to make certain that no snags lie in the path of the haul. This haul ended at a disintegrated bulkhead; so the catch was inspected with the net partially submerged. The catch included young kingfish, cunners, and an inshore lizardfish.

tool for collecting bait and scientific specimens the world over. A seine is nothing more than a long rectangle of mesh attached at both ends to sturdy poles. It is dragged through shallow water by two stalwart operators hoping to corral a few fish and avoid backache and sunburn at the same time. It all sounds pretty simple and for the most part, it is. But there are right ways and wrong ways to use a seine, and they can make the difference between a day of wasted effort and a collecting bucket swimming with future tank tenants.

The net can range in size from the four- to six-foot minnow seines that can be operated with ease by one person to the giant commercial seines extending up to a mile in length and hauled by boats or power winches. In between are the more practical seines, those from 10 to 100 feet in length, commonly referred to as beach seines.

These are the best nets for the aquarium collector and can be purchased for roughly a dollar a foot at most sporting goods and bait and tackle stores, making them one of the cheapest yet most effective fish-catchers available. Most smaller seines are made of treated cotton and have a life span of about two, possibly three seasons under normal use and with good care, particularly if used in saltwater collecting. Larger seines are almost always made of nylon and with normal maintenance will last for years. These are by far the best investment if you plan to stay in the collecting business.

Properly used, a seine is an extremely effective fishing tool, collecting virtually all living creatures (and a lot of assorted junk) that happen to find themselves in its path. For this reason, most states have laws governing the use of the seine—Pennsylvania, for example, restricts the net to the four-by-four-foot seine. These laws will be discussed in detail in the section on conservation and the law.

Seines are usually sold without poles, so your first task after buying one will be to outfit your net with a worthy pair. Common sense dictates that the larger the seine, the heavier the poles required, for they will take much of the strain of a loaded net. A fifty-foot, fine-meshed seine dragged through dense weed

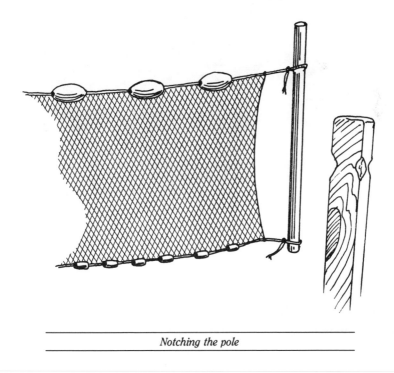

Notching the pole

beds will quickly pick up all manner of natural and man-made debris. This weight, in addition to the resistance offered by the water, will exert considerable pressure on both the operators' backs and the net poles. Thus, bamboo or tubular aluminum poles or broom handles are not a wise choice for any but the smallest seine. I've found that one-inch doweling works well enough for seines up to 20 feet long, while for those in the 50- to 100-foot range, lengths of two-by-four pine serve the purpose well. Most longer seines range from four to six feet in height, and their poles should be cut to allow a six-inch overhang on the top end. Notches should be cut at the points of tying to prevent the knot from slipping during use.

One-person operation of a minnow seine. This method is quite effective when working densely vegetated habitats. When moving along the edge of a weed bed, the inner pole is poked among the vegetation to flush hiding fishes into the net's path.

The next question has to be, "Where to seine?" The seine is not suited for use in rocky areas, those studded with sunken snags, or in water above the operators' chests. It is essentially a shallow-water net best worked over a sandy or weedy bottom free of protruding objects that might snag the net and either stop its forward progress (and release all those potential aquarium fishes) or tear a hole in the mesh. For this reason, the seine is most often employed in large, weedy lakes or in marine estuarine habitats. The ideal seining location is a shallow, weedy lake or bay with a gently shelving beach studded by small indentations or coves in which to end each run of the net.

The seine is equipped with a lead line and a float line. The former pulls the lower edge of the net to the bottom and the latter supports the net's top edge on the water's surface, forming a sort of aquatic curtain. The lead weights and styrofoam floats of the typical store-bought seine are usually inadequate for the job (they're usually too small or there are not enough of them), so you may wish to add extra ones.

With the exception of the gill net, a stationary net catches no fish, so the next step is to move the seine forward, and herein lies the rub in successful seine fishing. Most people associate net fishing with quick action and fast reflexes in order to bag an elusive, darting quarry, but in seining, speed is not of the essence. In fact, it may have the opposite effect. The reason for this lies in the seine's size and design. Moving through the water in the hands of experienced operators, a big seine is a juggernaut that engulfs all but the fleetest fishes (which are often the least suited to confinement in aquariums anyway).

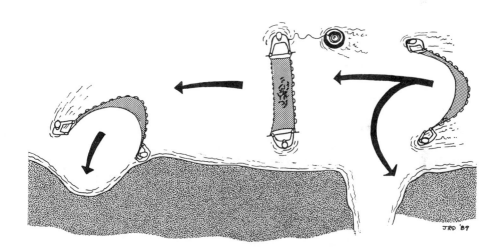

Aerial view of a seining sweep, showing preferred termination sites at a creek mouth and bank indentation. The catch can be inspected offshore (center) and any desirable specimens placed in the towed catch float.

Seining is one of the few methods of net fishing in which the quarry remains virtually unseen until the net is taken to the beach. Dragging a seine at a sloshing run raises the lead line above the bottom, and most fishes will escape under rather than over the net.

Mullet, needlefish, and a few other fast-swimming, open water species are among those that will leap over the float line when they sense the net closing in on them. Since these fishes do not adapt well to aquariums, they should be released if captured anyway.

This net is most effective in water no deeper than the net is high. It should be hauled by two persons who maintain a distance between themselves so that the seine forms a belly or a shallow U. This bag will corral and collect the fishes, rather than simply drive them before the advancing net. If it is pulled too taut, it will form a sort of moving fence. The net should be hauled at a slow walking speed, so that neither the lead line lifts nor the floats are dragged under. The lower ends of the poles should be angled forward and bumped over the bottom so that the lower edge of the net stays in close contact with it.

Most of the desirable aquarium species will be found on or near the bottom, so this seining technique is most important unless you're seeking the various high-swimming bait species.

A seine more than twenty feet in length worked over weedy terrain will tend to lift at its center so it's helpful to position a third person equipped with a pole or an oar at the middle of the net to hold the lead line on the bottom.

Each seine haul can be checked at two places; at the point of termination on the beach, and periodically offshore during the course of the haul. The former is the most frequently employed.

Many bait and recreational seiners drag the net up on the beach and flip it over, dumping the contents on the sand and sorting through the catch. The keepers are stowed in the collecting pail and the rest left to die in the sun.

The basic inhumanity of the act aside, this is a bad conservation practice, even if it does provide the gulls a free meal. The environmentally aware netsman will treat each haul of captives with tender, loving care, as though all were destined for the home tank, or, if unwanted, for immediate release.

To do this, haul the seine just above the water line. Then sort the catch in the net, removing any desirable fishes and those unwanted species known to perish quickly in exposure to air first and either consigning them to the bucket or placing them back in the water. As soon as you've determined that nothing you want remains in the meshes, walk the seine a few paces offshore and flip it over, releasing the rejects to life instead of slow, pointless death on shore.

The offshore check is practical only with the smaller, more maneuverable seines (twenty feet or under), but it is the best method if done right. When seining weed beds far from the beach, it's usually wise periodically to lift the net and look over the contents for possible keepers lest they escape over the long haul. To do this, the operators should stop and back away from each other, pulling the net taut and swinging it up to the surface, lead line first, so that the catch can be viewed in the belly. If any desirable specimens are noted, the net can be gathered in, hand over hand, until the collectors can easily remove the catch.

This is where a little inventiveness must enter the picture. Commercial clammers often tow a small raft fashioned from an inner tube or child's pool

Two young collectors hauling a ten-foot minnow seine through a weed bed in a lake in New Jersey's Pine Barrens. Note the position of the poles—they are held firmly in the direction of the haul and kept butted against the bottom. This haul ended in a sandy area between the shore-side weed beds and yielded all three species of Enneacanthus *sunfishes.*

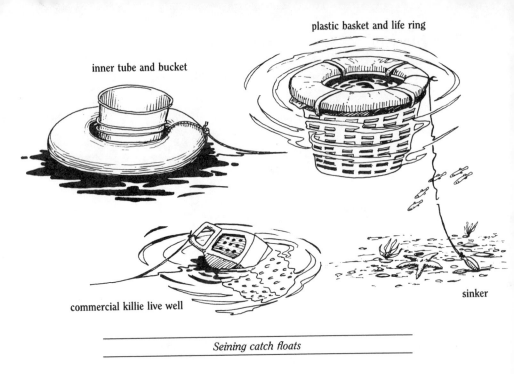

inner tube and bucket

plastic basket and life ring

commercial killie live well

sinker

Seining catch floats

ring as they rake the underwater clam flats, dropping the bagged bivalves into a bucket or bushel basket lodged in the tube's hole. This will work just as well for the fish collector, eliminating that long, tiring wade back to the beach, struggling fish in hand, to deposit it in that oh-so-far-away bucket. A floating live killie pot, tethered to the waist, works just as well, though it will hold fewer specimens than the tire tube "collecting barge."

Choose your seining terrain carefully, avoiding rocky areas or those studded with snags or other objects that will snag and damage a net.

Wear sneakers, waders, or other protective footgear when collecting. Virtually no water habitats—freshwater or salt—can be guaranteed free of cans, broken bottles, or other man-made delights. Play it safe.

Haul the net at moderate speed. An eager, aquatic footrace accomplishes little.

Keep your collecting buckets as close to the netting operation as possible to avoid prolonged exposure of the catch to air. Handle live fish with wet hands. Sort the catch as quickly as possible and promptly return all unwanted specimens to the water. Rinse your seine thoroughly after each use, especially in saltwater, and spread it to dry. Never roll up and store a wet cloth seine. It's the surest way to rot it.

Finally, any seining operation invariably collects a crowd of onlookers if other people are in the vicinity, so use the opportunity to talk up, and demonstrate, good conservation. It unfailingly pays dividends.

The Dip Net

After the seine, the dip net is probably the most commonly used fish-catching device. It is also the most varied in both design and size.

A dip net consists of a mesh bag attached to a metal frame attached to a long handle. The basic net has many variations, from the three-foot-wide party boat landing net equipped with a twelve-foot handle all the way down to the little braided wire aquarium hand net commonly employed in the capture of pet platys and zebra danios. In between are the dip nets best suited to the bait or aquarium fish collector.

Although most dip nets have circular mouths, they are also available in rectangular and triangular configurations, and some of the better nets are in the shape of a "D" on its side. These three designs are by far the best, as the flat side places much more of the net's frame in contact with the bottom, which is precisely what you want when sweeping it through prime terrain.

Although perfectly serviceable nets can be purchased from bait and tackle stores, these are usually made of tabular aluminum and are just not up to extended, hard use in rugged aquatic habitats. The user may spend more time bending his net back into shape than actually using it. Biological supply houses carry the best collecting nets. They may be expensive, about $60 at this time as compared to roughly $10 for a store-bought net, but they are designed for hard, sustained use and will last for many years with good care.

These collecting nets are made of heavy steel tubing securely attached to a stout, four-foot hardwood handle. In such a net, the only part that ever needs

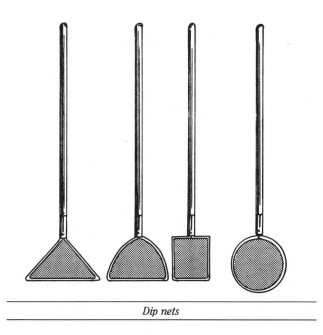

Dip nets

to be replaced is the nylon and canvas bag, which has a lifespan of about five years with average use. The strength of the frame at its point of attachment to the handle is the all-important aspect of any dip net, for it takes the lion's share of the stress when the net is used correctly.

Most beginners with dip net in hand for the first time make a fundamental

The "raking" method of dip netting, in which the net is placed against the bottom and pulled strongly and quickly toward the user. Unless you are aiming for a specific target, this is the most effective way to sweep a net through weed beds or other cover.

mistake. They either try a wild sideways sweep with the net or use an under-handed, upward jabbing motion, attempting to come up underneath the quarry and scoop it from the water. Unless they are very lucky, they are almost certainly doomed to failure, for most fish can move a lot faster than you ever suspected when they see a net bearing down (or up) on them. And contrary to the image created by the very term dip net, you don't "dip" with one if you expect to catch fish with it.

The most effective dip net action closely resembles that of raking leaves. Jab the net swiftly down to the bottom and pull it toward you with the same handholds as used in cleaning up the backyard. This movement gives the maximum amount of leverage and allows for much faster and more direct action than swinging the net from side to side or trying to lift it (along with the weight of the water itself) from an essentially off-balance position. Even fish that can be seen in the water can be caught by slowly passing the net over them and bringing it down and in towards you in one swift motion.

Dip nets outclass the seines hands down in terms of maneuverability. They are ideal for probing under bank overhangs and in other close quarters, and are an exceptionally effective tool for collecting secretive stream fishes. Wedge the net against the bottom and shuffle the rocks just upstream to spook any fish hiding under them. The current will quickly sweep them into the waiting bag.

Rinse the dip net of debris and allow it to dry before storing.

Mask, snorkel, swimfins, and hand net are the only equipment required for aquarium collecting around docks and sea walls. Such structures usually harbor heavy marine plant growth that provides shelter for many small fishes.

The Hand Net

The hand net differs from the dip net principally in size. A hand net is small enough to be maneuvered comfortably and easily with one hand; a dip net cannot be handled so easily. Most hand nets are made of light steel or braided wire framing and have handles between one and two feet long. Aquarium hand nets may vary in mouth-width from three to sixteen inches. The larger sizes make the best collecting hand nets, though their construction is on the flimsy side and thus their life span is rather short under sustained use.

The hand net is often employed by collectors using snorkeling or scuba gear. It is most effective in collecting species found on or near the bottom or in rocky and coral areas as it is light and easily manipulated in the often turbulent conditions found underwater. This net is least effective if the diver attempts to sweep a fish into it with a powerful swing. The resistance offered by the water will make it virtually impossible to bag anything but a dead fish.

Coaxing a sculpin into the net near a jetty at low tide. The fish had retreated under the rock and the smaller aquarium hand net was used for greater maneuverability.

The Drop or Cast Net

This ancient fish catcher almost always conjures up idyllic images of Polynesian fishermen casting for fishes over a tropical reef. Although it looks easy to fling this net out over the water so it blooms like a delicate flower before

The object of the cast net throw is to ensure that the net spins and flares to its widest extent before hitting the water. Cast nets are usually most effective in shallow water.

dropping into the sea, skilled use of it takes time and practice. Cast nets range in size from 6 to 20 feet in diameter. The small ones can be mastered without much trouble; the big ones are harder to handle.

The essential design is a large, flat, circular mesh purse that sinks to the bottom and then is drawn together by means of lines attached to the edges.

The cast net is a shallow-water net, functioning best in water no deeper than about six feet, depending on the net's diameter. Although the rim of a good cast net is usually well weighted with lead and the net sinks when thrown, the resistance of the mesh passing through the water slows it down enough so that most active fish can get out of its way if the water depth is greater than six feet. I've found that the six-foot net I use works best in three to four feet of water, bagging both free-swimming and bottom fish if thrown correctly.

The end of the net's line should be tethered either to an object on the dock or shore or to the thrower's wrist. Otherwise it may follow the net into the deep after a particularly heroic throw.

When handling a smaller net, think of a bullfighter holding his cape off to the right side. Grip the net in a wide-handed position. Swing your right hand first, then let go with the left hand, spinning the net. The cast net is similar to a giant, flexible Frisbee that must hit the water fully spread. Lean into the throw, almost as a discus thrower does, and the net should perform as designed.

Large cast nets can be mastered with patience and practice. Hold the net by its ring collar with your right hand and lift and grip the lead-weighted edge by the index finger of the same hand. With the other hand, grip a section of the net's edge several feet to the left, holding it out in a spread position. Swing

Prepare to throw a cast net by gripping it much as a bullfighter holds his cape. Then swing it back as far as possible and lean into the throw in a smooth motion; let the weight of the net do most of the work. the right hand crosses over the left, imparting a spin to the net and ensuring that it hits the water fully opened.

the net in a graceful pendulum motion, releasing all grips at once and letting fly. With a little practice, cast nets can be thrown near or far with considerable accuracy, and with little effort.

Cast nets are most effective when used in shallow water where there is little or no vegetation or underwater obstructions. They're more trouble than they're worth in close quarters, such as among dock pilings, rocky or snag-ridden waters, or along densely wooded stream banks where you don't have enough room to open it up, much less fling it.

The Lift Net

This net is commonly available in bait and tackle shops and most sporting goods stores. It is a square of mesh between 36 and 48 inches wide, supported at each corner by crossed rods, with lines runing from each corner to a central line.

This functions best in depths of four feet or less. Although a bait, such as a chicken neck or chunk of fish, is often wired to the center of the net, it can be lowered unbaited to the bottom where fishes are plentiful and moving about. Obviously, speed is of the essence when using the lift net, and for this reason, many collectors secure the line to a stout fishing rod or stiff pole for greater leverage and control. This net is an effective crabbing device and can be used to collect smaller crustaceans for the aquarium.

The Minnow Trap

Anyone who's done any sport fishing is familiar with that small wire-mesh cylinder with the inverted cones at either end. The killie trap or minnow trap, like the lobster pot, is a passive collecting device. It is baited, placed in a strategic location, and left there, either for a couple of hours or a couple of days. It sounds easy and it is, but the word "strategic" is all important, for an enticingly baited trap placed indifferently will produce indifferent results, to say the least.

The killie trap ingeniously employs the old "easy to get into, hard to get out of" rule. The small mouth of the inverted mesh funnel makes it easy for a fish to enter the trap, but the odds are against it finding its way out.

Killie traps can be placed unbaited in locations where the movements of fishes are confined or constricted in some way, such as narrow creeks and channels, small coves, or at bulkhead angles. Or they can be baited with bread, crab or fish meat, or other bait, and set in any area where fishes have been observed. A killie trap should not be baited unless you are specifically seeking killies, silversides, or freshwater cyprinids that are attracted by the bait. The best approach is to place the trap so that moving fish enter it simply because it's in their way.

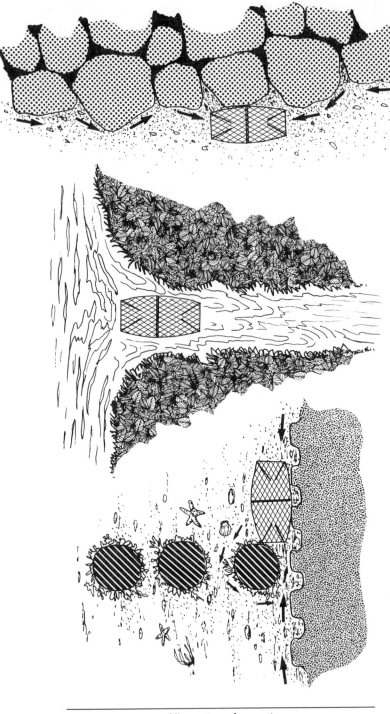

3. At groin or jetty

2. At mouth of creek or ditch

1. Next to bulkhead and pilings

Minnow trap placement

The familiar killie trap can be an effective collecting tool. This one is baited with crumbled crab meat.

An effective way to collect small marine specimens is to suspend a trap on or near the bottom close to a bulkhead wall. Small fishes are conscious of the appetites of big fishes and when moving about will almost always hug some kind of shelter. Thus, individuals are much more likely to enter a trap placed directly in their path than one in an open space only a few feet away.

Traps should be checked at least once a day, and more often if fishes are plentiful. Killie traps left unattended for days at a time invite pilferage by both natural predators and fishermen in the market for bait who find the trap by accident. I recently pulled up a trap I had been forced to leave unchecked for two days and found a very large eel coiled up inside. He looked well fed and was meaner than a junkyard dog.

Natural Traps

Stream fishes are often too active and agile to be easily collected with a dip net and their often-rocky habitats can make seining difficult, so other strategies must be used. For centuries, people have altered the contours of streams to force fish to move into positions in which they might more easily be caught for food. Fish weirs and pound nets are the descendants of those early, primitive, but highly effective fish catchers.

Stream traps can be made of the one material closest at hand and most obtainable—the rocks of the streambed itself. Build a rock trap in the form of a V, with either the stream bank forming one of the arms or the construction placed in midstream just below a pool where fish are congregating. In all cases, the wide mouth should face upstream and the point, open to a width of about a foot, should empty downstream. The rocks should be aligned and piled so that they form a pair of straight, converging walls that extend to or above the surface. Chinks and breaks should be plugged with smaller stones or other material.

As in the killie trap, fishes entering the V from upstream will be forced into an ever-narrowing path of travel, ending with either a waiting dip net, seine, or other device.

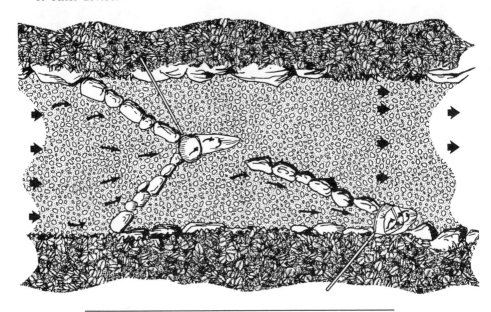

Two configurations of stream rock-weir construction, showing direction of current flow and placement of dip net. Such weirs present enduring barriers to fish movement if left in place and thus should always be completely dismantled after use.

Stream fish trapping is a cooperative venture requiring at least two collectors, one to handle the net at the end of the trap, the other to drive the fish into the trap from upstream or dislodge them from their hiding places by shuffling the rocks and stones so they are swept into the V by the current. The operation should be carried out with some dispatch, as swiftwater fishes will avoid the trap altogether, make a U-turn once inside, or slip through any gaps in the rock walls if given the chance. In other words, they are quick to sense a trap and thus should be chased into the funnel without pause. The net must be lifted at once when fish are in it. A killie trap placed at the funnel's exit often works well, though it sometimes constricts the pathway to such a degree that swiftly approaching fishes perceive it as a dead end and turn aside.

Dismantle a rock stream weir once it has served its purpose. Left in place, it mars the natural appearance of a waterway and may render the resident fish more vulnerable to predation by unnaturally restricting or concentrating their movements.

Stream Net Collecting

The seine and dip net can be used in shallow, swift-flowing streams. The stream current does most of the work; the nets are positioned in the right place to receive the quarry. Using a dip net, one person can work a stream by wedging the net among the rocks and then shuffling rocks directly upstream of the net's mouth. This action dislodges fishes, crayfish, and other aquatic animals and, if you're lucky, sweeps them into the waiting net. Working with a seine requires two, or ideally, three people—two to hold the seine in the moving water and the third to shuffle his way toward the net from upstream. Both methods are highly effective if carried out correctly and are the best way to collect such secretive stream fishes as sculpins and some darters.

The Drop Net

Divers often encounter tempting aggregations of small fish hovering about isolated coral heads and other natural or man-made objects, only to have them dart deep out of sight when approached. A drop net is an effective collecting tool under such circumstances.

Using a drop net. A Ping-Pong ball serves as a float to keep the net erect and more manageable.

This net is not often available commercially, but making one for yourself is no major undertaking. Use a circular piece of half-inch nylon mesh six to eight feet in diameter. Cut a wedge that is one-third of the circumference and comes to a point at the center, then sew the netting together to form a cone with about a four-foot wide mouth. Attach expandable rings to the edge and feed quarter-inch nylon rope through the rings. String seine weights, available in most sporting goods and tackle shops, every two or three inches on the rope to weigh the net down. Tie the rope, seal it by touching a flame to the knot, then trim it.

Carry this net to the bottom and drop it over the coral head, then poke the intricacies of the shelter until the fish flee from it—usually straight up into the net's cone. I've found that the net's form in the water can be maintained by using a Ping-Pong ball or other small floatable that will exert enough buoyancy to keep the cone's point vertical, but not enough to raise the net.

The Square Fish Trap

Larger, square fish traps can be constructed of either stainless steel hardware cloth or Plexiglass, with holes drilled in the latter to allow for the free passage of water. These box traps should be placed near natural or man-made objects that afford hiding places so that fish will approach and investigate them more readily. They can be baited with any kind of natural bait, but crushed crabs or a small, plastic mesh chum bag works best. Larger traps should be checked at least once a day to reduce the possibility of larger predatory fishes, such as moray or common eels, entering and devouring the prized aquarium specimens.

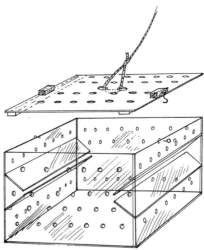

The plexiglass fish trap is durable, although the plexiglass tends to scratch and become opaque over time. Use silicone aquarium cement to assemble it.

Typical wire fish trap. Construction should be of coated chicken wire or hardware cloth, depending on the size of the specimens sought.

The Slurpgun

This ingenious device, usually a Plexiglas cylinder and piston operated by hand or spring loaded, has its boosters and detractors among professional fish collectors. The earliest slurpguns were homemade, but they are now manufactured and sold through most dive shops. The gun's greatest asset is in catching small fish that have retreated into tight, hard-to-reach quarters in rocks or coral. The nozzle is placed close to the fugitive and the piston handle pulled back sharply, drawing water and, you hope, the fish along with it, into the cylinder. Then the fish is quickly transferred into the collecting bag.

Some divers swear by the slurpgun; others claim the gadget is too hard to control while maintaining balance in the water, and that a good hand net and a small poke stick to coax a hiding fish into the net are all you really need.

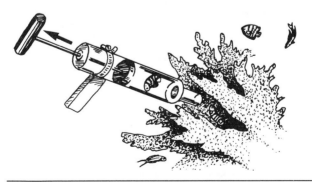

Typical slurpgun, showing operation and adaptability to narrow or tight spaces.

Transporting the Catch

A fish that arrives home dead is no good to anyone; it's a shameful loss that can be avoided by careful attention to how the captives are packed and transported.

Fishes collected on the spur of the moment can be carried home in just about any container handy if you have no choice. I once transported a tiny, beautiful blenny home in the ashtray of my car (washed out, of course), and carted a large tropical marbled eel out of the mountains of Trinidad in a rinsed-out pickle jar. These are obviously not the preferred approaches to the problem, so let's go over a few that are.

The best containers are either picnic coolers or heavy-duty styrofoam fish boxes that most pet shops will either sell or give you. These can be sealed so that the water remains constant—either cool or warm. Placing the captives in total darkness has a calming effect. This is important, as capture stress should be reduced as much as possible at this critical point.

Small, shallow-water trawls can be homemade of heavy wire, netting, a plastic jar, and a set of children's aluminum or Fiberglass skis. The wire frame is attached to the skis with pipe U-clamps and the live-specimen jar secured to the open end of the bag with a heavy rubber band. A large plastic bobber attached to the upper curve of the frame keeps the net upright and open during the tow, which should be done slowly from a small boat. This trawl is most effective in weed beds on smooth sand bottoms.

Do not crowd your fishes in the collecting containers. I collect all I think I'd like to take home and then cull about a third of them before leaving (assuming I've caught many specimens, of course). If the box is uncrowded and the water kept shallow, with a large air surface, you shouldn't need aeration over the short haul, say up to four or five hours. For longer trips, a battery-powered pump that diffuses air through an airstone, available at most bait and tackle shops, works very adequately. In most cases, though, I've found that the sloshing during travel aerates the water enough to ensure safe passage for carefully and prudently packed wild fishes, fresh- or saltwater.

An added touch that helps reduce stress in shy, retiring fishes is clumps of aquatic plants or algae in the collecting bucket and transport container. An object to hide under helps ease the strain of what has to be the most traumatic experience in the fish's life to date.

In transporting fishes at least two principles of sound aquarium management apply: Don't overcrowd and don't quarter a young largemouth bass with baby shiners, no matter how short the trip.

Drawing of Styrofoam fish box with cutaway showing sealed plastic bag containing the catch. The bag should hold only a few inches of water both to prevent the weight of shifting water from breaking the container and to allow some aeration of the water through sloshing. Most pet shops will give away, or sell at minimal cost, their extra shipping boxes.

A Home Away from Home

SETTING UP THE HOME AQUARIUM

"I was born upon thy bank river
My blood flows in thy stream
And thou meanderest forever
At the bottom of my dream."

Henry David Thoreau

Master, I marvel how the fishes live in the sea.
Why, as men do a-land: the great ones eat up the little ones.

Pericles

Removing an animal from familiar surroundings and placing it in a strange environment is a stressful, disorienting experience for it. Just ask any human family that has just completed a move from one city to another in pursuit of a better job or standard of living.

Fishes are a part of their environment perhaps more than any other group of living things. They not only depend upon it for food, shelter, and all of the other good things of life as the rest of us do, they are literally part and parcel of it, being suspended within it as a mote of dust hangs in our terrestrial air. A fish lives in a three-dimensional world where it can move at will and with little effort in any direction it chooses. And its medium, the water, moves through it as well, sustaining the fish and infusing it with life-giving compounds and elements much more directly than air does the land-based animal. If ever an animal, a living organism, perfectly illustrated the concept of Gaia—the earth as a single living organism and all its creatures merely cellular components of the whole—a fish does.

It has long been thought that an aquarium is little more than a container of water housing a few fish and some items of decor to render it presentable to the human eye. In all too many instances, even today, the typical home tank is little more than a chemical soup of preventive and corrective medications, multicolored gravels, plastic plants, and novelty air stones, the whole affair spotlighted by brilliant fluorescent light and tenanted by a beleaguered assortment of store-bought or wild-caught fishes thrown together with little thought given to their compatibility. That many fishes can and do endure this treatment has to be a testament to the fish as a survivor of some magnitude.

Not all that many years ago, setting up and maintaining a container to house fish and other aquatic life in the private home was something of a daunting

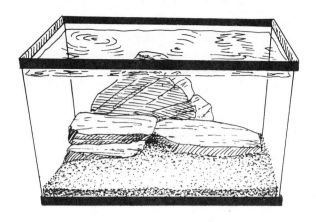

Typical tank set-ups:
Top: rocks and gravel only, for open-water fishes or substrata burrowers.
Center: rocks, bogwood, and artificial hiding places for shy or territorial
fishes. Bottom: Heavily planted tank, for shy, sensitive, or estuarine
fishes.

experience if one were to progress beyond the "goldfish in a bowl" level of commitment. A look at William T. Innes's *Goldfish Varieties and Tropical Aquarium Fishes* (1917 through many reprints) will reveal a task the dimensions of which might give pause to all but the most determined of hobbyists, or at best, those well-schooled in do-it-yourself heavy construction, glasswork, and water chemistry. In the early years of this century, the aquarium hobby was in its infancy. The budding aquarist had little choice but to make much of his own hardware, as there was little reliable equipment available on the market.

Heating and aerating a tank involved complicated, cumbersome, often unreliable pumps and heaters (or even primitive Bunsen burners!), and keeping marine fishes was an enterprise fraught with endless water changes (of natural seawater only) and a host of uncertainties. Few people even considered marine fishes and invertebrates as potential tank tenants in those days. They were deemed too difficult to keep alive.

Today, that's all changed. High-tech wizardry has kept pace with the growing interest in fishkeeping so that there is virtually no aquarium hard- or software, from the tank to the fishes to stock it with, that a hobbyist cannot purchase at a pet shop or aquarium store. Indeed, the question today is often how to avoid succumbing to the lure of sophisticated gadgetry and in the end overdoing a hobby that should ideally be an enjoyable, uncomplicated enterprise in an overly complicated world.

This chapter presents the basics of both freshwater and marine aquarium set up and maintenance using state-of-the-art but basic equipment. (Readers seeking further information will find several titles in the bibliography of this book which cover the subject in comprehensive detail.) I stress good old horse sense, in lieu of an unwise dependence on chemical test kits or a pharmacopoeia of chemicals and potions. The confines of an aquarium are not, nor will they ever be, a little piece of nature transplanted into your living room. There is simply no room to allow the countless and subtle cycles of nature to spin themselves out and produce the incredibly complex result so casually observed in a square foot of water outdoors. The aquarium is "nature" the way a wheat field is virgin prairie, but that's all right. We're providing an environment that will replicate the original as closely as possible so that the fish that must live in it are healthy and as free from stress as possible.

The hardware required will be discussed generically rather than by brand names (undergravel filters, submersible canister filters, etc.), leaving it up to the individual hobbyist to confer with a trusted aquarium shop on specific makes. Most of the larger manufacturers of aquarium hardware are quite reputable and will back up their products with some sort of warranty.

The preparation of quarters to house native freshwater and marine fishes differs from the tropical side of the hobby in only a few fundamentals:

• Duplicating the appearance of the natural habitat is the desired aim, thus bleached coral, dayglo red gravel, or mermaid air stones in a tank containing mudminnows and pirate perch is an esthetic no-no.

• Wild fishes, in particular the predators or highly territorial fishes, are subject to stress and crowding, thus the larger the tank, the better. This is much more important than in the goldfish-guppy side of the hobby, where the fish have spent their entire lives in an aquarium.

• The majority of wild-caught, native fishes will not thrive on, or even accept, the convenient, inexpensive prepared fish flakes or pellets. Prepare yourself for either the modest but additional expense of live or frozen foods or for the intriguing experience of raising or collecting food yourself.

• Farm-raised or wild-caught tropical fishes cannot survive if released into the wild far from home, but those natives collected nearby certainly can. Whenever possible, make the native fish hobby a two-way trip for your fish. Enjoy them, learn from them, and then release them where you got them. Believe me, there's a satisfaction to be gotten from this recycling approach.

The Freshwater Aquarium

Although you can buy old steel-frame aquariums at yard sales and flea markets for next to nothing, they're not offered for sale at pet shops anymore, having been superseded over the past 20 years by the all-glass tank. In spite of its fragile appearance, a well-made, all-glass aquarium is much more reliable, safer, and less likely to leak than the sturdy steel framers. They cost roughly a dollar a gallon, so the price of your most basic piece of equipment will not be at all unreasonable.

In purchasing a tank, there are more things to think of than its stated capacity to hold water and the dealer's willingness to take it back if it doesn't.

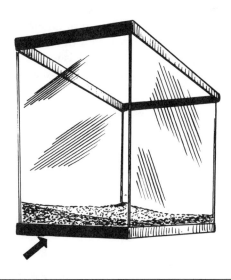

All-glass tank, showing plastic top-and-bottom support frame.

One of them is shape. The best tanks present the broadest expanse of the water's surface to the air for the most effective exchange of gases. This means that those tall, narrow aquariums that look so attractive in walls and office lobbies are not the kindest to the fish that must live in them. The best aquarium design is the long rather than the high tank, for this offers the wider water surface without sacrificing viewing area.

Glass tanks are made of plate rather than window glass and are damage-proof under normal handling. With water weighing 8.3 pounds per gallon, a filled tank should not be moved. The force exerted by the inevitable water shift may well stress it so that it will crack on the spot or spring a leak later. The better commercially made all-glass tanks are tested at the factory for leaks, and thus the chances of buying a leaker are small. I never have.

The 20-gallon tank is the best size for the aquarist with limited space. But for the neophyte native fish collector wishing to enter the hobby in a modest way and make any initial mistakes on a correspondingly modest scale, a ten-gallon tank is a good starter.

Many pet shops offer a ten-gallon tank complete with light hood, small vibrator pump and filter, a bag of gravel, a few other accessories, and sometimes even the stand to support the tank, at very reasonable cost. These packages are offered as an inducement to enter the aquarium hobby at minimal expense (and subsequently the store, as a return customer).

The location of the tank can be an important choice. It is often written that a window location should provide at least two to four hours of direct sunlight a day. But this is optional because modern aquarium lighting equipment offers a suitable alternative to natural light and makes the algae-growth problem easier to control—or to manage, if the fish are vegetarians. The tank's location can be any place in the house where the floor is level and will support the weight of the tank and its contents, and where the tank is not subjected to unusual temperature fluctuations, such as near an air conditioner.

New tanks should be thoroughly cleaned with a mild salt solution (no soap) and then rinsed with clean water. Once a tank is in position and contains sand or water, it should not be moved. Any movement may stress its seams.

The Substrate

The bottom of the native fish tank used for fishes with relatively unspecialized habitat requirements (sunfishes, shiners, catfishes, killies) can have a layer of medium- to coarse-grained, natural-colored quartz gravel. It's available in any pet shop. The gravel should be rinsed well and placed in the aquarium so that it slopes gently from a depth of two to three inches at the back to about one inch at the front. This will allow any waste and debris generated by the fish and plants to gravitate down the slope and accumulate at the front of the tank, greatly facilitating its removal. A greater rear depth also provides a better anchoring base for live plants, which should be arranged so they form a horseshoe-shaped wall along the sides and back of the tank. This leaves the front and center—or at least one-third of the tank's area—free as swimming room for the fishes and viewing space.

Stones and Other Items

Depending on the species involved, the decor can take a number of forms and serve an equal number of purposes. Nearly all setups will be enhanced by a gnarled, twisted cedar root or two as a centerpiece, surrounded by stones or rocks collected from the environment of your fish. Although it's assumed that the native fish-oriented aquarist will demonstrate leanings for things natural and thus shun ceramic divers, sunken ships, and busty mermaids, man-made objects such as old clay flower pots and ancient bricks can look attractive and will serve as hideaways for shy or nocturnal fish. In landscaping your tank, place taller items to the rear and smaller to the front. There's nothing wrong with using one of those underwater landscape-style tank backgrounds. They're far better to look at than a blank wall or electrical fixtures.

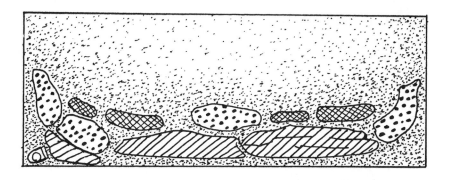

Front and top views of typical "rockscape" in an aquarium. The general rule: taller objects toward the back, swimming space front and center.

Cross-section of a landscaped tank, showing commercially available "rock wall" and use of larger stones as retaining walls for the substrate. Remember, taller objects toward the rear!

As with decor items purchased from a pet shop, scrub and rinse objects collected in nature before putting them in the tank to avoid the possibility of introducing parasites or contaminants. If there's any question about the water quality of the site where a root, rock, or other object was taken, soak it in a moderate aquarium dechlorinating solution overnight and rinse it thoroughly in clean water before setting it in the tank.

A good rule of thumb in decorating a tank is to avoid creating such a jumbled and complex habitat that the fishes or scavengers cannot reach the food that escapes them in the more open sections. The natural cycle and multitude of tiny organisms clean up leftovers (or dead animals) in nature. In the confines of the aquarium, the organic debris will quickly decompose, with very obvious esthetic and sanitary consequences.

Filtration and Aeration

Although a wide variety of filter units is available today, each laying claim to being the quietest, most reliable, and most effective, all have their good points. Choice of a suitable filter depends on the size of the tank, the degree of current and circulation required, and the needs and the number of the fish.

The filters in most common use include the undergravel filter, the outside power filter, the submersible canister, and the vibrator pump and box filter. The vibrator/box filter is the most primitive (substitute "cheapest"), but it is adequate for the smaller tank containing shy fish that prefer standing water and dense plant growth. They would not thrive in the powerful currents produced by an undergravel powerhead or a canister outflow.

The undergravel filter (the UG, in aquarium parlance) has enjoyed great popularity in recent years as, with the exception of its lift tubes, it is essentially an "out-of-sight" unit that uses the substrate itself as the filtering element and thus requires little maintenance. Properly set up, the UG is highly effective, though the gravel should be periodically stirred and washed with a siphoning device to clear it of the accumulated debris that will reduce its effectiveness.

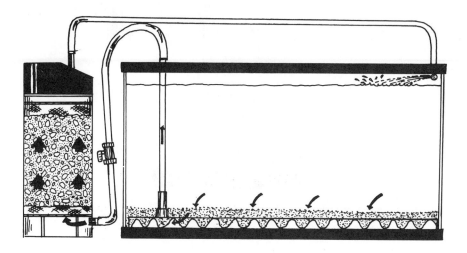

Diagram of typical canister/undergravel filter, showing dolomite or charcoal filter element in the canister and return spray bar in the tank. This system is one of the best for marine setups.

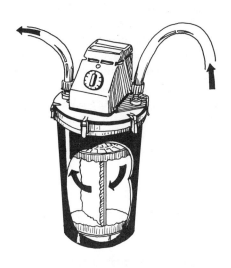

Canister filter, showing flow-through filter element. This is a powerful, efficient unit and may be used in conjunction with an undergravel filter. The water usually re-enters the tank through a perforated spray bar.

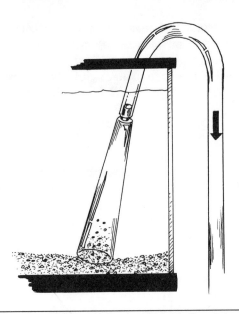

Siphon-type "gravel washer." The wide plastic funnel allows lighter debris to be drawn up and out without siphoning the gravel along with it.

Don't be lulled into purchasing a powerful, sophisticated, and expensive unit on the grounds that bigger or more complex has to be better. Very often, just the opposite is true. If you have any doubts or questions, ask your fishkeeping friends what they'd recommend or talk it over with a pet shop employee who has a reputation for candor and good advice.

Although most modern filter units aerate the water to a degree with spray-bars, powerheads, or filter outflows, additional aeration can be provided for a tank of fish requiring oxygen-rich water by airstones. These vary from small and inexpensive cylindrical stones of porous material to "airbars" and "bubble wands" available in various lengths. Airstones are connected to a standard vibrator pump through a flexible plastic air line and are effective for up to a year before they begin to clog with debris and need replacement. The most effective bubbles are medium-sized rather than misty or large.

The Water

To prepare a native fish tank, collect water in five-gallon containers at the habitat site when possible and use it to set up the tank in advance of the actual collecting.

This eliminates the need for aging tap water and adding chemicals to remove the other chemical additives present in drinking water that spell disaster for fishes.

The water requirements of wild fishes vary. A bluegill sunfish taken from a farm pond or city park lake exposed to myriad contaminants will display a far greater tolerance for raw tap water than will a darter or sculpin taken from a clear mountain brook or a bluespotted sunfish netted from a soft, acid-water pinewoods bog.

Sensitive fishes should always be at least acclimated to confinement in their native water and then slowly weaned over to conditioned and properly aged tap water if this is an absolute necessity.

If you must use tap water, condition it by either placing it outdoors in buckets for about 48 hours, allowing exposure to air and sunlight to cleanse it, or by aerating it with a vibrator pump and air stone for a day, permitting the chlorine and other gases to escape through the bubble action. Chloramines are added to public drinking water in most major cities and their environs. These are chlorine and ammonia compounds, used in place of chlorine to control bacteria, and they are toxic to fishes, as well as to their sperm and eggs. Chloramines are more difficult to eliminate from tap water than chlorine, but can be removed by the chemical sodium thiosulphate, which is available at most pet shops under several brand names. Use about three drops per gallon of water and dechlorimination will occur almost immediately. I'd rather avoid fooling around with drugs and go natural. A few bucketfuls of lake or river water is certainly safer.

Whatever the source, the water can be introduced into the empty but landscaped aquarium with the least disturbance to the decor by pouring it onto a

The most basic filtration/aeration setup: the inexpensive vibrator pump and corner filter. This arrangement is ideal for species requiring dense plant growth and quiet water.

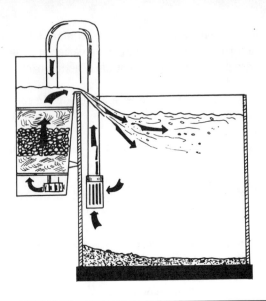

Diagram of typical outside power filter, showing flow of water through layers of charcoal and filter floss. Charcoal or activated carbon can be rinsed and reused for several months, although it loses it "water sweetening" ability within two weeks.

folded sheet of newspaper laid on the substrate or into a cupped hand. The latter eliminates the need for gingerly hauling a soggy slab of waterlogged Daily Planet from the tank.

Ideally, the aquarium, with its water and plants, should be allowed to stand for between six and ten days before fishes are introduced. This will allow you to keep a weather eye peeled for any potential problems such as heater or filter failures or contaminants in either the substrate or decor items that might not make themselves known immediately. It also enables the tank to develop a healthy bacterial culture before fishes are introduced.

Plants and Planting

The subject of aquarium plants—whether to go natural or artificial, wild or cultivated—has long been an object of discussion among experienced aquarists. There's no doubt that a tank filled with healthy, living plants is very attractive and is a closer duplication of nature than one filled with plastic.

The great majority of aquarium plants are tropical and substropical species that have been commercially propagated, and as they don't undergo seasonal cycles to the degree that temperate aquatic species do, they are better suited to the constant environment of the home aquarium.

Many of the temperate varieties of native species, such as *Myriophyllum, Elodea,* and *Utricularia,* undergo diebacks in the fall, and this seasonal event occurs in the aquarium as well, creating debris and a general mess. For this reason, I recommend that the person lacking a green thumb buy plants, deciding that exact duplication of the local environment is not practical and a healthy living plant of any kind is better than none.

Which way to go—plastic or the real thing? Artificial plants today are so convincingly made that it takes a close look to unmask the imposter.

Plastic plants are often scorned by serious aquarists, but they are the easy way out for the hobbyist either unable or unwilling to cultivate the real thing. Given the state of the art of the artificial today (most are astoundingly faithful copies of the originals), there is nothing wrong with going plastic, either to complement a few live plants, or as a total alternative. Because many fish species will either eat or uproot carefully positioned live plants, securely anchored plastic plants may well be the only alternative to a barren tank.

If you're contemplating maintaining live plants, bear in mind that the substrate assumes considerably greater importance. Most plants will not thrive in a substrate that is either too fine or too coarse; the former will pack down and prevent adequate breathing of the roots, as well as encourage fouling of the tank. An overly coarse gravel hinders the normal rooting of plants and also allows uneaten food items or other debris to fall beyond the reach of scavengers or cleaning devices. A medium grain aquarium gravel is best. Consult with your local pet shop and follow its recommendations.

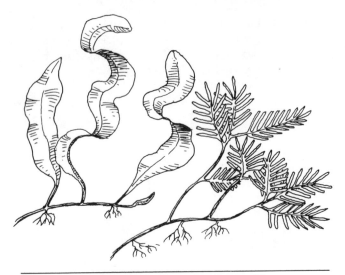

Variation in the leaf form of Caulerpa prolifera.

Common commercially available aquarium plants; bunched Anacharis, *potted* Crytocoryne.

Heaters

Most temperate native fish aquariums, both freshwater and marine, will not require a heater (in fact, the opposite may be true), but there are exceptions. Tropical marine butterflyfishes or angelfishes, collected in New York or New

Jersey in September in waters registering about 76°, should have that level maintained through the winter. Likewise, mollies or goldear killies collected in Mississippi or Louisiana and taken north to Ohio should not be kept at room temperature if this falls below 70° for any length of time. These fishes as well as other extreme southern forms are sensitive to low temperatures and will go off their feed and develop the shimmies and other disorders.

Most other temperate native species, in particular the sunfishes, will benefit from a period of lower temperatures during the winter, though it will be impossible, of course, to duplicate true winter dormancy levels in your living room. An exception to this would be an area where there is a considerable fluctuation of air temperature over hours or days, such as an office closed for the weekend or a home in which the heat is turned far down or off at night. In this case, a heater set at about 72° is advisable.

A number of types of reliable, inexpensive heaters are on the market today. I prefer the non-submersible, tank-rim type over the submersible because I don't like fiddling with an electrical appliance under water, no matter how safe it's supposed to be. But the choice is yours, for both types are reliable. If you have any doubts, ask your local fish dealer what he uses in his own display tanks, if his tanks are individually heated, and go by that, as pet shops can't afford unexpected heater failures that may chill (or boil) hundreds of dollars' worth of fish.

Turn off or unplug a heater if you plan to drain more than half the tank. I can say from personal experience that a rather impressive and potentially dangerous mini-explosion will be the result if you don't.

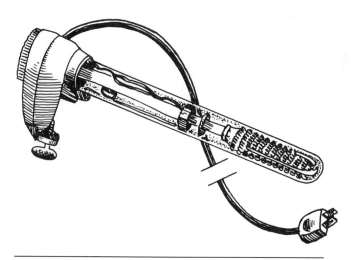

Tank clip-on, on non-submersible, heater. This design has been around for many years and is quite reliable, although a finger-dip check of the water temperature every day doesn't hurt—just in case.

A Home Away from Home—Setting Up the Home Aquarium 🐟 **43**

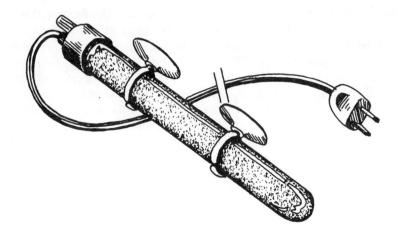

Typical submersible heater. These units are designed to be used totally submerged and may be attached to the tank's sides or laid on the substrate out of sight.

Aquarium Lights

The modern aquarium hood serves as both a light unit and snug-fitting cover. Unless you have custom or odd-sized tanks, you should use one. Light hoods are not expensive. They are made of corrosion-resistant plastic (most important in marine setups). Most models shield the bulbs from the water and any aeration spray with clear plastic panels. This eliminates most of the danger of rust in the sockets and circuits.

In most hoods, the light unit is centered over the tank, though models can be purchased with the lights positioned over the front or rear of the tank for different effects. The closer to the front, the better, for the fish will then be front-lit, rather than back-lit, which results in a school of silhouettes. Check the individual species accounts for the preferred light levels of each species and purchase the appropriate wattage in bulbs.

Incandescent bulbs throw a lot more heat than fluorescent tubes, so if you use the former in a tank containing, say, darters, trout, or freshwater or marine sculpins, all of which will perish at high temperatures, get the lowest wattage that will still illuminate the tank. I normally use two 15 or 25 watt bulbs in my cold water tanks and they do an adequate illumination job.

If you use higher wattages in a cool water tank, leave the cover slightly open at a place over the center of the tank, rather than near an edge, which is where most active fish will attempt a jump. This will allow most of the heat generated to escape and avoid a dangerous buildup, which won't take long during the warmer months. A temperate or cold water tank should not be lighted more than nine to twelve hours, particularly during the summer. Fluorescent lights are more satisfactory for maintaining lower water temperatures in cool water marine aquariums.

To reiterate: Shop frugally but wisely for the basic hardware. Don't allow yourself to be talked into buying complicated and sophisticated gadgetry that may cause problems later on. Instead, rely on a reputable pet dealer's advice. Allow plenty of space rather than opting for a too-small tank in the interest of saving a few dollars. It's far better for the fish, and a roomy tank is much more forgiving of chemistry catastrophes and other mistakes. Exercise patience when aging the new tank, and introduce the fishes a few at a time. Obey the time-honored "golden rules" of fishkeeping: Don't overcrowd, don't overfeed, and keep only compatible tankmates. That way, you'll have a good start on a fascinating and educating hobby.

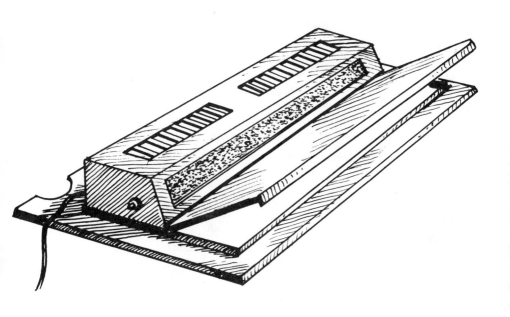

Inexpensive cover and light hood, showing lid for feeding and servicing.

Aging the Tank

One of the cardinal sins of the tropical fish hobby and the one that causes the most grief early on is impatience. The tank is set up and looks great. The water is crystal clear and the whole affair positively vibrates with color and symmetry. It looks squeaky clean, right down to those little tiny bubbles sticking to the glass and decor.

Now—right now—is the time to run out and either buy or collect the fishes and dump 'em in, right? That's wrong, of course, but new aquarium hobbyists find it almost impossible to wait for the tank to culture or break in, and they introduce the fishes much too soon.

Ideally, the new tank should be allowed to remain fallow and empty with all systems, including living plants, in place for about a week before introducing any fish, especially if tap water has been used to fill it. This way, harmful gases such as chlorine will have time to dissipate, the water has time to age and develop a healthy bacteria culture, and the reliability of the hardware can be established. For the native fish aquarium, you should fill the new setup with water from the place where you will get the fish. This will reduce the acclimation time somewhat, but it's still a wise move to allow the tank to settle in at least two to four days before introducing the inhabitants.

Introduce the fish into their new quarters in the evening and allow them to acclimate overnight, with the lights out and a minimum of outside disturbance, such as eager and anxious onlookers. The fishes should not be fed any cut or prepared foods for at least 24 hours. They will be under considerable capture stress and probably won't eat anyway. If fed, this poses an immediate problem of uneaten foods in the new tank. When offered food for the first time, most wild fishes will accept live brine shrimp or tubifex worms, which are active and as much like natural prey as any commercially available food. A small portion of live brine shrimp can be introduced into the tank the first night, as it will not spoil if uneaten.

The Marine Tank: The salt water aquarium technique differs only slightly from that of its freshwater counterpart, and the steps outlined for the latter can be followed—up to a point.

Culturing the new marine tank is only a bit more involved, but here the patience will pay greater dividends to the new aquarist.

The hobbyist has two options, depending on one's proximity to an ocean— using natural seawater or one of the commercially available marine mixes, which are perfected to the degree that they contain most, but not all, trace elements found in seawater.

When preparing a viable home for marine creatures, the environment must be as close as possible to that from which the fishes will be collected. Take water from the intended collecting site and fill the aquarium, adding some filamentous algae and a few hardy fish, such as mummichogs, as culturing agents. If, within two to four days, the tank is clear and the animals and plants healthy, it is ready for the addition of collected specimens.

Using artificial seawater mixes presents few problems with temperate and subtropical native marine fishes and invertebrates. With the exception of true reef fishes, which require stable salinity levels, most fishes are quite tolerant of wide shifts in salinity in the natural environment, especially near estuaries and inlets. As long as they are given an adequate period of acclimation, most marine fishes will suffer no ill effects when introduced into an aquarium containing artificial seawater mixed according to the manufacturer's instructions.

The new captives should be dripped before being placed in the tank. Run a length of quarter-inch airline tubing from the tank down to the bucket containing the fish and start a siphon. The dribble of the new water into the old will create a satisfactory mix in about 20 minutes and the fishes will adjust with no problems.

Accessories

The modern aquarium hobbyist has only to visit a pet shop or pick up a copy of one of the aquarium magazines to get a look at the virtual galaxy of equipment and gadgets available to one starting to keep fishes. While much of this gear is quite practical and essential to the successful operation of the home aquarium, some of it is not, and knowing the difference can be very helpful. Below is a list of the equipment that, over the years, I have come to accept as essential, or at least a good idea, for enjoyment of the hobby without overcomplication:

• Gravel washer or siphon. This is a half-inch plastic tube with a flared funnel at one end that allows the aquarist to remove debris and clean the substrate without siphoning up the gravel as well.

• Algae scraper. There are two types, the sponge cleaner and the old-fashioned type equipped with a safety razor blade. Both work well, though I prefer the latter because of its ease in handling and its thoroughness

• Hand nets. Keep a supply of various sizes on hand for the fish-catching challenges that will surely be presented you.

• Brushes. Stiff cleaning brushes are a must for scouring filters, lift tubes, and other gear during periodic cleaning and filter element changes.

• Plastic pitcher. Ideal for adding water. If you wash it in soap, rinse and dry it thoroughly before using it for aquarium water.

• Tank divider. This is inexpensive and will come in handy more times than you might imagine if you're keeping fish of something less than placid temperament.

• Observation shield. This can be inexpensive if made of heavy cardboard and taped to the front of an aquarium. It permits unobtrusive observation of sensitive or breeding fish (see illustration). While many wild fishes will tame rapidly under good aquarium care, most will not spawn or carry out more complicated natural activities if they are in a tank exposed to much human activity.

• Reference library. Many fine books on specific fish groups and the techniques of aquarium maintenance and care are available. A few of the more comprehensive and in-depth titles are listed in the bibliography.

Two popular algae scraper designs—the blade type and scouring pad. The latter requires more pressure to remove stubborn growth.

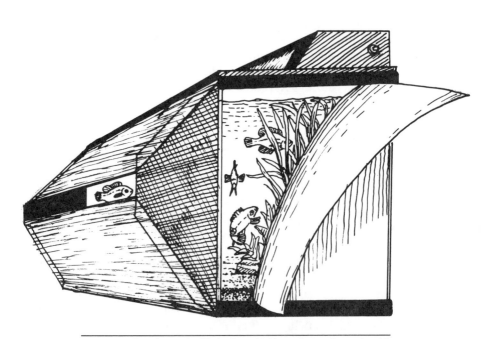

Aquarium observation shield. Such a shield can be easily made with heavy cardboard taped at the seams and hung from the front of the tank. The tank's sides can also be covered with brown paper to provide complete seclusion for the inhabitants.

Feeding the Fishes

The question of what, how much, and how often to feed fishes kept in aquariums has long been debated in aquarium literature. By far the most important requirement, however, is to use common sense when dropping food items into the tank. The individual food requirements of the species covered in this book are discussed in the species accounts in Chapter 4, but a few words on what has worked best for me over the years may be helpful.

The time-honored rule of thumb in aquarium circles has always been: "feed the fish no more than they can eat in five minutes without leaving leftovers." This is generally good advice, but as in all aspects of life, there are exceptions to the rule. The five-minute "golden rule" of feeding applies mainly to prepared or "dead" foods, such as frozen foods or cut fish or meat. These will quickly spoil if left uneaten for any length of time (depending on how warm the environment is). When offering any of these types of food, adhere strictly to the five-minute rule and you can't go wrong.

Live foods are another matter, though even here, pounds of live brine shrimp, tubifex worms, or feeder fish should not be dumped into the tank on the blissful assumption that the would-be diners "will get 'em all sooner or later." They may, or they may not; this is bad feeding practice that can create problems of oxygen depletion, food animals dying and sinking out of sight—or being sucked into the filtration system and lodging and dying there. You can be a bit more liberal in the introduction of live food items into the aquarium, but not much more.

Carnivore, omnivore, or vegetarian? This is, of course, the first determination that must be made for a particular species before determining the best food for it—and how to present the food so that it will be eaten. To varying degrees, newly-collected fishes can be difficult to induce to feed, but most will respond to the presence of live food. However, one must tailor the live food offered to the recipient; a five-inch pickerel will ignore a brine shrimp swimming by, while a least killifish will not only refuse to eat a feeder guppy but will likely be attacked by it!

Herbivorous fishes can usually be induced to begin (and continue) feeding by the temporary introduction of natural algae and other plant material and detritus collected from their original habitat. Once they are thoroughly acclimated, parboiled fresh romaine lettuce, mustard greens, cucumber rinds, or vegetable-based prepared foods are often an acceptable and accepted substitute for most vegetarian fish. Again, remove any uneaten greens within a day or two to avoid spoilage.

Live Foods

Given the variety of prepared foods available to the aquarium hobbyist today, live foods are generally considered more a supplement to the fish diet rather than the principal source of nourishment. Despite this, wild fishes benefit from a varied live food diet.

In the early years of the aquarium hobby and the science of aquaculture, live foods played a much more important role in fish nourishment than they do today.

My own philosophy is that given the low cost and near-universal availability of such common food animals as brine shrimp, tubifex, and bloodworms, offering living foods to predatory fishes that, for the most part, are accustomed to little else in nature, is the best course to follow. Most aquarium stores today offer a good selection of live (as opposed to frozen or freeze-dried) food, and if your involvement in the hobby is great enough, it will be simple to gather your own live foods when you're collecting fish or securing water for water changes. Either way, the ready availability of live foods and their reasonable cost make their use a wise and cost-effective move. By "live foods," I am referring to those smaller organisms such as tiny crustaceans and insect larvae commonly eaten by small to medium-sized fishes, rather than to such larger animals as bait minnows, nightcrawlers, or tadpoles normally fed to larger predatory fish.

Brine shrimp (*Artemia salina*) are without a doubt the single most widely fed live food today. Uncounted billions of the tiny crustacean are harvested in the saline lakes of Utah, California, and New Mexico, and artificially raised both commercially in large vats and by thousands of individual aquarists in gallon jars filled with salt solution and equipped with an air stone. For many years, brine shrimp have been sold through mail order as pets under the "some-stretch-of-the-imagination" term "sea monkeys."

Brine shrimp are an excellent live food, though they should not be fed exclusively as the nutrients provided by the hard-shelled, mostly calciferous little creatures are often inadequate for most active fishes. These shrimp can be readily purchased live, frozen, or freeze-dried from most well-stocked pet shops.

They can be easily raised from packaged eggs available at minimum expense. The procedure involves placing a quarter-teaspoonful of eggs in a gallon jar or slightly larger container containing fresh water dosed with two rounded tablespoons of seasalt mix. The temperature should be maintained at between 75° and 80° and the water subjected to gentle aeration with an air stone. At that temperature, the eggs hatch in about 24 hours, and the tiny young, or *nauplii*, can be concentrated at the surface for easy collection by directing a flashlight's beam at one side of the jar. Brine shrimp undergo 12 molts before reaching adulthood. They are about a quarter-inch in length in about three weeks.

Live brine shrimp can be purchased at most pet shops for between 50 cents and a dollar a portion, which is enough to give four to six four-inch fish a single feeding.

Tubifex worms, also called mud or sludge worms, are probably tied with

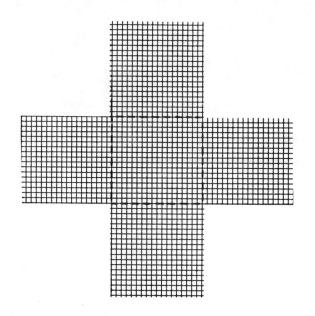

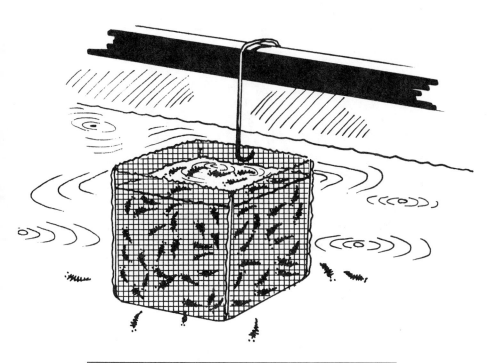

*A brine shrimp cage, made from plastic screening, slowly releases shrimp
for constant feeders such as puffers and filefish.*

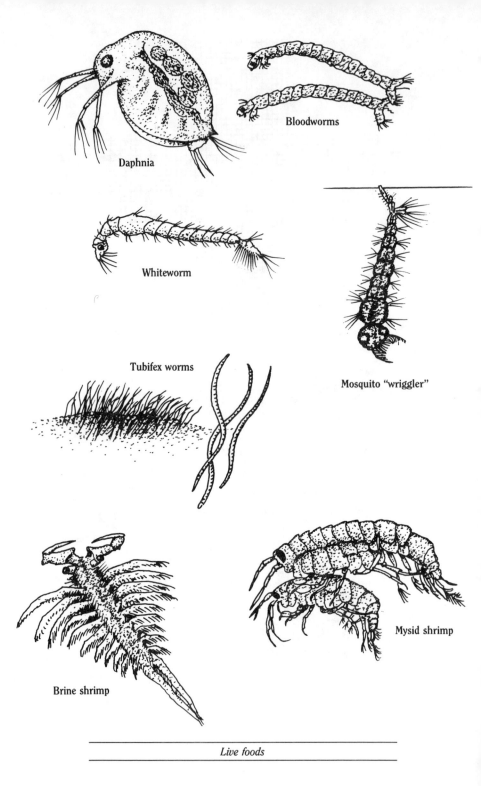

Daphnia

Bloodworms

Whiteworm

Mosquito "wriggler"

Tubifex worms

Brine shrimp

Mysid shrimp

Live foods

brine shrimp as a popular and inexpensive live food, and will be eagerly eaten by virtually all freshwater fishes and most marine species. Tubifex (sometimes incorrectly called "tubiflex") worms are creatures of degraded aquatic habitats, usually along watercourses containing raw sewage and other organic debris. The worms congregate in areas of quieter water flow and form large, dense colonies in the rank mud, slowly and rhythmically waving their lower bodies above the substrate so that the entire colony appears much as a vast, moving reddish carpet. Years ago, many serious aquarists grimly undertook the odiferous chore of collecting live tubifex, but with the ready availability of the animals in the hobby market today, that's seldom, if ever, necessary. Most pet shop tubifex are harvested in Mexico today.

Tubifex are an excellent, if somewhat rich, native fish food. Like brine shrimp, the worms should not be offered to fish exclusively but given with other live or prepared foods. Ideally, these worms should be rinsed after purchase and before each feeding as they may harbor disease organisms or parasites. Kept under refrigeration in a shallow, covered (a non-aquarist spouse will definitely appreciate that consideration!) container and rinsed daily, tubifex worms will remain alive for several weeks.

Bloodworms and whiteworms are not worms at all, but the larvae of midges (Chironomidae). Usually collectively called chironomids, they vary from bright red to nearly transparent in color and average ¼ to ¾-inch in length. These larvae creep over mud bottoms or can swim by using a twisting or wriggling motion, an action that at once attracts the attention of hungry fish. These worms are an excellent fish food and also may be purchased frozen or freeze-dried, the former offering the most nutritional value.

In spite of the obvious hazards involved in handling them and their intentional introduction into a home, mosquito larvae, or wigglers, are among the best natural fish foods and have been recognized as such for many years. They are collected by sweeping a fine-meshed collecting net through standing, fish-free water (especially woodland pools) where the wrigglers can be observed. The larvae can either be fed as collected or frozen for future use. Fish should be fed only the number of wrigglers they can consume within a few minutes, otherwise the survivors will metamorphose and seek an exit through any chinks in the aquarium hood and generally make life miserable and sleep impossible.

Daphnia pulex, also called "water fleas" or simply daphnia, are a live food seldom available at pet shops because they are rarely cultured commercially. They are easily collected in the wild if a population can be located. They are found in many aquatic habitats but only in those of higher and active organic decomposition will they be observed in any real abundance. Heavily fertilized waters, such as ponds near dumps, farming areas, or in parks, often contain daphnia in huge numbers. They can be dip netted with ease. Daphnia usually appear in cycles, or "pulses," and are best collected in spring or winter (often through the ice), and during the early morning hours when they are both more active and more easily seen before the sunlight becomes too bright and drives them lower in the water column.

Amphipods, mysid shrimp, and other smaller marine invertebrates often can be collected when they mass in spring and summer for breeding. They make excellent live foods for marine fishes. Mysid shrimp, in particular, are one of the best marine live foods. They often gather in huge swarms near the surface in quieter waters, such as in estuaries and around marina docks, where they can be dip netted with ease. They can be fed live, or frozen in small, shallow containers so that they form flat cakes that can be broken apart and fed to fishes later on.

The list of potential live foods is nearly endless and their availability is limited only by the individual aquarist's degree of motivation and willingness to either cultivate a supply or collect it in the wild. An extremely comprehensive and informative book on the subject is *Encyclopedia of Live Foods,* by Charles O. Masters, published by TFH Publications of Neptune City, New Jersey.

Releasing Native Fishes

If any aspect of the native fish hobby requires a strong environmental conscience, this is surely it. Imagine the dilemma: you collected an appealing one-inch bullhead last summer in a lake about 100 miles from home. For about six months the fish remained at a manageable size and got along with everyone else in the tank. One day, however, you take a hard look at things and notice that your other fishes seem to be dimishing in number. The bullhead has, in less than a year, become a seven-inch behemoth with a bottomless pit behind its mouth, and you suddenly have a problem—how to get rid of it. Your fishkeeping friends aren't thrilled by the idea of adding a monochrome grey, whiskered eating machine to their collections; the local pet shop owner slams his door in your face; and you really don't feel like driving 100 miles to dump an oversized catfish back in its home water. What do do?

This dilemma is a familiar one in the native fish hobby and one I have faced many times. For one reason or another, there will come a time when you will have to dispose of a few or all of your fishes. If you were a tropical fish hobbyist, you could usually take that unwanted oscar to your local pet shop and swap it for some live foods. Most native fishes, however, cannot be legally resold, and rank and file aquarium hobbyists do not want them. In addition, it is illegal and inhumane simply to dump a freshwater fish in any old freshwater pond, or a saltwater fish off any dock at any time of the year.

One of the basic tenets of the native fish hobby is that if you removed the fish from its natural habitat and placed it in an aquarium, you are responsible for its welfare while it is under your care—and for seeing that it is returned to its natural environment when you can no longer keep it. Whenever possible, the fish should be taken to its place of collection and released there, at a time of year (warm) when it will be able to find food and shelter. The casual release of a fish outside its natural range or its specific habitat (e.g., a park pond) may solve your problem but may present a terrible one to the fish and, just perhaps, to the environment.

Here are a few suggestions for making the disposal of an unwanted fish easier:

• Join a native fish association or tropical aquarium society. There just may be a member itching to get his hands on that two-foot, ever-hungry eel you are dying to get rid of.

• A public aquarium *may* be willing to accept an unwanted native species, depending on how valued or unusual it is, but call first.

• If you've collected a species known to put on size quickly, such as any of the bullheads, gars, or the bowfin, plan to keep the fish only through the summer months and release it in the fall—before icy weather makes it impossible to do so without killing the fish.

Conservation and the Law

(PERMIT, OFFICER? WHAT PERMIT?)

It used to be that going out and catching or killing anything in the woods, fields, lakes and the sea meant simply picking up a gun, a fishing rod or a net and going out and doing it—no questions asked, no limit imposed, and no accounting to anybody.

The fact that our ancestors did just that with so much joyful abandon and a regrettable lack of foresight and humanity is the principal reason why you can't go out and do that anymore. The literature is rife with depressing, indeed, horrifying accounts of slaughter and abuse of the landscape and the creatures that called it home. It's an endless dirge and very possibly what may end up on the epitaph of our own species.

Late twentieth century minds have only recently begun to look around, notice just what we've done to Mother Earth, and wonder whether there is time left to us to repair the damage and reestablish at least some modicum of harmony with our planet—the only one we've got—as ecologists have been telling us for years.

Henry David Thoreau stands today as a founding father of environmental conscience (and civil disobedience). He was a poet as well as the somewhat eccentric nature lover his contemporaries thought he was. Among his efforts was the ditty: "Any fool can make a rule, and every fool will mind it." It was that attitude that got him into hot water with the powers-that-be of his time. For Thoreau was a true Renaissance man who was outspoken about the natural world in a day when other men saw it as raw, forbidding wilderness, and worse, as a mere commodity, to be exploited and tamed according to biblical edict— pretty much as developers and corporate entities do today.

The man of Walden lived when fish and game laws were virtually nonexistent and the fishes were unmercifully hounded right along with the rest of animal creation ("pity the poor shad—who hears the fishes when they cry?"). Although Thoreau poked fun at his fellow man and their proliferating rules and regulations, and most especially at the constraints of city life that spawned them, he surely must have foreseen that distant day when those minor little irritations of modern society would become necessary to the very survival of the land and its creatures, including mankind.

So here we are, in the last decade of the twentieth century, and Thoreau's rules are very much the reality of our day. When it comes to collecting and keeping native fish, there are more than enough rules to go around. The would-be native fish aquarist should have a working knowledge of the yeas and nays, the wherefores and how-muches of the legal side of what used to be a most simple, almost idyllic pursuit.

State and Local Laws

Although many cities and counties, particularly in the South and Southwest, have regulations and ordinances pertaining to the keeping of reptiles and amphibians (especially those considered potentially dangerous if escaped or liberated), few are concerned with what you keep in an aquarium once it's safely there. In other words, some southern municipalities may be concerned that walking catfishes or piranhas may find their way into the local parks and waterways via fishkeepers' tanks, but the import, sale, and possession of these fishes are either prohibited or controlled primarily at the state and federal level.

All states and provinces have laws controlling the collecting, holding, and acquisition of native wildlife and most regulate the traffic in exotics (any fishes not native to a state or province). In 1989 Texas enacted legislation controlling

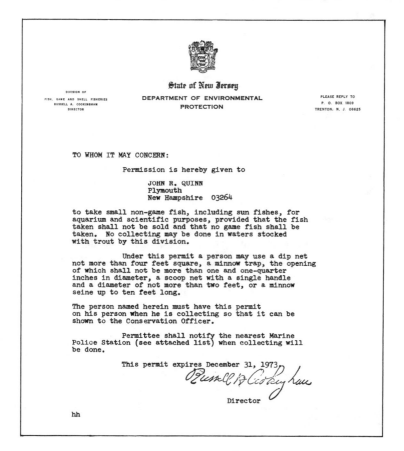

State of New Jersey

DIVISION OF
FISH, GAME AND SHELL FISHERIES
RUSSELL A. COOKINGHAM
DIRECTOR

DEPARTMENT OF ENVIRONMENTAL
PROTECTION

Scientific Collecting Permit

PLEASE REPLY TO
P. O. BOX 1809
TRENTON, N. J. 08625

TO WHOM IT MAY CONCERN:

Permission is hereby given to

John R. Quinn
85 Highland Place
Ridgefield Park, NJ
THE SQUAM LAKES SCIENCE CENTER

to take Johnny Darters and Mummichog from the waters of N. J.
Pine Barrens, selected lakes in Northern New Jersey and the
Ramapo River, by 10 Foot minnow seine and hand nets for
gathering material and observation for a forth coming book
on native fishes. No collecting may be done in waters
stocked with trout by this Division. All game fish must be
returned to the water unharmed.

The person named herein must have this permit on
his person when he is collecting so that it can be shown to
the Fish and Game Conservation Officer.

Permittee shall notify the nearest Marine Police
Station (see attached list) when collecting will be done.

This permit expires September 30, 1974, at which
time a report of collecting activities must be submitted to
the Division of Fish, Game and Shell Fisheries.

This permit does not convey the right to trespass.

Russell A. Cookingham

Director

RAC:pbo

enc.

cc--Capt. Henry
C O R. C. Klaus

---

or prohibiting the possession of certain fishes; Ohio considered, but has not yet enacted, similar legislation. Although this legislation was intended primarily to regulate fishkeeping on the commercial level, the ambiguous language confused both enforcement agencies and aquarists.

In most cases, the possession of a valid state fishing license will entitle you to collect *most* small, non-game fishes under the bait-collecting provisions. Certain restrictions are attached to this privilege, however. In New Jersey, for example, seines over 10 feet long may not be used in freshwater habitats without a scientific collecting permit, which costs $25. Although private individuals can secure this permit, it is much easier if you are associated with a non-profit scientific or educational institution and are collecting for research purposes or for public display.

In addition, no game fishes such as bass, pickerel, and trout, may be taken, and collecting is illegal in waters stocked with trout by the Division of Fish and Game, though special permission to collect in trout water may be applied for.

Most states also maintain their own endangered and threatened species lists, and the fishes (or reptiles and amphibians) included on them are off-limits to the private aquarist without a special permit.

In New Jersey, saltwater collecting or recreational angling is not regulated or licensed in any way, though two essentially marine species, the tomcod and the shortnosed sturgeon, are on the state endangered list. The state presumably could not legally prohibit private possession of either fish unless it could prove that the fish was collected in fresh waters under state jurisdiction. As both the tomcod and the sturgeon enter rivers and estuaries during the spawning season, if you bagged one of either species within state-administered waters and decided to keep it, you'd be in big trouble if stopped by a fish cop.

The safest and most environmentally sound course of action is to contact your fish and game agency and ask for its current regulations for both native and non-native fishes.

In most states, a scientific collecting permit requires the holder to submit a report of the year's activities. A collecting permit does not convey the right to trespass on private property, and specimens collected in the wild may not be sold on the open market.

This latter stipulation can cause some problems for hobbyists with an eye toward any mercenary possibilities that may exist in their hobby. Several species, including the Florida flagfish and the blackbanded sunfish, are highly popular with tropical fish hobbyists. In most cases it is permissible to trade or barter specimens within a native fishes association or aquarium club, but unless you can prove your stock was captive-bred or purchased from a dealer who can certify likewise, don't try profitably fish-farming rainbow darters or blackbanded sunfish. In all cases, check with your state fish and game or environmental protection agency for any regulations pertaining to the sale of any native fish species, wild-caught or tank- or pond-raised.

My advice is strict compliance with the law on every level. Establishing contacts within your state or provincial environmental agency will help you stay abreast of changes and will convince authorities of your sincerity, skill, and good faith in the pursuit of your interest.

Federal Laws

There are two major pieces of legislation that the native fish hobbyist must understand: the Lacey Act of 1921 and the Endangered Species Act of 1974.

The former is a still-enforced statute ruling that the aquisition of any plant or animal in violation of any state's law is also a violation of federal law. For the most part, the Lacey Act has been applied in cases involving foreign countries but it has at times been used in the interstate commerce of both native and exotic species. In other words, if you collected an endangered snail darter in Tennessee and sold it to a fellow hobbyist in California, and were arrested, you'd both be open to prosecution under the terms of the Lacey Act.

The Endangered Species Act states that no plant or animal species so listed may be collected or otherwise interfered with in any way, nor held in the possession of a private individual, unless special (very special) permission is granted by the U.S. Fish and Wildlife Service. Some 25 species of North American native fishes are on that doomsday list. The listing changes often, usually more unfortunate species are added as the habitat is diminished or degraded.

Conservation and the Law

Few serious, knowledgeable native fish aquarists will try to get around the Endangered Species Act. Most are familiar with the fishes included in the listing as well as their range and habitat, and thus immediately release them if they are accidentally collected. A copy of the current list of endangered and threatened species can be obtained from the U.S. Fish and Wildlife Service, Department of the Interior, Washington, DC.

The Injurious Wildlife Act prohibits the importation, sale, or possession of plants or animals determined to be dangerous, either through behavior or effect on the environment, and has included such notables as mongooses, piranhas, and the infamous walking catfish, now established in Florida. The act was passed too late to do anything about feral carp or English sparrows.

The walking catfish (*Clarias batrachus*) is one of the more recent cases of an exotic introduction gone wrong, but certainly is far from the only one. It was reportedly loosed upon Florida near Boca Raton in the mid-sixties. Since then, the fish has swum and plodded its way across a fair amount of the Sunshine State where average yearly temperatures are high and stable enough to support it, but it has not become the ecological nightmare everybody thought it would—not yet, at least. The blame for this one was laid on the doorstep of tropical fish importers, from whose holding tanks the catfish apparently fled—on fin.

The Injurious Wildlife Act is not often applied in cases involving the collecting of or trafficking in North American native fishes. Its implementation is far more likely in southern states with climates conducive to any non-native fishes or aquatic reptiles and amphibians securing a foothold. A copy of the regulations can be obtained from the U.S. Department of Agriculture, which administers the act.

International Laws

The United States and Canada are signatories to the Convention on International Trade in Endangered Species, familiarly known as CITES. This is an international treaty in which the signatories agree not to permit the import, export, or sale of any plants or animals listed in the International Red Book of Endangered Species. Participation is, of course, voluntary, and as Japan, the Netherlands, and Singapore declined to cooperate, they are frequently points of transfer or origin for illegal shipments of endangered animals. The provisions of CITES will not affect North American native fish hobbyists unless they attempt to ship or sell a fish species listed as endangered by their country to someone in another country that is a signatory to the treaty.

Most of the legal actions involving the collection or possession of wildlife species are civil actions, and unlike criminal actions, the burden of proof is on the defendants to demonstrate that they acted within the letter of the law. If you plan to do a good deal of native fish collecting in your own or in other states, or to swap specimens with aquarists in other states, learn the legal aspects of your activity.

In the 40-year span of my career as a naturalist and enthusiastic fish collector, I have been stopped and checked five times in three states and asked to present documents and to allow the conservation officer to inspect my catch. Three of the incidents were on saltwater so no permit was involved. The officer was checking for individuals harvesting blue crabs with a seine, a highly effective method that is illegal in New Jersey.

Collecting stream fishes deep in the mountains of central New Hampshire some years ago, I was surprised to see a game warden, complete with immaculate uniform and glossy shoes, step from the nearby shrubbery, hand extended for the required sport fishing license. I had none, but because I was working under a scientific collecting permit issued through an educational institution, all was well. Moral aspects of compliance with essentially common sense fish and game laws aside, enforcement in most states and provinces is quite effective today, and thus you never know just where or when you may be checked.

Threatened Species

The American Fisheries Society lists roughly 360 freshwater fish species, subspecies, and varieties as endangered, threatened, or "of special concern." This means that primarily due to habitat degradation, about one-third of the some 1,000 North American freshwater fish species, subspecies, and varieties are in trouble. The society notes that less than 3 percent of that total are in trouble because of recreational or even commercial fishing activities. But this is cold comfort to anyone who loves, respects, and interacts with the aquatic environment and the creatures in it.

Most of the present threat comes from continuing urban and agricultural development, chemical and runoff pollution, acid rain, and the introduction, whether accidental or deliberate, of exotic fish species. Many of Mexico's fishes are also threatened, due primarily to the explosive growth of population in that country, and the fisheries society says that about 62 percent of the species imperiled in the United States are in five of the desert states: Texas, New Mexico, Arizona, Nevada, and California, which is second only to Nevada (43 species) with 42 species reported in trouble.

Rather surprisingly, the heavily urbanized states of New Jersey and Connecticut are close to the bottom of the list, each having only two species listed as meriting real concern.

Canada, generally thought of as a nation still enjoying an unsullied and viable natural environment due to its much smaller human population and vast area, is experiencing serious declines in many fish species due to the acidification of lakes and ponds throughout the southern tier, according to the Canadian Wildlife Service in Ottawa.

The grim state of affairs in the environmental "aquasphere" worldwide in general and in North America in particular indicates a most pressing need for the study, appreciation, and skilled husbandry of our native fishes so that knowledge is gathered in time to save them.

The Species

The fishes presented in this section represent a cross section of the more common fish families and their species likely to be encountered by the beginning native fish hobbyist. I featured one or more species typical of a given family and did not include fishes currently listed as endangered or threatened, or those of restricted geographical distribution or extremely specialized food or environmental requirements. Recognized, or obscure, subspecies and races are avoided, as these are very often subject to taxonomic change within the scientific community, and many are very difficult to distinguish unless you are a trained observer. The bold indicator lines appearing on some of the figures highlight external physical features most characteristic of, or noticeable in, a given species.

Arrangement of Species

The freshwater and marine species covered in this book have been arranged according to the order of their evolutionary development, and not alphabetically, as might seem logical to the layman. This taxonomic system of classification is used throughout the biological sciences for all plant and animal groups. In a typical field guide to, say, birds, the listing always begins with loons, grebes, and flightless birds, considered more primitive, and ends with the sparrows and finches, the most advanced families. In the case of the fishes, the taxonomic nomenclature leads off with the most primitive forms—the jawless fishes such as the lampreys and hagfishes (not covered in this book)—then moves to the sharks and rays, which are often referred to scientifically not as true fishes, but rather as fishlike vertebrates. Teleosts, the bony fishes, by far the largest group, usually begins with the primitive "living fossil" on the marine side (the coelacanth, which because of its rare status is not included in this book) and the voracious bowfin on the freshwater side. Both of these creatures display anatomical features that link them to prehistoric forms. On the advanced side of the list are the marine puffers and filefishes and the freshwater perches and darters, considered among the more evolutionarily advanced fishes. You will not find every single fish species included in this book since many fish cannot be kept in aquariums, either because they are too big, too rare, or they simply do not live successfully confined in a tank.

Topography of a Fish

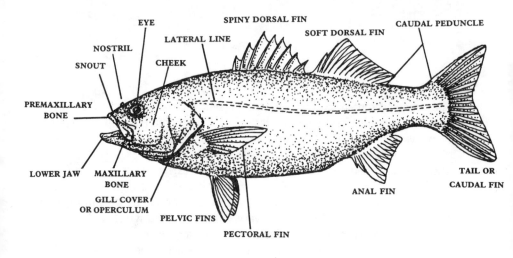

EYE
SPINY DORSAL FIN
CAUDAL PEDUNCLE
SOFT DORSAL FIN
LATERAL LINE
NOSTRIL
SNOUT
CHEEK
PREMAXILLARY BONE
LOWER JAW
MAXILLARY BONE
GILL COVER OR OPERCULUM
PELVIC FINS
PECTORAL FIN
ANAL FIN
TAIL OR CAUDAL FIN

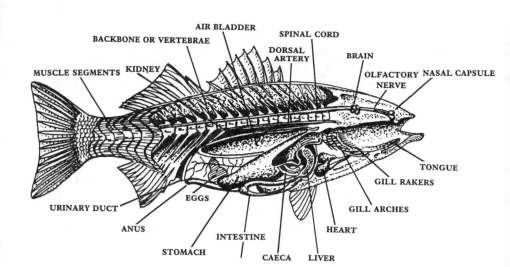

AIR BLADDER
SPINAL CORD
BACKBONE OR VERTEBRAE
DORSAL ARTERY
BRAIN
MUSCLE SEGMENTS
KIDNEY
OLFACTORY NERVE
NASAL CAPSULE
TONGUE
GILL RAKERS
URINARY DUCT
EGGS
GILL ARCHES
ANUS
HEART
INTESTINE
STOMACH
CAECA
LIVER

The external and internal anatomy of a typical teleost, or bony fish. A basic knowledge of the physical makeup of the fish will assist the aquarist in understanding the literature on the science of ichthyology, on aquaculture, and on the recognition and treatment of fish diseases.

What the Symbols Mean

The symbols shown in the following pages give you information on temperament, behavior, food, and environmental requirements for each fish.

The symbols give you very specific information, but you are warned that there are many variations on the theme of what may be expected of a fish in captivity. Thus, a fish listed as "peaceful" may be so only with fish of its own species or size and will, like most fish, readily eat any other fish small enough to be considered food. Some listed as "peaceful" may become less so as they grow in size.

 Generally peaceful. Can be kept in a community tank.

 A predator and generally aggressive. Cannot be trusted with smaller fishes.

 Prefers moderate to bright light levels.

 Prefers lower light levels.

 Moderately or heavily planted tank.

 Rock, coral, or bogwood decor.

 Open tank with sand or gravel substrate and few or no decorations.

 Generally active or a surface swimmer.

 Likes plenty of cover and hideaways.

 Generally accepts live foods only.

 Will accept live, frozen, or prepared foods.

Freshwater Fishes

BOWFIN
(Amia calva)

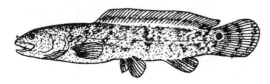

Range and Habitat: Throughout most of the Mississippi River drainage and east to Vermont and south to the Gulf of Mexico. It is found throughout the Great Lakes drainage except for Lake Superior and its tributaries. The bowfin, or dogfish, is a warm water species that prefers sluggish or standing water with abundant plant growth. It is found in larger rivers and their oxbows, and large lakes, where it both competes with and devours other, more desirable fish. Generally regarded as inedible, the bowfin is considered a pest by most anglers, though its size and power combine to make it a worthy adversary on hook and line. Efforts are underway in Louisiana to culture the species commercially as it has come under more intense fishing pressure for its eggs, which are sold as a lower grade caviar.

Field Marks and Collecting: The bowfin is a large, robust, cigar-shaped creature with a heavy, blunt head set with powerful, well-armed jaws. A large individual may reach two feet in length and weigh more than ten pounds. The very long dorsal fin is non-spinous; the caudal fin is rounded and has a dark ocellus, or eyespot, at the base near the dorsal edge. A distinguishing characteristic is a thin, platelike bone between the lower jaws called the gular plate. The bowfin is olivaceous to dark brown above, variously mottled on both the fins and body with black. The caudal eye-spot is bordered with orange or gold, brighter in the male. The fins are olive-green, with orange borders in breeding males. Young specimens are generally lighter in color, and the markings, similar to those of the adults, are more intense and contrasting.

Bowfins can be collected with a seine, a dip net, or a minnow trap (baited or not) set in weed beds. Young bowfins gather in dense schools guarded by the male for about a week before they disperse, and they can be easily netted at this time.

Aquarium Care: The late H. Ross Brock, a premier native fish collector, had this to say about the bowfin: "If you collect a bowfin, treat it well and you will have an unusual pet. Just remember this—they bite." That pretty much sums up the dogfish as an aquarium fish. It is a fascinating creature of ancient lineage that does well in confinement, but its appetite, disposition, and capacity for attaining large size make it a fish for the single-species tank. Bowfin quarters should be large (minimum 20 gallons, unheated, and decorated only with gravel and rockwork, as live plants will be moved about and uprooted by the fish's activities.

Bowfins will eat virtually all live foods small enough to swallow, with earthworms, nightcrawlers, live killies and feeder goldfish at the top of the list. They will accept strips of lean beef or fish, but remove all uneaten foods, for although the bowfin has a high tolerance for polluted, low-oxygen water, foul quarters will do them no good. If you keep more than one bowfin in the same tank, be sure they are the same size. The species is quite cannibalistic and will gulp down a sibling if it can.

LONGNOSE GAR
(Lepisosteus osseus)

Range and Habitat: Throughout the Mississippi River system and Mexico north to Montana and east through the Great Lakes drainage to Quebec. It is the most abundant and widely distributed of the ancient gar family, which contains seven North American species. Gars prefer quiet waters and are found in shallow lakes and bayous and in the backwaters and oxbows of larger rivers. The longnose is more tolerant of swift water than most gars and is often seen cruising and hunting in moderate currents.

Field Marks and Collecting: At first glance, the longnose gar is reminiscent of a pickerel or pike, but is distinguished from these by the much more slender body and snout, the latter studded with very capable teeth and the prominent, diamond-shaped scales. The adult longnose is olive above and silvery below with a few large spots anteriorly on the body. The fins sometimes have dusky streaks. The young (under four inches) are strikingly marked: olive above and clear white below with a dark stripe running from the eye to the base of the caudal fin. The fins are amber or orange with dark spots or streaks.

Adult gar readily strike a lure or live bait, but they are notoriously difficult to hook due to their hard mouths. The young hide in dense weed beds and among windfalls and other debris, much in the manner of pickerel, where they lie in wait for passing prey. They may be either dip netted or seined in such locations.

Aquarium Care: The various gars, especially this species and the spotted gar *(L. oculatus)*, have become somewhat popular for aquariums in recent years due to their exotic appearance and voracious nature. In spite of their appetite and ferocity, gars are quite sedentary, given to violent action only when food comes within sight. At other times, they lie quietly in the water and may then be annoyed or even harassed by large, aggressive tankmates. For this reason, it's best to keep them alone in a large, well-aerated tank, though they will coexist with large bass or sunfishes. The tank should have some plant growth to provide hiding places.

Very young gars feed on plankton and insect larvae and they can be offered baby brine shrimp in captivity. Larger individuals can sometimes be teased into striking a strip of fish or lean beef wiggled in front of them, but they usually spit it out once they realize it is nonliving food. The best and only real course is to offer them live fish, such as feeder goldfish or bait minnows. If the prospect of feeding live fish bothers you, don't keep a gar.

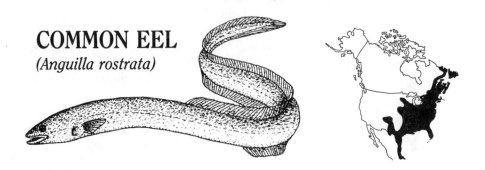

COMMON EEL
(Anguilla rostrata)

Range and Habitat: This wide-ranging fish is known from the Gulf of St. Lawrence to Brazil. It is virtually indistinguishable from the European eel *(A. anguilla),* which breeds in the same area of the Atlantic but returns to European shores and rivers instead. Eels spawn far at sea south of Bermuda, and approach the coast as tiny, transparent two- or three-inch juveniles, or glass eels. The females soon desert the estuaries and move inland to fresh water to mature and grow, while the males remain behind to await their return, often years in the future. The similar but unrelated conger eel can be told from the common eel by its larger mouth and dorsal fin that originates just behind the pectoral fins instead of much farther back on the body as in the common eel. The conger is strictly marine and never found in fresh water.

For most of its life, the common eel is a shoalwater and inland freshwater species that occupies a wide range of habitats from open sandy or muddy areas and sheltered areas around docks and jetties to rivers and lakes far from the sea. It is prevalent in boat channels in harbors and inlets, where it is trapped for food in eel pot fisheries.

Field Marks and Collecting: There's no mistaking an eel. It is a large (up to four feet) fish, snakelike in appearance, gray to olive above and pale gray to white below. The mouth is prominent and the lower jaw is underslung. The gill opening is small and semicircular, and is located just below and forward of each pectoral fin.

Eels may be collected many ways. The problem is not to get the fish in hand, but to keep it there, for an eel is extremely agile and every bit as slippery as that old, familiar saying would indicate. Small specimens (two to five inches and mostly males) commonly turn up in seine hauls in estuaries, and large individuals, all females, are netted in larger streams and rivers, often far from the sea. Eels readily enter killy traps, whether baited or not, and a larger one that squeezes in may attack and devour other fishes already caught in it. I recently had a 20-inch individual raid my trap set in a marina three times before I finally moved the fish and released it in another area. The eel was readily recognized by a distinctive scar on its head, and always entered the trap overnight, when eels are most active.

Aquarium Care: The eel ranks high as a voracious, fast-growing fish that will soon threaten other fishes quartered with it. Keep only the smallest specimen and plan to release it at the end of the summer season. Otherwise, the eel will become a dangerous, nocturnal predator, picking off its tankmates one by one. In the aquarium, eels quickly become active day and night and will eat all manner of foods, living or dead. They are ceaselessly active, and as they can be attracted to moving water, the area around filter inflow should be sealed off as this is where the travel-prone fish will exit from the tank.

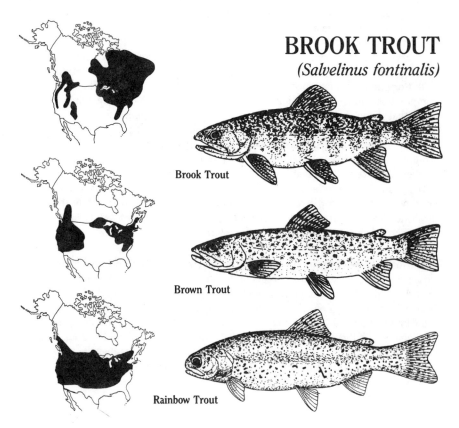

BROOK TROUT
(Salvelinus fontinalis)

Brook Trout

Brown Trout

Rainbow Trout

Range and Habitat: In clear, cool brooks, rivers, and lakes from Hudson Bay east to Labrador and south to Minnesota and in higher elevations to Georgia. Widely introduced elsewhere as a game fish, especially in the Pacific Northwest. The brookie or squaretail is the preeminent sport fish found in streams of cool, well-oxygenated water of good quality. It is intolerant of pollution and soon disappears, in the wild form, at least, from degraded waters. Several anadromous forms are known. The young fish, or parr, occupy the shallower waters or headwaters of the habitat while the adults are found in the deeper pools and among rocks and root tangles.

Field Marks and Collecting: The brook trout is an elongated, relatively slender, fine-scaled fish with a prominent mouth and the fatty, adipose fin present in all members of the Salmonidae. The color is dark olive green above with many wavy vermiculations of a lighter gold or olive. The sides may be bright orange or gold, silvery, or pale purple, and the body is sprinkled with yellow or red spots outlined in bright blue. Young specimens show six to nine prominent, oval dusky "parr markings" on the sides, the characteristic field mark. The dorsal and caudal fins are amber with irregular darker speckling or broken bands, and the pectoral, ventral, and anal fins are red or orange with a clear white leading edge followed by a black line.

The brook trout may not be taken by any method without at least a fishing license or a trout stamp, and cannot be collected live in any state or province without permission. Its habitat, if it is stocked with hatchery fish, is also usually off limits to collectors without a permit. The brown and rainbow trouts also come under this heading and are considered here as well.

Hatchery-raised stock can be purchased under permit for private stocking, but in most cases, this involves bulk shipments of hundreds or thousands rather than a few fish. Ask your state or provincial fish and wildlife agency how to secure permission to collect or purchase a few specimens for aquarium study. If you are affiliated with any non-profit scientific or educational institution, you should have little trouble. I have found that if you express your interest and intentions well, permission can usually be gotten for a modest collecting project involving most game species.

Adult wild trout are legendary in their wiliness and thus not easy to bag without an artfully presented bait or lure, as any true trout angler will tell you. Put-and-take hatchery fish are another matter, of course.

The young can often be dip netted from among shoreside rocks, roots, and debris, or cornered in the small streamlets they often occupy, out of the reach of their cannibalistic elders. Contrary to popular belief, small trout transport well as long as they are not crowded in the container and the water is kept cool.

Aquarium Care: The primary requirement of all trout, wild or otherwise, is cool, well-oxygenated water. They will decline and perish when the water temperature reaches or remains at 70° or more. Trout require large quarters. They are quite territorial and larger specimens may not get along with each other in confinement. Even smaller trout should be maintained in no less than a 50-gallon tank equipped with an undergravel filter and powerful pump and powerhead that will create a moderate to strong current. Low light conditions are advisable and plants are not necessary as they are not present in any number in the natural habitat. Live foods are recommended (brine shrimp and, tubifex for small fish; live minnows, worms for larger specimens), though most trout will learn to accept cut fish or meat and prepared foods in time.

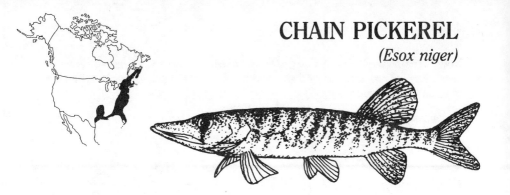

CHAIN PICKEREL
(Esox niger)

Range and Habitat: The familiar pickerel is one of the more popular and widely distributed of North American game fishes, found from the St. Lawrence drainage south along the Coastal Plain east of the Appalachians to the Gulf Coast and Texas. The fish occupies a wide variety of habitats, from quiet streams and rivers to large lakes, where it lies in wait for living prey among the weeds and windfalls of the margins. Pickerel are particularly prevalent among beds of water lilies where they attack and devour virtually anything small enough to be engulfed. The fish can often be spotted hovering motionless in the water, but it is a rare collector who is swift enough to bag one with a dip net.

Field Marks and Collecting: The streamlined, torpedo-shaped, sharp-snouted profile of the pikes and pickerels is familiar to any freshwater sport fisherman. The chain pickerel reaches a length of over two feet and weighs ten pounds or more, though most are smaller. Adults can be identified by the chainlike vermiculations on the back and flanks, while the young are vertically barred in dusky brown bands. The much smaller redfin pickerel *(E. americanus)* occurs along the Atlantic coastal plain from Maine to Florida. It displays a series of wavy, dusky bands along its sides. It seldom has red fins. The equally pint-sized grass pickerel *(E. vermiculatus)* occurs throughout the Ohio Valley south to Florida and Texas. It is very close to the redfin in appearance, but has a longer snout.

Pickerel from about two to six inches long can often be spotted and then cornered against the shoreline with a seine, but most specimens taken are the very young of between one and three inches. These are usually seined or dip netted in dense weed beds.

Aquarium Care: All pickerels have one requirement that will test the dedication of any aquarist wishing to keep them. They must have living (or at least moving) food, and lots of it. Although voracious predators, smaller pickerel will not thrive in an open tank filled with active, aggressive tankmates that may harrass them. They require heavily planted, quieter quarters that afford them plenty of hiding places in which to skulk and wait for passing prey. In the aquarium, this should ideally be small fish such as feeder guppies or young shiners, though very small specimens will usually accept live brine shrimp at first. As your pickerel puts on size, however, so will the size of the required prey, until this begins to include its tankmates. Add to this the fact that pickerel, if several are kept together, are decidely cannibalistic and will attack and devour each other if underfed, and you have a growing problem for the average aquarium hobbyist.

Note: The pickerel's status as a game fish nearly everywhere will usually preclude legally keeping one at home. Check first with your local fish and game authorities just to be on the safe side.

MUDMINNOW
(Umbra pygmaea and *limi)*

Eastern Mudminnow

Central Mudminnow

Range and Habitat: There are two American species in this genus, the eastern *(U. pygmaea)* and the central mudminnow *(U. limi)*. The eastern species occurs in bogs and slow-moving streams of the Atlantic coastal plain from Long Island to Florida. The central mudminnow is found in similar habitats from the upper Mississippi Valley and Great Lakes north into Canada. A third species, the Olympic or western mudminnow *(Novumbra hubbsi)*, occurs in a very restricted range in Washington State (see note below).

Field Marks and Collecting: Mudminnows of both species look and behave somewhat like blunt-nosed little pickerel, and the genus is in fact closely related to the Esocidae. The fish has a way of hovering in mid-water, pectoral fins furiously beating alternately. It turns deliberately towards an object of interest and studies it intently before striking swiftly, like a pickerel.

Both mudminnows are small, elongated, cylindrical fish of warm brown coloration. The eastern species displays horizontal dotted lines of darker brown, while the central mudminnow is vertically crossed by eight to ten dark, indistinct bands. Both may reach a length of five or six inches, but most collected specimens are about half that size.

The mudminnows' habitat will present the only major obstacle to collecting. Both species are found in soft-bottomed, densely weeded, sluggish or standing water that often makes the use of a seine impractical. A sturdy dip net is usually the best approach. As the mudminnow is almost never spotted before capture, the process involves sweeping the net through shoreside masses of submerged vegetation and pawing through the resultant mess in the bag.

Aquarium Care: It is in the aquarium that this little fish's personality really shines. Mudminnows adapt readily to confinement and normally accept food quickly. Although they prefer moving prey, such as live brine shrimp or tubifex, they will accept the frozen version in time. They particularly like live bloodworms, available at any well-stocked pet shop. The fish are most content in heavily planted, dimly lit quarters, but, as they are not overly introverted by nature, they usually get along well in more open community tanks. Although mudminnows will occasionally show some aggression toward other fishes, in particular their own kind, their mouths are too small to inflict damage, and injuries are rare.

Note: The Olympic mudminnow is rare in the Pacific Northwest and classed as Of Special Concern. It occurs primarily in the Chehalis and Deschutes Rivers and the Cook Creek drainages in Washington. Although the Olympic mudminnow is quite abundant in many localities within its limited range, discretion should be used in retaining any mudminnow collected in Washington.

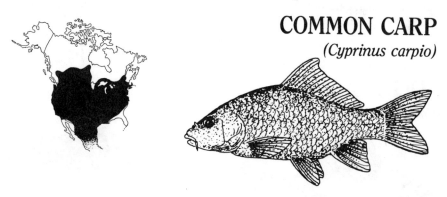

COMMON CARP
(Cyprinus carpio)

Range and Habitat: The carp's natural and original range includes much of Asia and perhaps Europe. It was introduced into North America as a potential food fish in the late 1800s and has since spread throughout the continent, from central Canada to southern Mexico in suitable habitats.

In many places, carp will be found in virtually every river, lake, and pond that will support fish life, but it prefers shallower, weedy areas and dislikes clear, fast-moving water.

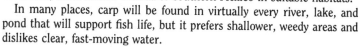
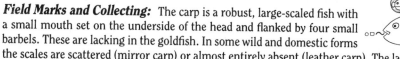
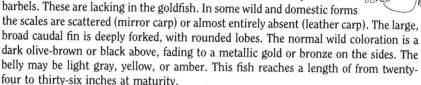

Field Marks and Collecting: The carp is a robust, large-scaled fish with a small mouth set on the underside of the head and flanked by four small barbels. These are lacking in the goldfish. In some wild and domestic forms the scales are scattered (mirror carp) or almost entirely absent (leather carp). The large, broad caudal fin is deeply forked, with rounded lobes. The normal wild coloration is a dark olive-brown or black above, fading to a metallic gold or bronze on the sides. The belly may be light gray, yellow, or amber. This fish reaches a length of from twenty-four to thirty-six inches at maturity.

Carp are most apparent during the spring spawning season, when hundreds of big breeders approach the shoreline to the accompaniment of much splashing and commotion. This is a very prolific species, with large females producing up to two million eggs. Young carp can be seined in shallow weedy areas near shore or can be caught easily in minnow traps set in aquatic vegetation and baited with bread. In known carp ponds, check the trap every two or three hours. A large number of fish jammed into the trap may damage or stress each other, making them poor risks as aquarium specimens.

Aquarium Care: The carp, like the familiar goldfish, is a hardy, adaptable creature that often defies the well-meaning efforts of inexperienced fishkeepers to kill it. But the fact that it can live in overcrowded quarters and in water that is grossly polluted due to overfeeding doesn't make that the right approach to keeping them. Give them a roomy tank (or better yet, an outdoor pond) to allow for growth, and well-filtered water, and don't overfeed so that excess food spoils, and carp will survive 50 or more years.

Carp quarters should have a medium-fine sand substrate to allow for some rooting. Providing artful decor, such as driftwood and live plants, is a waste of time because the carp is an active, powerful fish that will quickly rearrange things in its rooting and blundering about. Carp will accept just about anything remotely edible, but good, all-around foods are the goldfish and koi flakes and pellets available at any pet store.

GOLDFISH
(Carassius auratus)

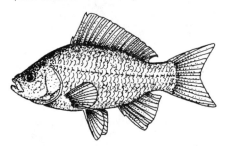

Range and Habitat: Of Asiatic origin, the goldfish has been widely introduced into North America, where thriving wild populations now exist in many regions. The fish has established itself in all but the northernmost states and Canada, where severe winters have not been conducive to the establishment of breeding populations. Goldfish favor smaller, warmer bodies of water with abundant vegetation and soft substrates. They are often seen foraging near shore, where the bright orange or gold color of recently liberated individuals makes them highly conspicuous, no matter how murky the water may be.

Field Marks and Collecting: Although, as the world's most popular aquarium fish, the goldfish is familiar to nearly everyone and would seem to need no description, the identity of the nondescript wild form is often not so obvious. The goldfish is very much like the carp in appearance, but has a slimmer, more graceful profile. The mouth is small and lacks barbels, and each nostril has a prominent tubercle. The body is covered by large, metallic scales, and the tail is forked and the lobes rounded. Recently liberated goldfish display the cultivated colors of their particular strain, but over succeeding generations in the wild, these hues are lost and replaced by the bronze-gold or browns of the wild form. Domestic pond and feral goldfish reach a length of between eight and fourteen inches at maturity, though they may breed at much smaller sizes under crowded conditions.

Like the carp, the goldfish may be collected by seining in weedy areas near shore in favorable habitats. They enter baited minnow traps readily, and larger specimens are often taken in farm and park ponds by youngsters using hooks baited with bread or doughballs.

Aquarium Care: The goldfish has been the favorite aquarium fish for centuries, and a vast body of literature exists on its care and breeding. It was on the subject of the venerable goldfish that virtually all of the time-honored principles of aquarium maintenance were formulated. The three principles are: Don't overcrowd, don't overfeed, and make periodic water changes. These especially apply to the goldfish, for it's an active, hearty eater that generates a lot of waste, and its environment must be kept free of contaminants if it is to thrive. A goldfish tank should have a 25 percent water change every two weeks and the substrate should be stirred and siphoned frequently to avoid the accumulation of wastes. Many perfectly adequate goldfish foods are available today, and as the fish is distinctly vegetarian (it will eat aquarium plants), an occasional leaf of parboiled spinach is appreciated.

FATHEAD MINNOW
(Pimephales promelas)

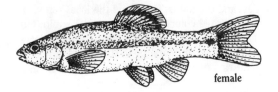

female

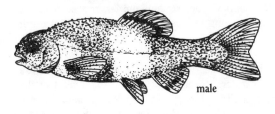

male

Range and Habitat: This widely distributed little fish is found from north-western Canada east to Quebec and Maine, south through the Ohio River Valley, and southwest into Mexico. It is absent on the Pacific slope and along the Atlantic Coastal Plain from about New York south to the Gulf of Mexico, except in the many places where it has been introduced either accidentally or deliberately.

In the northern part of the range, the fathead inhabits boggy lakes and swamps; further south, it is a fish of shallow lakes, ponds, and even ditches, where an absence of natural predators often allows them to become abundant.

Field Marks and Collecting: The fathead minnow is an elongated, rather robust little fish most easily identified by its blunt, rounded head and dark color. Females and nonbreeding males are dark olive or brown above and silvery-green on the sides with a dusky or bluish lateral stripe. The tail is quite broad and the lobes are rounded. The breeding male is very distinctive. He becomes very dark, almost black, except for two broad vertical bars, one just behind the gill covers and one at midbody, that are a pale buff or gray. A gray pad of rough tubercles develops on the back just forward of the dorsal fin. The male uses this to stroke and clean the eggs once they are laid, usually on the underside of a solid object. The fathead grows to about three inches long and is at senility's doorstep in its third year.

The fathead is raised commercially as a bait fish on a vast scale, with large industries in many states such as Arkansas and Minnesota. In the latter state alone, Eddy and Underhill (*Northern Fishes,* 1976) estimated that in the 1970s there were some 3,000 bait dealers and more than 350 fish farmers dealing principally in the fathead, or at least heavily dependent on it. The hobbyist wishing to try a few fatheads in his aquarium need only visit the nearest bait dealer.

In 1985, a xanthic, or golden, color morph of the species began turning up in the ponds of a few Arkansas breeders. In addition to being offered on the bait market, this new strain was sold through pet shops as the golden minnow.

Collecting the fathead in the wild presents few problems. The fish may be seined or dip netted wherever it is abundant, or collected in a minnow trap baited with dog food.

Aquarium Care: The fathead's legendary tenacity on a fishook is carried over into an inherent hardiness as an aquarium fish if given adequate care. This means clean, well-filtered water, no overcrowding, or overfeeding. This fish will coexist with most other cyprinids, though it will, of course, be eaten by any larger predators kept with it. The fathead will eat all standard aquarium fare, live or prepared, and will make itself at home in most community tanks without conflict. This species will breed in confinement if given enough room, a varied diet, and objects such as bog roots or broken flowerpots on which to deposit the adhesive eggs. It is one of the few cyprinid fishes to offer parental care and guardianship to the eggs and fry.

COMMON SHINER
(Notropis cornutus)

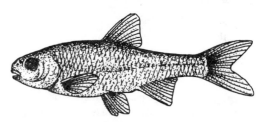

Range and Habitat: From Saskatchewan and New Brunswick south to the Carolinas and Tennessee. The common shiner frequents a wide variety of habitats, such as larger lakes, ponds, and rivers, but for the most part it is found in streams with a fast flow and gravel or sand bottoms. Shiners congregate in the deeper pools beneath bridges and below dam spillways. In central New Hampshire's Baker River, I found this fish very common in shallow, rocky areas where it was easily collected using the rock fish trap described in the collecting section.

Field Marks and Collecting: The common shiner is a bait fish well known to most sport fishermen. It is a robust, moderately compressed fish with large scales and a blunt, rounded head. The tail is moderately forked and has rounded lobes. The non-breeding fish is a dark slate blue or olive-brown above fading to silvery on the sides and belly. The fins are transparent, though they may display touches of red or dusky. Breeding males are beautiful, with the sides and fins suffused with bright gold, orange, or red. Prominent tubercles develop on the head of the male at this time.

This active, agile fish can be a challenge to collect in larger streams. In rocky areas, the fish trap is most effective for corralling adult specimens. Young fish can often be cornered in pockets and bagged with a dip net. A baited minnow trap will work well in quieter backwaters, but should not be used in fast water as these large, active minnows will quickly find themselves jammed in it by the current and killed.

Aquarium Care: The common shiner is an undemanding fish in confinement and thus makes a good beginner's native fish. Although it tames rapidly and becomes something of a pet over time, this fish will decline if not given enough swimming room and variety in the diet. This means a minimum of 20 gallons for a half-dozen adult (four- to six-inch) shiners, and a diet that includes live foods as well as vegetable-based goldfish or koi foods, as this fish is decidedly omnivorous. The shiner tank should be as open as possible, with the only recommended decor being a large root and a few plants.

EMERALD SHINER
(Notropis atherinoides)

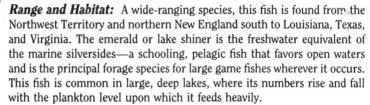

Range and Habitat: A wide-ranging species, this fish is found from the Northwest Territory and northern New England south to Louisiana, Texas, and Virginia. The emerald or lake shiner is the freshwater equivalent of the marine silversides—a schooling, pelagic fish that favors open waters and is the principal forage species for large game fishes wherever it occurs. This fish is common in large, deep lakes, where its numbers rise and fall with the plankton level upon which it feeds heavily.

Field Marks and Collecting: The emerald shiner is a long, slender fish with a rather delicate appearance. The head is angular in profile and the eyes are large. It is a dusky emerald green above, fading to a pale metallic green or silver on the sides. There is a narrow black lateral band running the length of the body, and the belly is a clear white. All of the fins are transparent and the strongly forked tail lobes are triangular.

Emerald shiners are both cultivated and collected in vast numbers for bait. Why this is the case is a mystery to me, for I have found them to be highly susceptible to handling and stress. These fish will enter a minnow trap placed in shallow but open water and baited with bread or crumbled fish. They can also be taken with a fine-meshed cast net. Fry can be carefully dip netted from shoreside weed beds. Make sure that they are exposed to as little stress as possible as they are as delicate as they look.

Aquarium Care: The emerald shiner makes an active, though somewhat uninspiring aquarium fish, being devoid of color, especially in confinement. They are quite susceptible to careless handling and also to sudden changes in water temperature. These active, schooling fishes should be quartered in a large tank equipped with a filter that provides some current. As is the case with most schooling fishes, they should be maintained in groups of between six and 20. They are primarily plankton and very small fish eaters. The best foods are newly hatched or adult brine shrimp, depending on the size of the fish. They can be trained to accept prepared foods and will grab them until they reach the bottom. Young fry are vegetarian and should get parboiled spinach or lettuce in the diet. If kept under low-light conditions and fed a variety of foods, the emerald shiner will retain what color it has. This combined with its ceaseless action, will create a pretty picture.

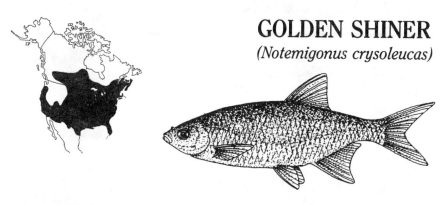

GOLDEN SHINER
(Notemigonus crysoleucas)

Range and Habitat: Numerous subspecies found from Saskatchewan east to Quebec and south to Florida and Texas. It has been widely introduced elsewhere as a bait and forage fish for game species. The golden shiner occupies a wide variety of habitats, from small farm ponds to larger lakes and rivers, where it is primarily an open water, schooling fish. It tends to gather in loose schools near the surface, though never far from the protection of weed or water lily beds.

Field Marks and Collecting: This fish, also known as roach, bream, butterfish, and pond shiner, depending on the locality, is very likely the species almost everybody has in mind when they think "shiner." The golden is a trim, deep-bodied fish, strongly laterally compressed, and of an attractive, reflective brassy or bronzy color in healthy adults. The mouth and head are small and the anal fin has a concave, sickle shape, even in young specimens. In the adults, the large scales are outlined in black, giving the fish a crosshatched or chain-link appearance, and the fins are usually a soft brown or orange.

Young golden shiners usually gather in large, loosely organized schools in shallow water near shore where they may be seined or dip netted with relative ease. Since this species is also one of the most widely sold bait fishes, larger specimens can be purchased from bait dealers. Because fish destined for the hook are not treated with much concern for long life, any shiner or other species brought this way should be checked carefully for injury or fungus. This approach may not endear you to the shop owner, but it will greatly reduce the risk of trouble in your tank later on.

Aquarium Care: William Innes wrote that this fish "is one that takes easily to the aquarium and is quite hardy under any reasonable conditions . . . in the sunlight, flashing its bright silver sides, it is a very pretty member of the aquarium family." It is a relatively large (up to 12 inches), active minnow, so a larger tank should be provided to give the fish ample swimming room. The golden shiner is omnivorous, taking all manner of animal and some vegetable (algal) fare. Primarily a surface feeder, it will accept prepared flake foods as well as all live foods. A tank housing shiners of any species should be securely covered as nearly all are confirmed jumpers.

SPOTTAIL SHINER
(Notropis hudsonius)

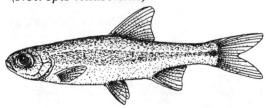

Range and Habitat: This is a wide-ranging northern species, occurring from the Yukon Territory south throughout central Canada to North Dakota east to the Hudson River and south to Georgia and Kentucky. This is one of the most ubiquitous of the weed shiner types, found in all suitable habitats ranging from coastal streams of considerable brackish content to ponds, streams, and lakes of the interior. The favored situations are shallow, open water with sand or gravel bottoms interspersed with scattered weed beds. The young are usually seen in large schools over sandy areas and among weed beds near shore.

Field Marks and Collecting: This pale, little fish can be difficult to distinguish from the myriad other weed shiners. The spottail is pale tan above with a dusky or pale pink lateral band running from the gills to the caudal fin. The band terminates in a dusky brown or black spot slightly smaller than the eye. The fins are transparent or may show touches of brown or dusky pink.

The spottail shiner is easily collected in a minnow trap set among weeds at the edges of open areas. It can either be baited with bread balls or placed unbaited in a strategic location. A ten-foot minnow seine works well with this species if the collector can maneuver the fish into an indentation in the lake shoreline; otherwise, they are often too swift and agile to be encircled by anything but the larger seines, which may be illegal.

Aquarium Care: This species, and most of the weed shiners, are among those native fishes that will readily accept prepared fish foods, feeding as they do on similar matter in the wild state. Although shiners patrol the entire water column from surface to substrate, they prefer the surface and, as such, will readily eat floating flakes or small pellets. This diet can, of course, be varied with live foods such as brine shrimp or tubifex worms.

The spottail shiner, like all schooling fishes, should be given plenty of room in the aquarium—no less than 20 gallons for six to eight adults. A dark gravel substrate and subdued frontal lighting will show off these ceaselessly active little fish to best advantage.

BLACKNOSE DACE
(Rhinichthys atratulus)

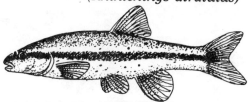

Range and Habitat: Several subspecies are found from Manitoba and North Dakota east to Nova Scotia and south to North Carolina and Nebraska. Although it is occasionally found in lakes in the western part of the range, it is primarily a stream fish, preferring smaller watercourses with gravel or rock bottoms. They can be found in all streams except the very fastest races and rapids, and often collect in small, loosely-formed schools in quieter backwaters. The fry and juveniles are usually found near shore.

Field Marks and Collecting: The blacknose is an attractive little (up to four inches) minnow that can be told by its ocher or rich brown back, clear white belly, and the black lateral stripe running from the snout to the base of the caudal fin that separates the two areas. The lower part of the body is often speckled with dark spots, usually the larvae of mussels that parasitize the fish without apparent ill effect. Breeding males have a dusky red lateral band, and the pectoral and ventral fins are often bright red. Males also have longer pectoral, ventral, and anal fins than the females. The mouth is terminal rather than under the snout.

The blacknose is one of the swiftest of stream fishes, and it can usually outmaneuver a collector with a dip net with ease. It can best be caught using the seine-rock shuffle method or with the rock stream trap. Adult dace are usually the best for aquariums as the young fry are so fragile that even careful handling often stresses them beyond their endurance. Although it is quite hardy, it should not be crowded in the transport container. If possible, the container should be provided with a battery-powered air stone during the trip home.

Aquarium Care: The blacknose acclimates well to aquariums after a short period of some difficulty adapting to standing water. Its equilibrium is geared to the water action of the natural habitat so that balance in the aquarium is maintained with some effort for the first week or two unless a powerful filtration current is provided. The fish soon makes itself right at home, however, and behaves normally and feeds readily on virtually all live foods and many prepared flakes and granular foods. Algae in the tank can be beneficial as the fish is strongly herbivorous, though it can get along without greenery if it has to.

This fish, like most North American stream fishes, requires clean, well-aerated, unheated water and a substrate that at least approximates the original—coarse gravel, pebbles, and smaller rocks will do nicely, with a large cedar root or two added for decoration. As with most cyprinids, this dace can be a jumper, so its quarters should be tightly covered, particularly near an outside power filter inflow, as this will be the most likely spot for an exit attempt. Dace should not be kept in the company of such predators as bass, large sunfish, or pickerel.

LONGNOSE DACE
(Rhinichthys cataractae)

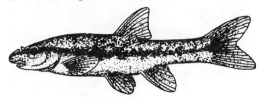

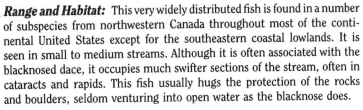

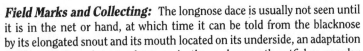

Range and Habitat: This very widely distributed fish is found in a number of subspecies from northwestern Canada throughout most of the continental United States except for the southeastern coastal lowlands. It is seen in small to medium streams. Although it is often associated with the blacknosed dace, it occupies much swifter sections of the stream, often in cataracts and rapids. This fish usually hugs the protection of the rocks and boulders, seldom venturing into open water as the blacknose does.

Field Marks and Collecting: The longnose dace is usually not seen until it is in the net or hand, at which time it can be told from the blacknose by its elongated snout and its mouth located on its underside, an adaptation to feeding very close to the substrate also seen in the suckermouth catfishes popular in the tropical fish hobby. The longnose is a slightly longer (up to five inches), slimmer, and less strongly patterned fish than the blacknose dace. It is a soft brown color above, silvery or brassy below, and the sides are marked with a dusky, irregular band rather than a more intense lateral stripe. Breeding males are flushed with reddish-gold on the sides and fins.

This fish can only be collected by shuffling the rocks of swifter stream sections and catching the dislodged specimens in a seine or dip net just downstream. I have taken a few in a minnow trap placed among the rocks at the bases of waterfalls, but they sometimes damage themselves in their efforts to escape, so this is not recommended.

Aquarium Care: Coming from such a wild and wooly habitat, the longnose dace could not be expected to adapt to the placid confines of a fish tank. But they do, and quite readily. Maybe they're grateful for the peace and quiet. Whatever the reason, this dace has virtually the same aquarium requirements as the preceding species, with the exception that a moderately strong current is desirable in order to allow the fish to pluck food from the flow as they hide beneath rocks and roots. In my experience with specimens collected in New Hampshire's upper Baker River, they soon abandon their rock-hugging ways and move much more freely about the tank, though they do not school as the blacknose will. A dace tank can be decorated with roots and bunches of *Fontinalis,* a cold-water plant that can be collected in streams and which does well in cool, clean, well-filtered water. Like the blacknose dace, this fish is undemanding in food preferences and will accept all live foods and most commercial flakes.

REDBELLY DACE
(Phoxinus species*)*

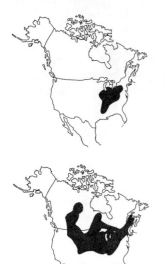

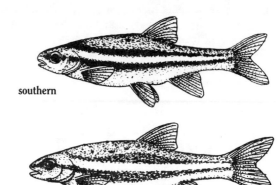

southern

northern

Range and Habitat: There are three species: the northern redbelly dace *P. eos),* found from northern British Columbia to Hudson Bay and Nova Scotia south to Colorado, Minnesota, and Pennsylvania; the southern red-belly dace, *(P. erythrogaster),* occurring from southern Minnesota and Pennsylvania to northern Alabama, Arkansas, and Oklahoma; and the mountain redbelly dace *(P. oreas),* a small population inhabiting the Upper James, Roanoke, and Kanawha Rivers.

The northern redbelly is found in spring-fed bogs and ponds and the quieter portions of smaller creeks and streams. The southern form is more often found in faster brooks and streams where it is usually near bank undercuts and windfalls, which provide it with some protection from the voracious brook and brown trouts, which often share the habitat.

Field Marks and Collecting: The northern and southern species of this fish are similar in appearance. The principal distinguishing characters are the respective ranges and the intensity of the colors (brighter in the southern form). Both are elongate fish with a slight hump that peaks at the insertion of the dorsal fin. The mouth is small. The back is dark brown to olive and the sides and belly are pale yellow to bright red, depending on the season. There are two dark lateral stripes on the sides, and in the southern form, these are separated by a bright pink or reddish band. There is usually a series of small spots along the upper back of the southern redbelly. The mountain redbelly dace is similar, but may show a series of larger, darkish blotches along the ridge of the back. All species attain a length of about three inches at maturity.

Redbelly dace are active, agile little fish that can usually avoid a dip net unless they are cornered in a confined area of the stream. The dip net is best worked beneath bank overhangs and among streamside vegetation where the fish frequently hide. A seine can be used (where legal) with good effect in quieter backwaters where the fish may tend to school up.

Aquarium Care: Redbelly dace possess all of the attributes of the first-rate aquarium fish that have been sought for years by hobbyists. They are active, peaceful, hardy, and very colorful if maintained in good health. They should be quartered in a larger tank, 55 gallons and up, in groups of six or more or with other schooling stream fishes. Filtration should be on the strong side and the tank rockscaped, with bogwood added for accent. Heat is not rquired for this species and may wash out their colors. Redbelly dace are displayed to best effect in much the same manner as neon and cardinal tetras, in a dimly lit tank against a dark substrate. Black aquarium gravel is a good choice. This fish will accept a wide range of foods once acclimated, from live foods through most of the prepared varieties. The redbelly will live in aquariums for between three and four years under good care.

STONEROLLER
(Campostoma anomalum)

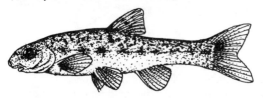

Range and Habitat: Several subspecies from Minnesota and the Great Plains states east to New York and south through the Appalachians to Texas. It is a fish of varied habitats, with most eastern forms found in lakes and larger rivers, and western subspecies occurring in smaller streams and creeks. They are usually encountered in stream sections having gravel or pebble rather than sand substrates.

Field Marks and Collecting: The stoneroller or hornyhead is a large, robust minnow, reaching a length of eight to ten inches. It is a brownish-brassy color, mottled with darker browns, and the dorsal and anal fins are marked with a dark crossbar. There is sometimes a dusky lateral band, and the body is often speckled with darker spots. The mouth is under the snout, and the upper lip is thick and fleshy. The lower lip has a prominent cartilaginous ridge inside. In breeding males, the fins and body are flushed with varying shades of yellow or orange, and there is a triangular spot at the base of the caudal fin.

The stoneroller is a large enough minnow to be collected easily on a barbless hook baited with angleworms, though, as I've noted, this is not the preferred method. Smaller specimens can be lured into a baited minnow trap or seined in stream pools or back-waters, where they often congregate in large numbers.

Aquarium Care: The stoneroller is a bottom feeder that patrols its environment much like the popular algae-eater of tropical aquarium fame. Although it will accept live and frozen foods without complaint, either algae should be allowed to grow in the tank or the fish should be offered boiled lettuce or spinach on a regular basis, for the stoneroller is of strongly vegetarian leanings. Otherwise, this is an undemanding fish that can be kept in a tank suitable for other stream species. Don't invest a lot of time or money on live aquarium plants for they will only be uprooted by the stonerollers' foraging or eaten outright. Go plastic if you must have permanent greenery in a stonerollers' tank.

CREEK CHUB
(Semotilus atromaculatus)

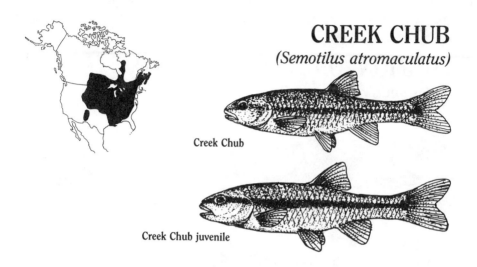

Creek Chub

Creek Chub juvenile

Range and Habitat: This wide-ranging fish is found from Montana east to the Gaspé Peninsula and southward into the Gulf States. A very similar subspecies, *Semotilus a. thoreauianus*, occurs in the southeastern states. The creek chub lives up to its name, favoring creeks and small streams and rivers, and only occasionally being found in larger lakes or rivers. It is an active fish, usually found in open water and in deeper pools and backwaters over gravel bottoms.

Field Marks and Collecting: This is a robust, sturdy minnow that reaches the adult length of 13 to 14 inches, enough to make it a lively adversary on light tackle. A creek chub's swift strike and subsquent fight has fooled many a neophyte trout angler. The nonbreeding adult is dusky silver with a darkish lateral band and a prominent black spot at the forward base of the dorsal fin. Breeding males are variously hued in bright blues, purple, and orange on the sides and have prominent, rough tubercles on the top of the head. The tail is broad and strongly lobed.

Creek chubs, also called horned dace, are quick fish capable of great maneuverability. They can easily dodge a dip net in open water. They are best collected by cornering them in a natural stream indentation with a seine (check with authorities first in trout waters) or by building a rock fish trap.

Aquarium Care: This fish is very hardy and adapts quickly to aquarium life, though it must have clean, cool, well-aerated water in order to duplicate somewhat the stream environment. A 55-gallon tank is best, with a gravel and rockwork substrate. Cedar roots and bogwood may be included for esthetic effect. Creek chubs will eat virtually all standard aquarium fare, from live foods to most prepared flakes and pellets. They may be kept with other stream fishes close to their own size without conflict, though the males may become aggressive in spring. The species has never been spawned in aquariums. Like most cyprinids, the gregarious creek chub likes the company of its own kind, so several should be kept together, both out of consideration for the fish's social tendencies and for the striking visual effects of an active school in a large tank.

COMMON, OR WHITE, SUCKER
(Catostomus commersoni)

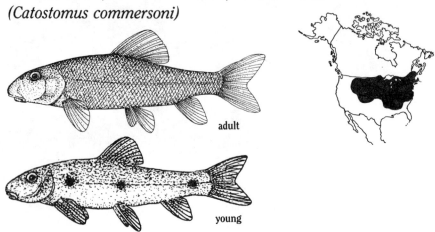

adult

young

Range and Habitat: This widely distributed fish is found east of the Rockies from northwestern Canada east to the Maritimes and south to Colorado, Missouri, and Georgia. It has been widely introduced outside the original range.

The common or white sucker inhabits larger streams and rivers, sharing much of its habitat with trout. They are prevalent in the deeper pools and backwaters. I have found them especially abundant beneath bridges and below smaller dams in some streams in New Hampshire. The younger fish are often seen in shallow water near the shoreline, where they industriously root about in the substrate and among weed beds. They are quite wary and alert, however, and not easily approached. I have not known them to school but rather travel about in small groups or singly.

Field Marks and Collecting: The common sucker attains the adult length of between 16 and 19 inches. It is olive or brown above, fading to silvery-pink on the sides to pure white on the belly. The snout is rather long and the mouth is on the underside of the head as in most bottom-feeding fishes. The scales are fairly large and prominent, and the fish has an overall shiny or reflective look. Breeding adults become much more rosy in color with reddish lower fins.

Smaller suckers may be collected with a seine in natural stream indentations. They will enter a minnow trap set in a sheltered area and baited with compressed bread (to keep it from disintegrating in the current's flow) or dog food. Medium-sized fish can be caught on hook and line using worms.

Aquarium Care: Suckers are hardy fish that will thrive in the aquarium as long as they are provided with plenty of food. This should include some vegetable-based items such as algae or parboiled spinach as the sucker is strongly vegetarian. Allowing a good crop of algae to bloom in their quarters will benefit them, unsightly as the plant may be to human eyes. Suckers are peaceable creatures that will not molest other tankmates. The males may become aggressive in spring if they are approaching breeding size, but this is rare behavior in the confines of the aquarium. The sucker tank should be large and well-filtered, for these fishes are grubbing, rooting, messy feeders. They will uproot or eat plants, so plastic is recommended for a sucker tank.

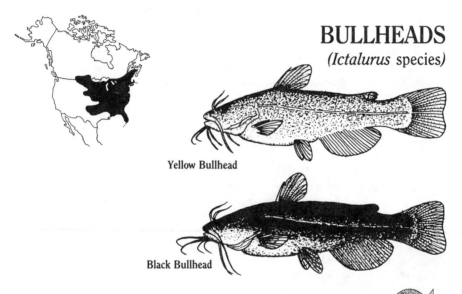

BULLHEADS
(Ictalurus species)

Yellow Bullhead

Black Bullhead

Range and Habitat: The catfishes of the genus *Ictalurus* commonly called bullheads have a very wide distribution. The black bullhead, or horned pout *(I. melas),* occurs from North Dakota east to New York and south to Texas. The brown bullhead *(I. nebulosus)* ranges from North Dakota and Saskatchewan to Nova Scotia and south to Florida and Mexico. The yellow bullhead *(I. natalis)* is found from east of the Rockies to New York and south to the Gulf of Mexico. The flat bullhead *(I. platycephalus)* is a coastal species occurring from the Roanoke River in Virginia south to Georgia. All but the flat bullhead have been widely introduced outside their natural ranges as food and game fishes.

Bullheads occupy a very wide variety of habitats. Their very adaptability and hardiness have been the key to their success in not only surviving but thriving in the face of a host of man-caused trials and tribulations, not the least an intense recreational fishery and the growing pollution of many North American waters. In general, though, bullheads of any species are nocturnal scavenger/predators that favor quieter waters such as ponds, lakes, and larger rivers and streams. Virtually any body of water capable of supporting fish life will prove satisfactory to bullheads as long as there is adequate plant growth for shelter and abundant prey animals and organic detritus.

Field Marks and Collecting: Bullheads are large-headed, robust catfishes with squared or slightly forked tails and an adipose fin. The pectoral and dorsal fins have sharp spines that can inflict a mildly painful wound on the unwary collector. The brown bullhead is usually a mottled dark brown fading to white or grayish on the sides and belly. It reaches a length of about 18 inches. The black bullhead may be yellowish brown to black, depending upon the habitat. Both the upper and lower barbels are dark. The yellow bullhead reaches a length of 16 inches or more. It is highly varied in color, ranging from light brownish-yellow to nearly black, but the lower barbels are always white. The flat bullhead is a mottled olive-brownish color; the underjaw barbels are normally paler than those of the upper jaw and snout. The body profile is elongate and the head is rather broad and flat.

Young bullheads may be collected along shallow, weedy shorelines with a dip net or seine. A minnow trap baited with pieces of meat and left near shore overnight in a known bullhead pond will almost certainly collect all the little horned pouts you could possibly use. Baby bullheads are shepherded about in a dense crowd by one or both parents for the first couple of weeks of their free-swimming life. A sweep with a dip net will always bag a few from such an aggregation, though I try to avoid this approach as it may disperse the school prematurely and leave the young exposed to undue predation.

Aquarium Care: Bullheads are one of the easiest native fishes to maintain in aquariums, their requirements being little more than water of acceptable quality and lots of food. They will thrive in almost any tank, perhaps a little too well. When small, they make good tank scavengers and will subsist on all prepared foods plus all live or meaty fare. The problem is that little bullheads metamorphose into big bullheads with truly amazing speed, at which time they will become a real threat to tankmates. This is a fish that ideally should be collected small in the spring and then released in early fall before the waters cool below the danger point.

CHANNEL CATFISH
(Ictalurus punctatus)

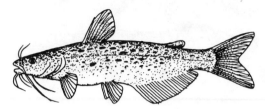

Range and Habitat: From the Great Lakes and Saskatchewan south throughout the Mississippi valley to the Gulf and Mexico. It is widely cultured as a food fish and introduced elsewhere, including Hawaii, as a game fish. The channel cat is found in larger rivers and lakes, though it has become established and thrived virtually wherever it has been deliberately introduced, including small bodies of water along the New Jersey shore, where it is actively fished for. Adults are deep-water prowlers, while the young may be found at most levels nearer the shore, especially in heavily weeded or debris-laden areas.

Field Marks and Collecting: The channel cat may reach lengths of up to two feet and weights of 20 pounds or more, though most are half that size. It is a relatively slim catfish, bluish-gray on the back and silvery to white below. The sides are usually speckled with small, irregular black spots. The head is rather long and somewhat flattened dorsally, and the tail is strongly forked. The young are a slightly darker gray above and more intensely spotted. A cultured albino form is quite popular in tropical aquariums.

Young channel cats can be seined in weed beds or caught in a minnow trap baited with a chicken neck or other such ripe bait. Since this species, like the bullheads, will put on size faster than you will have thought possible, it's best to collect the smallest specimens possible and plan to release them as soon as they become a problem to feed and house.

Aquarium Care: The channel cat is a hardy, adaptable fish that will survive reprehensible conditions before expiring, and it will eat virtually any organic fare. Small specimens make ideal scavengers for the community setup, though, like all catfishes, it cannot thrive on mere leftovers or fish waste, as catfish are often expected to do by neophyte tropical hobbyists. They must get an adquate diet if they are to thrive. Keep in mind that it is an active nocturnal predator as well. As it grows, it will pick off larger and larger fishes in its tank.

MADTOMS
(Noturus species)

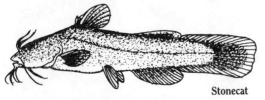

Stonecat

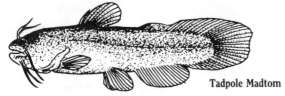

Tadpole Madtom

Least Madtom

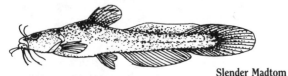

Slender Madtom

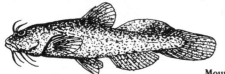

Mountain Madtom

Range and Habitat: There are roughly 12 species in this genus. The tadpole madtom is by far the most widely distributed and best-known, occurring from the Dakotas to Quebec and south to Florida and eastern Texas. Its life history, collecting, and care in the aquarium are representative of the group.

Madtoms are primarily stream catfishes, found for the most part in watercourses with stony or rocky beds that provide plenty of cover for these nocturnal fishes. The tadpole madtom also occurs in larger lakes where it prefers heavily vegetated shorelines and bog margins.

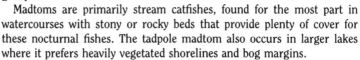

Field Marks and Collecting: Madtoms are small, slender catfishes that appear rather like tadpoles when first seen. They have a long adipose fin that is either continuous with the caudal fin, or separated from it only by a moderately deep notch. In all species, the tail is either rounded or squared off. The stonecat *(N. flavus)* is the largest species at a length of between six and ten inches, while the least madtom *(N. hildebrandti)* of southwestern Mississippi is the smallest at two to three inches.

The two most effective methods of collecting these secretive little fish are the rock-shuffling technique and the minnow trap. The trap should be baited with the rankest meat you have the courage to handle. Place the trap among rocks or vegetation at the stream or lake edge. In good habitat it should yield a number of fish.

Aquarium Care: Like other North American catfishes, madtoms are hardy creatures that require little special care to keep them in good condition. However, no catfish is a garbage can, able to subsist on the leavings (if there are any) or waste of other fish. Adequate nutrition is a must. Madtom quarters should contain enough rockwork to give these retiring fish plenty of hiding places. Although nocturnal, they will often come out of hiding when the lights are on in the tank once they have been thoroughly acclimated to confinement.

BURBOT
(Lota lota)

Range and Habitat: From New England and Pennsylvania west to the Columbia River and thence northward to Alaska and the Arctic Ocean. It is a cold-water lake and stream fish that favors clean, well-oxygenated water. In northern streams it is found in the deeper holes, while the young may be in the shallows poking about in a search for anything edible.

Field Marks and Collecting: The burbot, also called the lawyer, eelpout, and dogfish, is the only strictly freshwater member of the codfish family. It is a dark olive-brown variously mottled with even darker markings. The body is elongated and rather compressed posteriorly, but the fish can appear quite big-bellied when well fed. The head is small and flattened and the eyes are tiny for the size of the fish (up to twenty-six inches long and weighing about ten pounds). The skin has tiny, embedded scales but feels smooth. The fish closely resembles the marine eelpout *(Zoarces)* and has an appetite and temper equally as impressive.

Very young burbot, five inches and under, are the only individuals of this species that could even be considered as aquarium fish. Although they are not very common, they are easy to spot as they are very dark in color and move about in shallow water seemingly without fear. I have collected this species in central New Hampshire's Baker River using a dip net and even an empty glass jar. They are that easy to approach. The adults spawn in late winter (even before ice-out) and young of between two and four inches can usually be found in streams by late May.

Aquarium Care: The burbot is a voracious fish and will attack and devour any fish or other creature small enough to swallow. They will down fish close to their own size. For this reason, a burbot should be either kept alone or with fish considerably larger than it is, such as bass or large perch. This fish, like the common eel and most of the bullhead catfishes, will surprise the aquarist with its speed of growth under the favorable conditions and ample food supply of confinement. It is another fish that should be kept for a while and studied and then released at the point of collection. As with any obviously temporary tank tenants, plan ahead before you find that the creature has become a real problem in the dead of winter, when it cannot be released without killing it.

PIRATE PERCH
(Aphredoderus sayanus)

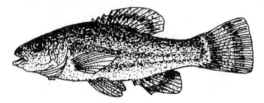

Range and Habitat: In two principal regions, the central Mississippi valley from southern Minnesota southward and the Atlantic coastal plain from New York south to eastern Texas. The pirate perch is found in densely weeded stream and bog margins, where it hides among thickets of aquatic vegetation such as sphagnum moss or bladderwort. In the east, this fish prefers the soft, acid waters of cedar swamps, and it is abundant in the tea-colored waters of the New Jersey Pine Barrens.

Field Marks and Collecting: The pirate perch's most conspicuous field mark is its color. It is an almost uniformly dark fish, either olive-brown or, in the many eastern specimens I have examined, blackish-purple fading to a smoky gray on the underside. Its most remarkable physical attribute will be found in its specific name—when you say anus, you note this fish's outstanding anatomical character. The fish's vent migrates forward from the typical location near the anal fin in very young specimens to a point on the throat in adults. Reaching a length of about five inches, the pirate looks like a rather big-headed, large-mouthed, dusky fish with darkish fins.

The pirate perch is rarely seen before it is collected. It is yet another of those very secretive fish that is caught primarily by hauling a seine or sweeping a dip net through dense weed beds and sorting through the mass of vegetation for the quarry. It can be best collected in areas where the water is filled with plant life and detritus from the surface to the substrate, and beneath bank overhangs along slow-moving streams.

Aquarium Care: This fish is a rather morose, somber oddball that moves about very little in the aquarium, preferring to lodge itself among the plants during the day, at least, for the pirate perch is essentially nocturnal in habits. At night, the fish becomes an active, voracious hunter, eating anything small enough to swallow. It should not be kept with fish much smaller than itself, no matter how inoffensive it may appear. Well-planted, dimly lit quarters should be provided, and the softer the water the better. Most pirates steadfastly refuse dead or prepared foods and thus should get liberal feedings of live brine shrimp, tubifex worms, small earthworms, or young fish. They will sometimes accept pieces of fish or lean meat placed in front of them. They are unhappy in an open tank with a turbulent filter current, doing best in near-standing water thick with plants.

TROUT-PERCH
(Percopsis omiscomaycus)

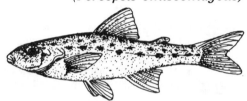

Range and Habitat: This genus includes two species: the trout-perch occurs from Alberta to Quebec and southward to Kansas, Missouri, and Virginia, and *P. transmontana* is found in the Columbia River basin. This fish prefers clear lakes and larger rivers and creeks, where it is found on gravel or sand substrates. It is a secretive, essentially nocturnal fish that hides in dense weed growth during the day, emerging at night to feed.

Field Marks and Collecting: The trout-perch resembles both a trout (in that it has a fatty adipose fin) and a perch (it looks vaguely like a small yellow perch or a young walleye). It is a pale brown to white, almost translucent color, with a horizontal row of between 9 and 12 dusky spots along the upper back and a second row along the midline. The adipose fin is finely marked with black along its upper edge. The tail is strongly forked. The trout-perch reaches a length of between three and five inches.

Being nocturnal, trout-perch are best collected at night with a light. A seine run through shoreside aquatic growth will usually get results, as will a minnow trap baited with dog food and set in submerged vegetation overnight. As the species often spawns in smaller streams, specimens can be collected with a dip net near sand or gravel bars at night.

Aquarium Care: This species does best when kept in a spacious tank with a sand or gravel substrate and some plant growth or roots to provide daytime hiding places. The tank should be dimly lit and filtration kept moderate to gentle. The trout-perch is reported to be very temperature-sensitive (considerable die-offs often occur in summer, at least in Minnesota, due to the sudden warming of lakes) so abrupt fluctuations of the water temperature should be avoided. This fish will accept most live foods and can be induced to take prepared foods. They are peaceful creatures and will not bother tankmates of like size and temperament.

GOLDEAR TOPMINNOW
(Fundulus chrysotus)

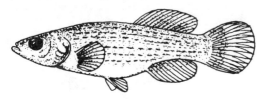

   Range and Habitat: Coastal swamps and streams from South Carolina to Florida, Louisiana, and Oklahoma. This fish is very common in the numerous drainage ditches that crisscross the southern coastal states. Most are spotted in open water near the edges of dense weed beds, though many are also collected from the bottom debris.

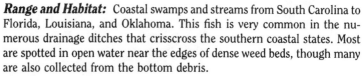 **Field Marks and Collecting:** The goldear is a trim, cylindrical fish in the best killifish tradition and is readily recognized when seen from above by the bright metallic spot on each gill cover, which shows up as twin flecks of gold in darker waters. The male is olive-green above, fading to a pale green on the sides and belly. There are rows of red, reflective spots on the sides and between six and ten dark crossbars. The median fins of both sexes are finely speckled with dusky brown. In some local races there is some degree of blackish mottling. A population with nearly solid black sides has been reported from the vicinity of Coral Gables, Florida. Females are much plainer, though they, too, usually show rows of metallic spots on the flanks. The goldear reaches a length of about three inches.

Goldears are best collected (in my own experience with the species in Mississippi) with a large-mouthed dip net, as the habitat is often too mucky to permit effective handling of a seine. When you approach them, they dart under bankside vegetation, and can be caught with an overhand sweep of the net.

Aquarium Care: The goldear has long been a favorite both with American and European aquarium hobbyists and does well if its few needs are met. It should get a fairly roomy tank well stocked with such bushy plants as *Anacharis (Elodea), Myriophyllum,* and bladderwort, and the temperature maintained at between 70° and 75° as this is a warmth-loving fish. Like most killifishes, the goldears will accept a wide variety of the conventional live and prepared foods, and they are particularly fond of live *daphnia*. The species has spawned regularly in aquariums, the only requirements being dense plant growth to receive the eggs, a slight elevation of the temperature to between 75° and 78°, and plenty of live foods to condition the breeders. The fine, hairlike roots of the water hyacinth or commercial spawning mops available at pet shops make good egg-laying media.

BLACKSTRIPE TOPMINNOW
(Fundulus notatus)

Range and Habitat: From Iowa and Ohio south to Tennessee, Mississippi, and Texas. This fish is common in the shallower waters of lakes, ponds, and slower-moving streams. They are abundant in weedy drainage ditches where they occur with the goldear killy and gambusia. The black-stripe is a surface fish usually observed in large schools at the edges of dense weed beds.

Field Marks and Collecting: Varies from a reddish brown to olive above, with a broad black or purplish band running from the eye to the base of the caudal fin. The lower flanks and belly are a clear white. This is an elongate, long-snouted fish with a larger eye than most killies have. The dorsal and anal fins are far back on the body. The tail is fan-shaped and usually finely spotted in black. This fish reaches a length of about 3½ inches.

The blackstripe, like most killifishes, can be collected by a variety of means—dip net, seine, minnow trap, or lift net—wherever they occur in abundance. The species seems to be most active in the early morning and late afternoon.

Aquarium Care: An undemanding fish, the blackstripe topminnow will thrive under the conditions given for the goldear—a roomy tank, plenty of plants, and peaceful tankmates. It will accept most live foods. As it is a surface feeder in nature, most prepared flakes suit it very well. The blackstripe will coexist with most other fish that occur with it naturally, but gambusia should be avoided as these will harass and pick at it (along with most other fishes in the tank).

LEAST KILLIFISH
(Heterandria formosa)

Range and Habitat: Southeastern United States, from South Carolina south along the Coastal Plain to about the New Orleans area. The least killie is found in swamps and weedy roadside ditches, usually in pockets of local abundance. It is very secretive and rarely observed in open water, always being found among dense weed beds.

Field Marks and Collecting: Until the discovery of the near-macroscopic Philippine goby, the least killifish held the title of the world's smallest known fish. At the maximum length of about one inch—males are even smaller—the distinction is easy to see, for a fully grown male is hardly larger than a newborn molly. The least killie is a rich golden brown or olive above (depending on the habitat). A dark, broken band runs from the snout to the base of the tail, where it terminates in a prominent spot. The underside is usually clear white or pale yellow. There is usually a black spot basally on the dorsal and anal fins, and some individuals show between four and six faded, dusky crossbars.

The very small size of this fish is the only real obstacle to easy collecting, for it can be hard to spot in a net full of debris, and is so small that it can easily slip through the meshes of a seine. A fine-meshed dip net is thus the only real way to go. Several colleagues and I, collecting the species near Bay St. Louis, Mississippi, found that sweeping the net through dense weed growth and then keeping the bag in the water so the fish could swim free of the plant tangle was the best way to secure specimens without unduly exposing them to the air while we pawed through the net on the bank.

Aquarium Care: The least killifish is the classic single species tank fish in that there are virtually no other fishes with which it can be quartered with safety. The species is so small, shy, and secretive that any other fishes kept with it would only intimidate it and force it into perpetual hiding. The least killie does well in small containers and has been kept and bred with success in five-gallon tanks. It is a livebearer, and the miniscule fry will usually escape being eaten by their parents as long as a heavy plant growth is maintained in the tank. Gentle filtration and lower light levels are also recommended for this timid fish. Smaller live foods (baby brine shrimp or *daphnia)* are best, for large brine shrimp or tubifex worms may be beyond the tiny male's ability to subdue and eat. Being principally a surface feeder, the least killifish will usually accept most prepared flake foods without trouble.

PYGMY KILLIFISH
(Leptolucania ommata)

Range and Habitat: In marshes and bogs in Georgia and Florida, mostly in coastal areas. It is usually associated with the *Enneacanthus* and *Elassoma* sunfishes and shares their habitat preference—densely weeded, quiet areas that afford these small, shy fish some degree of security from predators.

Field Marks and Collecting: Also called the swamp or lemon killie, this fish vies with *Heterandria formosa* for the title of the smallest North American fish. Adults stretch the tape at one inch. The pygmy killie is pale gold or tan. Both sexes have a dark lateral stripe that is paler in the female. Both male and female show a dark spot at the base of the caudal fin, and the female has another spot on the body just above the insertion of the anal fin. Males may have 9 to 11 dusky crossbars on the sides.

A dip net swept at random through a mass of aquatic growth in the fish's habitat is the best way to collect the pygmy killie. Most specimens are small enough to slip through the ¼-inch mesh of a seine. Their pale, nondescript color may make individuals a challenge to spot among the tangle of weeds in the net, so search the bag thoroughly before upending it.

Aquarium Care: This species is most definitely a candidate for the single species tank for it is so shy and retiring that most other fishes will only stress or eat it. Exceptions to the "no tankmates" rule would be the pygmy sunfishes, the least killifish, and perhaps small individuals of the *Enneacanthus* group of sunfishes—fellow shrinking violets all.

The pygmy killie is one of the few fishes that will do quite well in a very small tank. A dimly-lit, five-gallon tank heavily planted in *Anacharis* or *Cabomba* and subjected to gentle aeration/filtration will suit them fine as long as they are not crowded.

BLUEFIN KILLIFISH
(Lucania goodei)

 Range and Habitat: Bogs and swamps of Georgia and Florida. The bluefin prefers clear, standing water with abundant vegetation, water that is slightly hard and darkly stained by organic debris.

 Field Marks and Collecting: In nonbreeding colors, the bluefin is a somber little fish, being olive with a black lateral band ending in a dark caudal spot. The dorsal and anal fins are transparent or pale amber with black edging. The male has a broad black band basally on the dorsal fin. In breeding condition, the male's dorsal and anal fins become bright, almost iridescent blue, strongly bordered with black. The bluefin reaches a length of about 1½ inches.

This fish is a highly secretive, nervous little creature that is found in or near heavy plant growth. In most cases, a random sweep of a dip net through favorable habitat will yield a mess of weeds and a bluefin or two. The favored habitat doesn't lend itself to effective seining.

Aquarium Care: Dr. Robert Goldstein, who has had considerable experience with this species and with killifishes in general, has this to say about keeping the bluefin: "Difficult to maintain in good health, bluefins do not breed easily [in aquariums] and require good water conditions with no rotting or fungal growth on the bottom. The greatest problem with the fish is its deportment, this fearfulness interfering with normal husbandry practices." The bluefin killie should be maintained in a heavily planted tank with no tankmates of any kind for best results. A ten-gallon tank with lush plant growth and illuminated by low-watt incandescent bulbs is recommended. Smaller live foods should be offered.

DIAMOND KILLIFISH
(Adinia xenica)

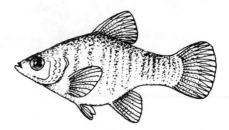

Range and Habitat: In coastal brackish and occasionally freshwater habitats from Florida and along the Gulf Coast to Texas.

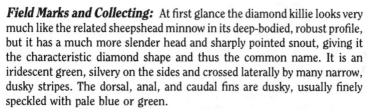

Field Marks and Collecting: At first glance the diamond killie looks very much like the related sheepshead minnow in its deep-bodied, robust profile, but it has a much more slender head and sharply pointed snout, giving it the characteristic diamond shape and thus the common name. It is an iridescent green, silvery on the sides and crossed laterally by many narrow, dusky stripes. The dorsal, anal, and caudal fins are dusky, usually finely speckled with pale blue or green.

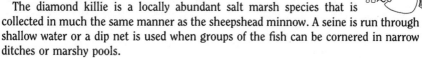

The diamond killie is a locally abundant salt marsh species that is collected in much the same manner as the sheepshead minnow. A seine is run through shallow water or a dip net is used when groups of the fish can be cornered in narrow ditches or marshy pools.

Aquarium Care: Being of rather limited and sporadic distribution, the diamond killie is not as well known to aquarists as are other members of the large killifish family. Although it has been reported from nearly pure fresh water, this fish must have some salt in order to thrive, thus it does best in brackish water; one tablespoon of roniodized salt per gallon of water will suit it. It is an active little fish, but unlike the sheepshead, it will not normally harass or attack other fish kept with it. The diamond killie will accept all live foods as well as graze on algae and any edibies it can find.

BANDED KILLIFISH
(Fundulus diaphanus)

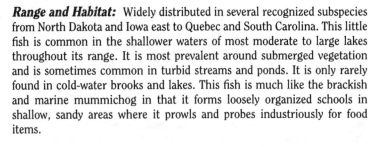

Range and Habitat: Widely distributed in several recognized subspecies from North Dakota and Iowa east to Quebec and South Carolina. This little fish is common in the shallower waters of most moderate to large lakes throughout its range. It is most prevalent around submerged vegetation and is sometimes common in turbid streams and ponds. It is only rarely found in cold-water brooks and lakes. This fish is much like the brackish and marine mummichog in that it forms loosely organized schools in shallow, sandy areas where it prowls and probes industriously for food items.

Field Marks and Collecting: The banded killie looks like the typical *Fundulus* killifish except that it is more slender and has a more pointed head and snout than most members of the genus. It is a rather drab fish, being olive with silvery sides and belly and crossed with about 18 narrow black vertical stripes. The back and sides are usually spotted in rose and light blue, and the fins in nonbreeding fish are plain. In breeding males, the colors are intensified and the dorsal fin is irregularly banded in dusky or black.

The banded or freshwater killifish replaces the marine mummichog in shallow, weedy, shoreline habitats inland and exhibits similar behavior—that is, it forms loosely organized schools that patrol the edges of weed beds and sandy areas in search of the small invertebrate fare it feeds on. Banded killies usually dart into the vegetation or substrate debris when disturbed, unlike the mummichogs, which usually make a dash for deeper water. Thus I've found it best to sweep a dip net through weed growth where the fish were last seen. This will usually bag at least a few specimens. Otherwise, they may be seined.

Aquarium Care: The banded killie thrives in strictly fresh water and thus does not require the addition of salt for good health as do most others of the genus. Although it is related to and somewhat resembles the mummichog, this fish lacks the former's hardiness and can be quite sensitive to rough handling and poor water conditions. It should not be crowded, either in the collecting container or the aquarium, and must be given water of the best quality. The tank should be well planted and rather brightly lit in order to encourage some algal growth. Once acclimated, this killifish will accept nearly all commercially available live and prepared foods, especially those that float on the surface, as this is primarily a surface-feeding fish.

AMERICAN FLAGFISH
(Jordanella floridae)

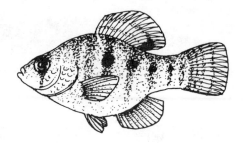

Range and Habitat: In coastal swamps, lagoons, drainage ditches, and ponds from Florida to Yucatan. The flagfish prefer heavily weeded areas where they may occur in great numbers.

Field Marks and Collecting: The common name stems from the color and pattern of this little fish supposedly resembling Old Glory, and the alternate rows of red and blue-green dots adorning its sides do in fact bring the flag to mind. The flag killie is a robust little fish (2½ inches at maturity) that is best identified by the arrangement of colors given above, combined with a large, diffuse spot just below the dorsal fin. In young specimens a series of dark spots is centered in four to five diffuse vertical bars which eventually give way to the single spot present in adults. Females are less colorful than males, and have an additional black spot at the posterior edge of the dorsal fin.

Flagfish are best collected with a dip net as their densely weeded habitat does not lend itself to use of a seine. They can also be caught in a killie trap baited with bread or other bait, such as dog biscuit.

Aquarium Care: The flagfish has been known to European aquarists for many years and has enjoyed much more popularity there than in its native land. The fish is available through aquarium stores in the United States and Canada, most of them being imported from Europe or Singapore, although some are still collected in the wild in Florida.

This fish is hardy and undemanding, though it prefers a thickly planted tank that may, in fact, serve more than mere decorative whim, for it can be aggressive and males will fight among themselves with vigor. They can also spell trouble for other, slower-moving species that can't get out of their way or avoid them. Thus for best results they are ideally kept alone. Flagfish can be spawned in aquariums with relative ease. Provide plenty of cover, a temperature between 70° and 75°, and ample food with an emphasis on algae, and the fish will take care of the rest. The young are fewer in number than in most killifishes and are large at hatching so that most will survive if the tank's plant thickets offer them enough hiding places.

GAMBUSIA
(Gambusia affinis)

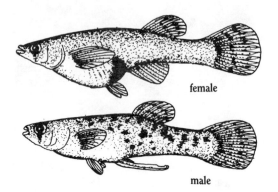

female

male

Range and Habitat: Exists in many subspecies, a few of them severely threatened. *G. affinis* occurs in two races, from southern Illinois and Indiana south to Alabama and Mexico and from New Jersey south along the Coastal Plain to Alabama *(G. affinis holbrooki)*. At least six other species, some of extremely limited distribution, occur in Texas and Mexico. These are: Largespring gambusia *(G. geiseri);* Clear Creek bambusia *(G. heterochir);* Pecos gambusia *(G. nobilis);* Blotched gambusia *(G. senilis),* and the Big Bend gambusia *(G. gagei).*

Gambusia, also known as mosquito fish, potgut, or pusselgut minnow (in Florida), prefer warm, sluggish streams, drainage ditches, or standing waters with abundant vegetation. The species has gradually been extending its range into cooler regions. There is a thriving population in Teaneck in northern New Jersey from which I've collected numerous specimens over the years.

Field Marks and Collecting: At first glance, the mosquito fish resembles nothing more than a nondescript guppy. It is a livebearer and the male posseses the specialized anal fin known as the gonopodium. This serves as an intromittent organ for the transfer of sperm to the genital pore of the female. In most forms, the gambusia is a plain grayish-olive above and silvery below, but the males of some southern populations are often heavily pigmented with black blotches and speckles. The fins may be transparent or show traces of dusky or blue. Pregnant females usually display the dark gravid spot common to familiar tropical poecilids such as guppies, platies, and swordtails. An adult female gambusia is large at 2½ inches; the male is smaller, 1½ to 2 inches.

Gambusia are active, alert little critters that can be hard to collect in spite of their abundance and wide range of habitats. They are generally too small to be bagged in a minnow trap and often slip through a seine as well, so the best approach is a dip net and a willingness to slog about in the often mucky, boggy environs. I have found that they can be baited to a particular area with bread or prepared fish flakes and then bagged by sneaking up on them through shoreside vegetation as one would stalk the noble trout.

Aquarium Care: As might be guessed, the adaptable gambusia presents few problems in an aquarium. They will eat a wide variety of foods from live to prepared, and will freely breed in a well-planted tank. The one problem centers around the fish's behavior, for the mosquito fish can be an aggressive animal. This scrappy behavior involves others of their own kind for the most part, though they will often harrass other fish kept with them. They will also eat their own young at every opportunity. In view of this, the mosquito fish is best kept in a single-species tank heavily planted in *Anacharis, Myriophyllum, Cabomba,* or other such dense floating vegetation. If you wish to breed the species, a standard livebearer breeding trap, available at any pet shop, can be used to house the female while she gives birth to her large, rather well-developed fry.

SAILFIN MOLLY
(Poecilia latipinna)

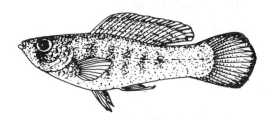

Range and Habitat: The sailfin is one of the few North American fishes that is considered a tropical fish and is popular in the aquarium that occurs naturally within the continental United States. The fish's range extends from South Carolina along the Gulf Coast to Mexico in coastal fresh and brackish areas, often being found in seawater. I treat it as a freshwater fish here as I have found it most abundant in bayous, bogs, and roadside ditches in Louisiana and Mississippi, where considerable numbers are collected. The mollies favor weedy areas with expanses of muddy bottom in which they root about for the minute prey and vegetable matter they eat.

Field Marks and Collecting: The male sailfin molly is a familiar fish to virtually everyone who has even dabbled in the aquarium hobby. The great dorsal fin, normally carried folded against the fish's back, is an exquisite organ when spread in the courtship display, being liberally spangled with black spots and sprinkled with a veritable rainbow of colors. The overall color is olivaceous above and silvery to white on the sides and belly. The broad, rounded caudal fin is orange bordered with black in the adult male. The female is similar in form but lacks the large dorsal fin and shows the dark gravid spot characteristic of livebearers. Her fins are transparent or faintly dusky. The molly is a robust fish with the mouth situated at the top of the snout, indicating a surface feeder.

Mollies can be collected with a seine where they are found in more open situations and with a dip net in more heavily weeded areas. They will enter a minnow trap baited with bread or dry dog food.

Aquarium Care: Mollies are warmth-loving fish and should be kept in a tank of at least a mildly brackish composition in which algae growth is encouraged. This may not present the prettiest picture, but no molly ever thrived in a sparkling clean, sterile aquarium with intensively filtered, polished water. In the absence of adequate algae growth, the fish should be offered periodic feedings of boiled spinach or lettuce as a substitute. Molly quarters should be maintained at a temperature of between 78° and 82°. If kept cooler or in fresh water, the fish go off their feed and engage in a shimmying movement. If conditions are not corrected, the fish will emaciate and die.

Like guppies, platies, and swordtails, mollies are livebearers but the number of young delivered at one time is smaller and they are larger at birth than those of platies and swordtails. If kept in a lushly planted tank and fed adequately, mollies will seldom molest their own young. They are rather peaceable creatures, although males sometimes squabble over females.

MOTTLED SCULPIN
(Cottus bairdi)

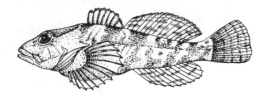

Range and Habitat: From Labrador and Northwest Territories south to the Ozarks and the Appalachians. It is represented in the West by several subspecies. Most sculpins are marine but species occurring in fresh water inhabit clear, cool water lakes, streams, and rivers, and prefer rocky substrates with minimal vegetation. They are secretive fishes never found far from the protection of rocks, roots, and bottom debris, from which they make periodic forays after prey animals. The large (12 inches) Pacific staghorn sculpin (*Leptocottus armatus*) is an essentially marine species that enters coastal streams from Alaska south to Baja California.

Field Marks and Collecting: The mottled sculpin is a big-headed, almost tadpole-like fish that tapers to a rather slender, laterally compressed body. The pectoral fins are large and fanlike. Spines are present on the gill covers and the moderately large eyes are high on the sides of the head. The color is a warm reddish brown fading to yellow or clear white on the belly. The body and fins are variously mottled and blotched with darker browns or black. The overall effect is like that of an undersized freshwater toadfish.

Given the rocky nature of the fish's habitat, the sculpin collector is limited to two methods for bagging sculpins: the minnow trap and the seine. The former can be lodged unbaited among the rocks and left overnight, while the seine can be held or lodged in position in the stream bed while another person approaches from upstream shuffling rocks.

Aquarium Care: Like their marine counterparts, freshwater sculpins have a higher oxygen requirement and a distinct need for cooler water temperatures, two factors that make them difficult at best to maintain under average aquarium conditions. The aquarist interested in serious observation of this group should invest in a commercial aqua-chiller in order to maintain the 50°–70° range sculpins require, otherwise they will perish as soon as the room temperature rises much above 75°. That problem aside, the sculpins need clean, well-aerated water with a moderately strong filtration current. The substrate should duplicate the rocky stream bed, and plants are not necessary. Although some aquarists report that these fish will in time learn to accept prepared foods, live fare is by far the preferred, with blood and tubifex worms, earthworms, and small feeder guppies the most available. Sculpins can be kept with any other cold-water stream fishes as long as the latter are not small enough to make a meal for the sculpin, which will readily ambush them at night.

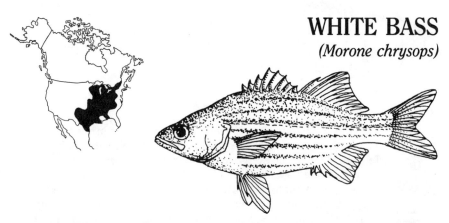

WHITE BASS
(Morone chrysops)

Range and Habitat: The white bass is typical of the temperate basses, and collecting and care is similar for most of the group, which includes the yellow bass *(M. mississippiensis)* and the white perch *(M. americana).* The white bass ranges from Minnesota east through the lower Great Lakes and St. Lawrence drainages and south to northern Alabama and Texas. It has been transplanted elsewhere as a game fish.

The temperate basses are freshwater forms of the seagoing basses (the Serranidae). They favor larger, deeper ponds, lakes, and rivers, where they form large schools near the surface. The young gather in similar shoals near shore over a wide range of bottoms.

Field Marks and Collecting: The white bass is a moderately deep-bodied, laterally compressed fish; the overall color is light olive or tan on the back and a bright silver on the sides and belly, with seven to nine irregular black lines running the length of the body. The snout is elongate and tapered with the upper jaw ending about midpoint of the eye. The dorsal fins are separate. In younger specimens, the fins are sometimes dusky or tinted with a reddish hue.

This species is best collected in early summer when the young have attained a size suitable for aquariums. They are most easily seined in shallow waters near tributaries entering lakes and ponds, where the adults have spawned.

Aquarium Care: This group needs no special care other than adequate room, for the temperate basses will put on size fast if fed adequately. Although not overly aggressive, the white bass should not be kept with fish small enough to be considered food. All of the live foods available at pet shops, plus chopped smelt or lean beef, will provide an adquate diet for this fish and others of the group.

PYGMY SUNFISHES
(Elassoma species*)*

Range and Habitat: There are three recognized species in this genus: the banded pygmy sunfish *(E. zonatum)*, occurring from southern Illinois to Texas and Florida; the Everglades pygmy sunfish *(E. evergladei)*, found in cedar and cypress swamps in southern Georgia and Florida; and the Oke-fenokee pygmy sunfish *(E. okefenokee)*, occurring in the Okefenokee Swamp in Georgia and northern Florida. All three species prefer quiet, near-standing, heavily vegetated waters of soft, acid composition. The banded species is quite widely distributed, often found in roadside ditches in the southern parts of the range.

Field Marks and Collecting: These are the smallest of all the North American sunfishes and basses, reaching a maximum length of about 1½ inches at maturity. All three are of very similar appearance, the main differences as follows: The banded pygmy sunfish is olive with 10 to 12 vertical bars on the flanks. It has a squared-off tail and a black spot about the size of the eye on the side just below the insertion of the dorsal fin. Breeding males are often very dark, almost black, while the females become pale yellowish-brown. The Everglades pygmy sunfish is also olive overall with a slightly reddish cast and irregular vertical markings. The tail is more rounded than in the banded species and there are irregularly distributed blue-green dots anterior on the body. The Okefenokee species is a rich brown with variable dark markings and blue spots; it is very similar to the Everglades species and can be told with certainty only by examination of the dorsal fin rays (it averages more than the former) and by the top of the head, which is scaleless in *E. okefenokee*.

The pygmy sunfishes are so small and secretive that they are usually collected incidentally in seine hauls or dip net sweeps through dense vegetation. They will enter a killie trap placed in suitable habitat and left for a day or two.

Aquarium Care: Ideally, these tiny centrarchids should have a tank of their own, densely planted and with lower light levels. They are unhappy in open tanks crowded with active tankmates. Smaller live foods such as live brine shrimp, bloodworms, and mosquito larvae are the best foods, although specimens I had in a five-gallon tank for some time eventually came to accept some prepared fish foods. The banded pygmy sunfish has spawned in suitably set up aquariums.

BLACK BASSES
(*Micropterus* species)

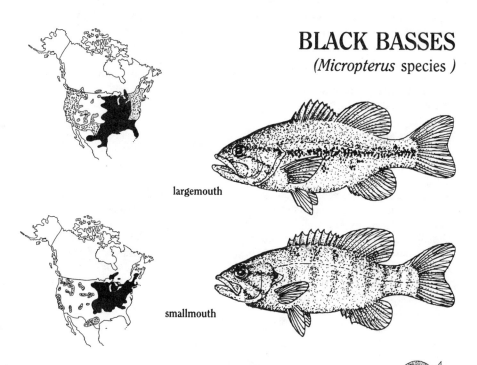

largemouth

smallmouth

Range and Habitat: The largemouth bass *(M. salmoides)* occurs from southern Canada through the Great Lakes drainage to central Mexico, and from Maryland to Florida on the East Coast. It favors warmer water than the smallmouth *(M. dolomieui),* which occurs from Minnesota to Quebec and south to Alabama and Arkansas. Both have been widely introduced elsewhere, including Hawaii. An intermediate form, the spotted bass *(M. punctulatus),* is found from southern Illinois, Missouri, and Ohio south to eastern Texas and the Gulf states.

The largemouth and smallmouth basses have distinct habitat preferences, the former favoring shallow, warm ponds and lakes with abundant vegetation, the latter frequenting cooler, deep lakes and rivers with rocky substrates and plenty of root and blow-down tangles. Adult bass hug such shelter while they wait for passing prey while the young often cruise about wherever there is suitable cover. Like pickerel, bass are highly cannibalistic.

Field Marks and Collecting: The best field mark for the largemouth is the angle of the upper jaw, which extends past the rear margin of the eye; in the smallmouth, it extends to about the center of the orbit. The largemouth is dark greenish olive above, with a darker irregular lateral band. The sides and belly are a clear white or brassy color. The smallmouth is greenish above and a dusky silver below, the body plainer in pattern than the largemouth, but often faintly banded vertically. The eye of the adult is a carmine red. The young of both species usually display a strong dark lateral stripe, which fades or breaks up with age. The spotted bass has the same coloration as the two former species but shows more irregular mottling and has a more prominent opercular spot.

Most bass, even relatively small ones, are caught by angling, usually with live bait or lures. With care, such individuals can be acclimated to aquariums, but if there are severe hook injuries they should be released as they are prone to persistent mouth infections that can be difficult to cure. Young bass can be collected by surrounding an aggregation with a 20-foot seine, moving in, and hoping for the best, for they are very swift and agile. Very small fry can be collected by sweeping a dip net through vegetation. Before collecting any, check with your state fish and game department, for these are game fishes and their capture and possession are regulated almost everywhere.

Aquarium Care: The black basses are for those aquarists who like to keep such exotics as piranhas and snakeheads. They are fearsome predators that must have living prey and lots of it. These are not fish for the casual hobbyist or one who doesn't like the sight of blood or one animal eating another one, nor for those unprepared both to provide such fare or to keep the bass by itself in a large tank. Bass are best suited as display animals in science centers or public aquariums. If you must keep one, give it roomy quarters with clean, well-aerated water and live foods such as feeder guppies and goldfish, nightcrawlers, or small crayfish. Very small individuals will accept live brine shrimp or tubifex worms, but only until they put on some size, at which time they will ignore such small fare. Bass of equal size usually get along well in the same tank. They are classic examples of fish that should be kept only for a while and then released before they become a problem to feed and house.

BLACKBANDED SUNFISH
(Enneacanthus chaetodon)

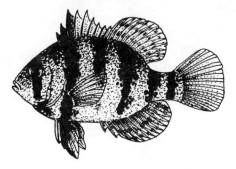

Range and Habitat: In scattered locations from southern New Jersey to northern Florida. Prefers coastal plain, acid-water situations, normally pine barrens and cedar swamps. Often very local in abundance; considered fairly rare and quite sensitive to human alterations of the habitat. Look for this very beautiful little sunfish in quiet, weedy bogs and slow-moving streams stained dark red-brown by tannic acid and organic debris. They are quite prevalent in beds of beaked rushes and under most circumstances are found close to the protection of the shoreline. In areas where they may appear abundant, it is very likely an isolated population that would suffer from overcollecting. Retain only a few specimens for your aquarium.

Field Marks and Collecting: Adults reach 3½ inches. This fish is unmistakable: It looks much like the familiar tropical angelfish, with dark, irregular bars against a silver-gold background, accented by a carmine-red eye and delicate salmon-pink or orange ventral fins. Rarely observed in open water, but when alarmed, it moves off in a slow, deliberate manner before suddenly vanishing among the dense sphagnum moss fronds.

This little gem may be either seined or caught with a dip net, depending on the terrain. Numerous sunken snags can make seine collecting a challenge in the typical habitat. Among the best locations are weedy overhangs at lake margins, beaked rush beds, and the quiet backwaters of slower-moving pine barrens streams. This fish, even more so than most species, should not be crowded in the collecting bucket or subjected to undue stress in handling. A styrofoam ice chest or other such container that seals out light will calm the captives and make the trip home easier for them.

Aquarium Care: The blackbanded sunfish acclimates well to captivity if handled gently; otherwise they are prone to fungus infections. Most individuals refuse all but live foods at first, though they will usually come to accept most frozen and freeze-dried foods in time. Soft, acid water is a must if the wild-caught fish are to remain in good color and health. Due to their shy temperament, a heavily planted, dimly lit tank suits them best.

Note: This fish has proven so popular with aquarists, particularly in Europe, that many more are raised commercially overseas than are collected in their native land.

BLUESPOTTED SUNFISH
(Enneacanthus gloriosus)

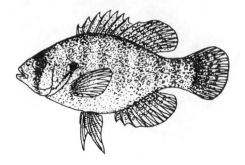

Range and Habitat: In quieter waters of the coastal plain from New Jersey and eastern Pennsylvania to northern Florida. This fish favors acid water heavily overgrown with sphagnum moss and other submerged or emergent vegetation. It is almost always found very close to shore and often in association with the black-banded and banded sunfishes.

Field Marks and Collecting: This fish, at 2½ to 3 inches, the smallest of the three midget sunfish species, is one of the most dainty and gentle of the centrarchids, a family not exactly renowned for its timidity. Although often confused with the banded sunfish, it can be told from that fish by its slimmer profile and more pointed snout, and by its black opercular spot, which is smaller than the eye and has a tiny, silvery spot just in front of it. The body of this species lacks bands or is only faintly barred and is usually of a plain olive or, in acid water, a reddish-brown color. Except for the anterior portions of the dorsal and anal fins, the entire fish is liberally speckled with iridescent blue spots during the breeding season, giving it its other comon name, diamond sunfish.

The bluespotted sunfish is collected in the same manner as are the other *Enneacanthus* sunfishes, and it ranks with the blackbanded in fragility. Take few specimens, handle with great care, and don't overcrowd, either in the collecting bucket or in the aquarium.

Aquarium Care: This species will decline if kept in an open, brightly lit tank with active or aggressive tankmates. As with most shy fish, it should be given a thickly planted tank and kept in low light. This species is shown off best when kept in a tank containing cleaned cedar roots and black aquarium gravel. In these conditions, the colors retain their intensity to a much greater degree. The bluespotted sunfish prefers live foods, being less likely to accept prepared fish foods. Quarter it with other non-aggressive species, such as mudminnows, banded and blackbanded sunfishes, or smaller pirate perch.

BANDED SUNFISH
(Enneacanthus obesus)

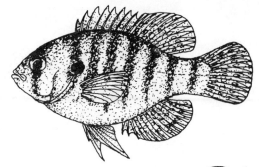

Range and Habitat: Found in slower-moving streams and lakes in the coastal lowlands from Massachusetts to Florida, becoming more common in the central and southern portions of the range. This attractive midget sunfish shares its habitat preference with the genteel black-banded sunfish—quiet acid water lakes, bogs, and stream margins in pine barrens and cedar swamps. It favors heavily vegetated areas such as sphagnum bogs and is rarely found far from the protection of the shoreline. The banded, or sphagnum, sunfish is a bit bolder and more adventurous than the other two *Enneacanthus* species and may be observed actively swimming in more open areas.

Field Marks and Collecting: This is a chunky little (three inches) olive fish, liberally spangled with dots of iridescent gold, green, and purple. The body is crossed vertically by 6 to 8 irregular dark bands, and the opercular spot is as large as the eye, an important field mark in differentiating this species from the similar blue-spotted sunfish, with which it shares much of its range.

The banded sunfish can be collected in shallow water in which aquatic plant growth affords hiding places. Bank overhangs in sphagnum bogs are usually very productive spots. They are the commonest of the three *Enneacanthus* sunfishes wherever they occur together and the one most often turning up in the seine when a person is seeking the black-banded sunfish. This species is hardier and more tolerant of stress and handling than either the black-banded or blue-spotted species, but should be handled with care and not crowded in the collecting pail.

Aquarium Care: In spite of its family relationship to the powerful, predaceous black basses, this is a relatively timid little fish that will decline in the face of excessive aggression and competition on the part of the tankmates. As such, it requires a heavily planted tank best kept under lower illumination and is ideally quartered only with relatives of the same genus. Soft, acid water is best, and it's helpful if periodic water changes are made using water collected at the site of capture. Although it prefers live foods, the banded sunfish is highly adaptable and will come to accept most standard aquarium fish foods, up to and including pellets. Like most native sunfishes, this species will retain much of its natural color and vigor if kept at room temperature and allowed a period of cooler weather dormancy, if possible. Given these conditions, the species will breed in aquariums; hybrids between it and *E. gloriosus* have been reported.

MUD SUNFISH
(Acantharchus pomotis)

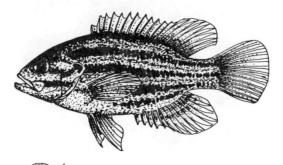

Range and Habitat: Lowland streams and bogs on the coastal plain from southern New York to northern Florida. The mud sunfish is distributed rather irregularly throughout its range and is not an abundant fish anywhere. It is quite rare at the northern extreme of the range, and should not be kept if collected in New York. This fish favors acid-water habitats, such as cedar swamps and pine barrens country, and is often found with the black-banded, blue-spotted, and banded, or sphagnum, sunfishes. It is found in sluggish or standing water in which there is heavy plant growth, such as water lily beds.

Field Marks and Collecting: The mud sunfish is a moderate-sized centrarchid that reaches the length of about seven inches in very large individuals. It is a robust, chunky, dark greenish to olive fish with five indistinct longitudinal bands along the pale gold flanks. It is best told from the other smaller sunfishes by its heavy head, large mouth, and dark brown eye.

This species is rare and this makes it very popular with native fish aquarists in spite of its unimpressive colors. I have found it locally abundant in pockets in the New Jersey Pine Barrens, where it favors the quiet backwaters of smaller lakes and bogs. Most mud sunfish come to net incidentally during collecting operations. The seine is most effective in covering more prime mud sunfish habitat than could be worked with a dip net, though dragging the seine through the habitat can be arduous.

Aquarium Care: In spite of its robust physique and decidedly predatory nature, the mud sunfish is a retiring creature that does not fare well in an open, brightly lit tank. It is sensitive to harrassment by aggressive tankmates and will remain in hiding if kept under such conditions. This is a fish for the "pine barrens tank," with neutral to soft water and decorated with plenty of gnarled cedar roots and thickets of aquatic plants affording hiding places. This fish will accept all of the standard live foods, as well as most meat and fish fare. It generally ignores prepared fish foods unless very hungry.

PUMPKINSEED
(Lepomis gibbosus)

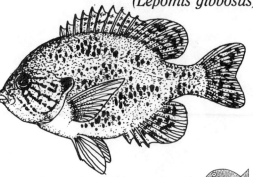

Range and Habitat: This common eastern centrarchid has a very wide range, occurring naturally from Manitoba and North Dakota east to New Brunswick and south to Iowa, Ohio, and South Carolina. It has been widely introduced elsewhere as a panfish. The pumpkinseed is far from choosy in its habitat requirements, being found in virtually any standing or moving body of water that will support fish life. It favors small lakes and ponds containing abundant vegetation, and quickly makes itself at home in streams and even large rivers where adequate shoreside cover exists.

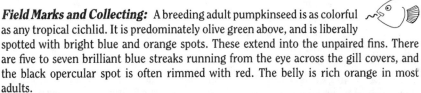

Field Marks and Collecting: A breeding adult pumpkinseed is as colorful as any tropical cichlid. It is predominately olive green above, and is liberally spotted with bright blue and orange spots. These extend into the unpaired fins. There are five to seven brilliant blue streaks running from the eye across the gill covers, and the black opercular spot is often rimmed with red. The belly is rich orange in most adults.

Pumpkinseeds may be collected by virtually every method available. Where they are abundant, small fish will readily enter a killie trap baited with bread and set near docks and other such man-made shelter, and they are rather easily caught with a lift net placed in the same surroundings. A seine will bag all the "sunnies" you can use if the vegetation is not so heavy that it impedes its use. Pumpkinseeds nest in the sandy substrate close to shore in late spring and early summer, the males guarding the conspicuous depressions. The adults should not be collected when observed guarding eggs or newly hatched fry, as these will quickly perish or be eaten by predators without the custodianship of the parent.

Aquarium Care: The pumpkinseed is the archetypal native aquarium fish, and its beauty has made it extremely popular with aquarists both in North America and in Europe, where it is in great demand and is bred regularly by hobbyists. It makes few demands on its keeper except that it should have clean, well-aerated water and be given plenty of room, for the species is aggressive when adult and will bully tankmates if given the chance. Generally, they coexist well enough if of equal size, but they should not be kept with more timid fishes, such as shiners, dace, or any of the *Enneacanthus* sunfishes. The young adults seem to be the most pugnacious, with older fish becoming more agreeable as they mature. This sunfish should get as much live food as possible if it is to maintain health and color, with chopped or whole earthworms or strips of lean beef particular favorites.

BLUEGILL
(Lepomis macrochirus)

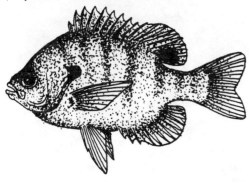

Range and Habitat: Very widespread, occurring naturally from about Minnesota east to Lake Champlain and south to Florida and Texas. Widely introduced elsewhere, including California and Hawaii. Like the pumpkinseed, the bluegill makes itself at home wherever there is water that won't kill it outright. It is popular for farm ponds, where it often reproduces itself out of house and home in the absence of predators, resulting in severe stunting. The bluegill is also found in most natural ponds, lakes, and slower-moving rivers within the range. The bluegill prefers heavily vegetated areas affording plenty of cover. In waters free of bass or pickerel, adults will often be seen swimming in open water.

Field Marks and Collecting: The bluegill appears rather dusky at a glance, being a dark olive-green, with blue streaks on the operculum. The body has five to seven vertical bands. The belly is often a suffused gold or orange. The opercular spot is a solid black and rather large, often larger than the eye, and there is a prominent black spot posteriorly on the dorsal fin in most younger individuals. The bluegill is one of the larger sunfishes, reaching a length of ten inches or more and weighing two pounds. It is a very popular gamefish throughout its range.

Use the dip net for collecting bluegill as they can be wily and will hug the protection of submerged vegetation and thus can be difficult to bag with a seine. Smaller young fish can often be enticed to enter a baited killie trap set in shallow, weedy areas, or, with patience, herded into a fish trap constructed of rocks on sandy lake beaches.

Aquarium Care: This fish will present the aquarist with few maintenance problems, but it may prove troublesome to other fishes as it grows large. It can be kept with any of the other, larger centrarchids as long as they are all of roughly equal size and are given enough space to set up roughly defined territories.

REDBREAST SUNFISH
(Lepomis auritus)

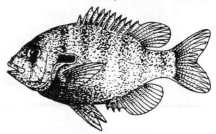

Range and Habitat: New Brunswick to Florida and along the Texas coast. This fish is found in a wide variety of habitats, from deep, clear water lakes in the north to weedy sloughs and ponds in the southern part of the range. They are particularly prevalent in water lily beds in the shallower waters of large, clear lakes, where great numbers of small, often stunted individuals may be observed. I have found them especially abundant in the Squam Lakes—Lake Winnipesaukee complex in central New Hampshire.

Field Marks and Collecting: The best field mark is the bright carmine red belly of the breeding adult. The undersides of juveniles and non-breeding fish are a pale yellowish-gold. This fish is olive on the back and sides, liberally spotted with red and with bright blue streaks on the cheeks. The opercular lobe is quite long and may be either black or of a plain dark brownish color. This is a rather elongate little sunfish, rarely reaching eight inches in length; most average about half that size.

This is the popular "kivvie" of New England. Most are caught with a hook and line. Even the smallest eagerly take a bait and, if handled very carefully, can be acclimated easily to aquariums. Very small individuals can also be collected with a dip net in shallow water near shore as they are fond of congregating and feeding in sunlit, sandy areas. I have found boat launching areas to be especially good spots to look for this species.

Aquarium Care: The redbreast is a good aquarium fish that requires no special treatment beyond the usual. Avoid overcrowding or keeping with overly aggressive tank-mates. This sunfish is rather peaceful for a centrarchid and does well in the community setup. It prefers open, well-lit situations and although the very young feel more secure in heavily planted surroundings, the adults are active schooling fishes that prefer swimming room. The redbreast is not strongly territorial, but no more than four adults should be kept together in the 10 to 20 gallon tank to avoid frequent squabbling. This fish is quite catholic in its food preferences, and will accept most aquarium foods without complaint.

ROCK BASS
(Ambloplites rupestris)

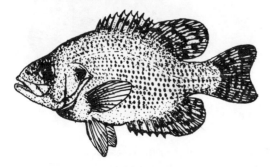

  Range and Habitat: Widely distributed from Vermont and Saskatchewan south to Mississippi and Louisiana. Rock bass favor shallow water in clear, cooler lakes and rivers. They are prevalent near dense weed beds and windfalls of brush, fallen trees and natural debris.

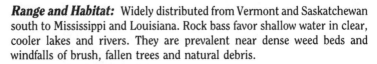 **Field Marks and Collecting:** The rock bass, also called the redeye bass or goggle-eye, is a moderately deep-bodied, robust centrarchid with a prominent mouth and large red or orange eyes. It is dark brown above and brassy or gold on the sides, with several irregular saddle-shaped markings along the back. Darker scales form a series of seven or eight very irregular rows on the sides, and the unpaired fins are light brown and banded or barred in dusky. The tail is broad and slightly forked. The rock bass reaches about ten inches at maturity.

Rock bass spawn in shallow water in spring, sometimes in concentrations. As with most sunfishes, the male takes charge of the eggs and stands guard over the fry for a week or so after hatching. After the young begin to disperse they remain in shallow water among suitable cover and may be dip netted with relative ease. A small seine run through weed beds will almost always bag a few along with other aquarium species.

Aquarium Care: Like most centrarchids, the rock bass can be aggressive and is an enthusiastic and sometimes cannibalistic predator, so tankmates should be chosen carefully. Other larger sunfishes or perch are suitable. All of those should be roughly the same size to avoid conflict. Ideally, as with all larger predatory fishes kept together, the fish should be collected as juveniles and raised together. The tank should be large, and decor should include rockwork and adequate plant growth to provide territories and cover for smaller fish. The rock bass will accept nearly all commercially available live foods, along with earthworms, small crayfish, and bait minnows. In time, the rock bass, along with most other larger sunfishes, will learn to accept cichlid pellets.

WARMOUTH
(Lepomis gulosus)

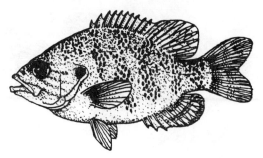

Range and Habitat: From southern Minnesota, the Great Lakes, and Virginia south to Texas and Florida. This species prefers sluggish or standing water that is shallow and thick with aquatic plant growth. River oxbows and backwaters as well as swamps studded with submerged logs and stumps are favored habitats.

Field Marks and Collecting: The warmouth, also called the goggle-eye, mud bass, and stumpknocker, is a dark brownish-olive above, brassy or gold on the sides, and pale yellow or white on the belly. The sides are marked with irregular, broken dark bands, and the dorsal, caudal, and anal fins are dark and variously spotted or banded. The warmouth is a dark, mottled sunfish with a large head and mouth. The eye is usually a deep brown or red and the mouth is large, the maxillary reaching to the posterior edge of the eye. The species reaches the length of about ten inches.

Small specimens may be collected with a dip net in densely weeded areas. They will also enter a minnow trap baited with a chicken neck or dog food.

Aquarium Care: The warmouth can be aggressive when larger, and cannot be trusted with any fish much smaller than itself. Young specimens may squabble until territories are set up and a pecking order is established, after which they can coexist tolerably well as long as there is enough space and cover for the submissive fish to avoid the dominant. Depending on size, warmouth will accept virtually all live foods, from brine shrimp and bloodworms up to nightcrawlers and small fishes. The tank should be decorated with plants and rockwork to afford adequate cover and maintained under moderate to low illumination to bring out what color there is in a warmouth.

SACRAMENTO PERCH
(Archoplites interruptus)

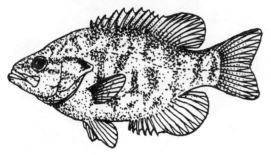

Range and Habitat: This is the only centrarchid native to the region west of the Continental Divide. A fossil species, *Archoplites taylori,* has been described from middle Pleistocene of east-central Washington. The Sacramento perch is a relict species found only in the Sacramento, San Joachin, and Pajaro River drainages in central California. It has been introduced into other river systems in California and Nevada.

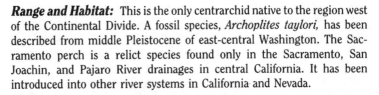

Field Marks and Collecting: The Sacramento perch reaches a length of about 20 inches and weighs up to ten pounds. It is black above, with mottled brownish and black sides, and usually has six or seven vertical dusky bars. Like most centrarchids, it has the large mouth of a predator and is, in fact, an enthusiastic one. Unlike most sunfishes, the Sacramento perch does not build a nest to receive its eggs but attaches them to the substrate or plants and abandons them to their fate. This habit has worked against the fish in that introduced exotics have played havoc with the survival of the eggs and reduced the number in some areas.

Specimens under four inches that are taken on hook and line can be acclimated to aquarium life without too much trauma if handled carefully. That's far from the ideal method of capture. The young can be seined or dip netted in weedy or rocky shallows wherever the species occurs in any numbers.

Aquarium Care: Tank conditions for this fish are the same as for other larger sunfishes—a roomy tank with plenty of rockwork or bogwood cover, clean water, and an abundance of live foods or cut fish or meat. Young perch will accept live brine shrimp and tubifex with relish, while larger individuals should be given live bait minnows or crayfish. They are territorial in nature and grow fast, so peace and serenity in a perch tank may well be a passing thing as the fish grow.

OTHER SUNFISHES
(Lepomis species)

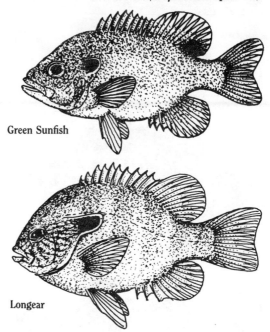

Green Sunfish

Longear

Range and Habitat: The longear sunfish *(L. megalotis)* occurs from Iowa and Quebec south to South Carolina and Mexico. The green sunfish *(L. cyanellus)* is distributed from the Great Lakes region south to Mexico. These are typical sunfishes in that they are found in a wide variety of shallow water habitats, from clear lakes to more turbid streams. The green sunfish is often collected in drainage ditches and small ponds, where it often has been introduced, either deliberately or accidentally.

Field Marks and Collecting: The green is a large sunfish, reaching the length of about 8 inches. It is a robust, large-headed fish that is dark olive green above, paler below, and crossed by a series of dark brownish bars. The longear is very deep-bodied. It is dark brown or greenish above, bluish green on the sides, and sprinkled with numerous pale yellow or green spots. On breeding males the vertical bars are dark blue with a bright orange ground color and brilliant reddish belly. To add to the confusion surrounding common names, the longear is often called pumpkinseed and creek perch locally.

   Both of these species favor shallow water habitats, in particular the margins of weed beds and areas of lush waterlily growth. Small specimens are best collected with a dipnet as the bottom in such areas often makes seining difficult.

Aquarium Care: The tank conditions are virtually the same as for the other Lepomis sunfishes: give them ample room and hiding places and you should avoid trouble, at least until individual fish grow larger than others in the tank and begin to harass the smaller ones.

CRAPPIES
(Pomoxis species*)*

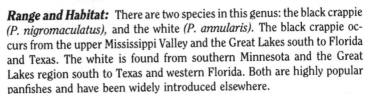

black

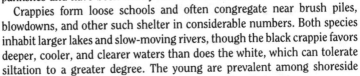

white

Range and Habitat: There are two species in this genus: the black crappie *(P. nigromaculatus),* and the white *(P. annularis).* The black crappie occurs from the upper Mississippi Valley and the Great Lakes south to Florida and Texas. The white is found from southern Minnesota and the Great Lakes region south to Texas and western Florida. Both are highly popular panfishes and have been widely introduced elsewhere.

Crappies form loose schools and often congregate near brush piles, blowdowns, and other such shelter in considerable numbers. Both species inhabit larger lakes and slow-moving rivers, though the black crappie favors deeper, cooler, and clearer waters than does the white, which can tolerate siltation to a greater degree. The young are prevalent among shoreside root tangles and vegetation where they form aggregations like their elders.

Field Marks and Collecting: Crappies are trim, attractive fish, and the species are very similar in profile but differ in coloration. They are deep-bodied but more elongate than most sunfishes and have large, flaglike dorsal and anal fins. The eye is moderately large and the mouth has the large gape of the predator. The black crappie is dark olive-green above; the sides are pale green or bronze. The entire fish, with the exception of the pectoral and ventral fins, is strongly marked in rows and broken bands of dusky or black spots. The white crappie is dusky olive above, fading to yellowish-green and white or cream on the belly. There are five to ten dusky vertical bars on the sides. Both species reach lengths of up to 12 inches.

Multitudes of crappies are caught on hook and line every summer. Their one unfortunate physical feature, a tender mouth, has lent them the nickname "papermouth." Those caught this way are useless for an aquarium. The ideal crappie habitat, all those stumps and snags, makes the use of a seine for collecting a very iffy proposition, so the skillful use of a dip net or lift net is probably the best bet. Crappies are nervous fish, so they should not be crowded in the collecting pail, and the container should be kept covered to calm the new captives. The crappie is a game fish, so explain your interest to your local game warden before bagging any.

Aquarium Care: Crappies are active creatures and thus should be given ample room in the aquarium. Use drift or bogwood as well as attractive additions to the decor as these fish like to hover among such natural objects and make swift dashes after food items. Clear, clean water is imperative, and the tank should be kept securely because the fish are inveterate jumpers. They will accept most live, frozen, and even prepared fish foods when thoroughly acclimated. Black crappies I kept for some time were especially fond of live mealworms and crickets, readily purchased at most pet shops.

YELLOW PERCH
(Perca flavescens)

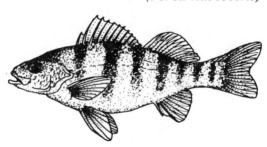

Range and Habitat: Widely distributed from north-central Canada south to Kansas, Ohio, and South Carolina. The familiar perch occupies a wide variety of habitats, from deep, cool lakes in the north to warmer ponds and streams in the southern part of its range. It is a hardy fish, quite tolerant of acidity and poor water conditions, though it does best where environmental conditions are optimal (deep, cooler lakes). Perch occupy virtually all sectors of their environment, from the depths of the lake to its shallow, weedy shorelines, the latter as fry and juveniles. In the absence of natural predators in smaller bodies of water, these efficient, adaptable fish will thrive and reproduce themselves into stunted multitudes of breeding mini-perch.

Field Marks and Collecting: The yellow perch is a spiny creature, as is well known to any angler who has ever attempted to remove a hook from one. It is an elongate though robust fish with two prominent spines on the angulate gill covers. The color is olive-brown above, fading to yellow on the sides and white or pale yellow on the underside. The dark color of the back is extended on the sides in six to seven dark vertical bars; the dorsal and caudal fins are dusky, and the pectoral, ventral, and anal fins may be dusky orange to bright red. The yellow perch averages ten to fourteen inches in length at adulthood.

The active, always hungry, and inquisitive perch responds readily to the presence of a baited minnow trap. This is probably the easiest way to collect small individuals for aquariums. This can be placed in weedy areas or beneath docks where the small fry often abound. They can also be dip netted among weed and water lily beds. Larger perch (four to six inches) bite readily and can be caught on a barbless hook baited with virtually any cut bait.

Aquarium Care: The yellow perch is not the widespread, successful species it is today because of a shy, retiring disposition. In the aquarium, the perch is not overly aggressive but neither is it a fish to be kept with any other species small enough to make a meal for it, or of a timid nature. The ideal perch setup would be a large (20–50 gallons) tank containing several sunken roots and a fair amount of plantings. Yellow perch can be kept with most sunfishes of equal size, though they should not be quartered with cyprinids or darters, as these will surely be harrassed and eaten. Perch should be kept well fed or they will emaciate over time. This means keeping fewer specimens and offering them ample feedings of larger live foods or pieces of cut fish or lean beef. A small bullhead or madtom can be housed with them to take care of any leftovers.

TESSELATED AND OTHER DARTERS
(Etheostoma olmstedi)

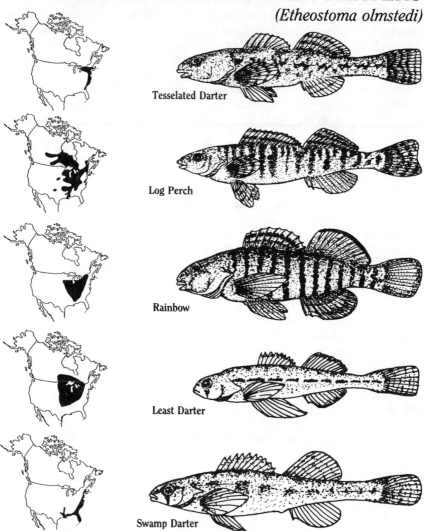

Tesselated Darter

Log Perch

Rainbow

Least Darter

Swamp Darter

Range and Habitat: The tesselated darter is found from the Lake Ontario drainage south to North Carolina. This is primarily a Coastal Plain fish, replaced to the west by the very similar johnny darter *(E. nigrum)*, which occurs from Hudson Bay south throughout the Mississippi Valley and the Great Lakes drainage basin to northern Texas and Florida.

Both species are common in the quieter sections of smaller fast- and slow-moving streams and in cool, clear lakes. They prefer sand or fine-gravel bottoms and are usually found in water less than three feet deep and near beds of aquatic vegetation.

Field Marks and Collecting: The colors and patterns of these darters closely match those of the habitat. The ground color is a pale brown or straw, paler below. There are six or seven dark saddle-shaped marks along the back and a series of seven to twelve W- or M-shaped markings longitudinally on the sides. All of the fins except the ventrals are pale tan, finely banded or speckled with dark brown. The tesselated darter differs from the johnny primarily in the number of dorsal fin rays (less than 13 in the johnny, 13 or more in the tesselated), and in the paler colors and less intense and defined markings of the tesselated darter.

Darters may be told at once from the sculpins that share their habitat by their more slender forms, smaller mouths, and more pointed snouts. Their fanlike pectoral fins are not as large or as apparent as those of the sculpins when the fish are viewed from above.

There are some 120 species of darters in three genera currently recognized, from the six-inch log perch *(Percina caprodes)* all the way down to the pint-sized least darter *(E. microperca)* adult at 1½ inches. Some of the more colorful species commonly kept by the native fish hobbyist are the greenside darter *(E. blennoides)*, the bluebreast darter *(E. camurum)*, the orangethroat darter *(E. spectabile)*, and the rainbow darter *(E. caeruleum)*. Many of the darters are extremely local in distribution, being restricted to single drainages or even a single river or stream within that drainage, such as the famous (or infamous, depending on your leanings) snail darter *(Percina tanasi)*.

With the snail darter and a number of other darter species now protected by state and federal law firmly in mind, make it a point to contact your state fish and game agency before wetting a net in darter turf. This particularly applies in the south-central states, such as Tennessee and Kentucky, where there are more species with very small, fragmented ranges.

Since most darter species occupy similar habitats, they are collected by essentially the same methods. Shuffling rocks and stones upstream of a dip net or seine will usually turn up darters, as will a smaller seine dragged over sandy or pebbly areas in streams. Be aware, though, that most darter habitat is also trout habitat, and you will definitely be stopped and questioned if a game warden sees you hauling a seine around in waters stocked with this game fish. Most darters can pass through the wire mesh of a standard killie trap, and the very small species, such as the least and swamp darters, can easily slip through the quarter-inch mesh of the typical seine, so a dip net may be called for here.

Aquarium Care: In spite of their small size and generally somber non-breeding colors, the darters have become very popular with native fish aquarists, and many species have been successfully kept and even bred in captivity in recent years. Some darters are among the most colorful of freshwater fishes when spawning. The darters are specialized fishes in that they are primarily bottom-dwelling and require cool, well-aerated water in order to thrive in confinement. Species normally found in warmer, standing waters, such as the swamp and least darters, will do quite well in the lushly planted, moderately filtered tank, but for the most part, if you hope to keep darters for any length of time, you must be prepared to duplicate the stream habitat as closely as possible. This means a "stream tank" equipped with plenty of rock and pebble cover, perhaps a few gnarled roots of bogwood and plastic or hardy live plants, and efficient filtration that both cleans the water and provides it with some degree of forced oxygenation. In this respect, either an undergravel filter with powerheads or an outside canister filter with spray bar is recommended.

Although darters are peaceful fishes that will coexist with nearly all other smaller freshwater species, the serious darter aquarist should maintain them by themselves.

This not only makes better sense esthetically but serves a practical purpose as well, for although darters will actively pursue food on or above the substrate, they generally lose when forced to compete with more active, aggressive fish plucking food from the water column above them. The natural behavior of this facinating group of fishes can be studied much more effectively when they are kept alone, or at most with a few other fishes, such as sculpins or dace, found in the same habitat.

The darters will accept nearly all smaller live foods and, depending on the species (or individual), may learn to take prepared fish foods, though these are not ideal.

Endangered or Threatened Freshwater Species

The following freshwater fishes are under severe pressure, and most are classified as endangered or threatened in some areas. They should be left alone or released if encountered or caught during a collecting expedition. Their pictures and range maps are shown here to help collectors avoid species under pressure. A sighting of an endangered or threatened species should be reported to a local conservation organization, such as the state chapter of the Audubon Society, and to the state or provincial fisheries office (see Appendix III).

PADDLEFISH
(Polyodon spathula)

Increasingly rare throughout its range.

HOG SUCKER
(Hypentelium nigricans)

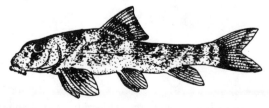

Listed as Endangered or Threatened in several midwestern states and Pennsylvania.

DESERT PUPFISH
(Cyprinodon maculatus)

Threatened throughout its range; currently under surveillance and management.

SAND DARTER
(Ammocrypta pellucida)

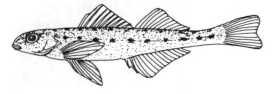

Threatened or Of Special Concern in several states.

TULE PERCH
(Hysterocarpus traski)

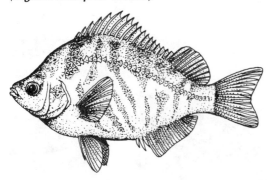

Listed as Threatened in several localities in its range in California.

LEOPARD SHARK
(Triakis semifasciata)

Range and Habitat: Oregon south to Baja California. It is a common fish in shallow bays in southern California where it is frequently caught by sport fishermen.

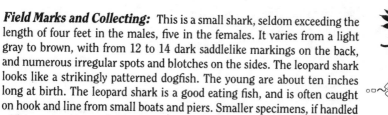

Field Marks and Collecting: This is a small shark, seldom exceeding the length of four feet in the males, five in the females. It varies from a light gray to brown, with from 12 to 14 dark saddlelike markings on the back, and numerous irregular spots and blotches on the sides. The leopard shark looks like a strikingly patterned dogfish. The young are about ten inches long at birth. The leopard shark is a good eating fish, and is often caught on hook and line from small boats and piers. Smaller specimens, if handled with care, can be acclimated to aquariums. This shark should be placed in as large a transport container as possible and aeration provided with a battery-powered air stone as it will perish quickly otherwise. Cover the container to calm the fish and lower its respiration rate.

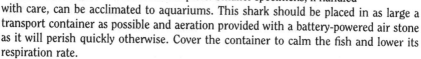

Aquarium Care: The leopard shark should be housed in as large a tank as possible and provided with clean, well-aerated water. A 100-gallon tank would be the wise choice, even for a ten- to 15-inch young one, as the fish needs lots of swimming space and will grow quickly if provided with ample food. A leopard shark can usually (and I stress that word) be housed with other fish its own size without problems, but it will attack and eat any fish or invertebrates much smaller. It will eat most meat and fish, especially chunks of fish, shrimp, lean beef, or live bait killies. As with all sharks, no matter how small, this species should be approached and handled with caution, for it has been implicated in at least one attack, on a skin diver in California.

SKATES
(Raja species)

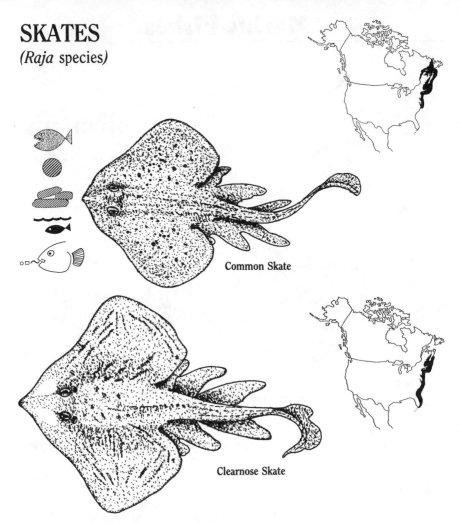

Common Skate

Clearnose Skate

Range and Habitat: The common or little skate *(R. erinacea)* is a shallow water species occurring from Cape Hatteras north to about Halifax, Nova Scotia. It is most common in offshore shallow, sandy areas from Cape Cod to New Jersey. The clearnose skate *(R. eglanteria)* is known from Florida to the Gulf of Maine but is most common in the area of the Middle Atlantic States. Other, similar Raja species include the big skate *(R. diaphanes)*, the briar skate *(R. senta)*, and the large barn door skate *(R. stabuliforis)*, the latter being a deepwater species the young of which are seldom seen inshore.

The smaller skates are usually found close inshore on sandy bottoms, either in bays or just off the surf zone where large numbers are taken in summer by anglers using clam or squid baits. Young individuals are sometimes taken in seines hauled in shallow bays. The black, rectangular empty egg cases of the common and clearnose species, sometimes called "mermaids' purses," are familiar objects on beaches in summer.

Field Marks and Collecting: The little (maximum 24 inches) skate is a spiny creature that may vary in color from gray to a rich reddish-brown with darker mottlings or spots. The underside is clear white. Three rows of tubercles, or thorns, run along the back from the eyes to the tail. The snout is blunt, as opposed to the clearnose's snout which is sharply pointed with triangular pale or translucent areas on either side of the midline. The clearnose reaches the length of about 36 inches, though most are between 24 and 30 inches. It is a warm reddish-brown to pale tan with numerous dark, broken bars interspersed with both dark and pale spots. A single row of tubercles runs along the midline of the back.

Smaller individuals (8 to 12 inches long) of both species are frequently taken on hook and line using clam or squid baits. The very smallest of these can be acclimated to a large aquarium. The young occasionally turn up in seine hauls made over sandy bottoms or eelgrass beds, I have collected a few of them over the years in Cape Cod Bay in mid to late summer.

Aquarium Care: Skates require large tanks with broad, open areas of sand or fine gravel. A tank housing these fishes alone needs no items of decor for these will only interfere with their movements or create angles and corners where the fish may become lodged. Very young skates, about four inches long, can be tricky to keep as they sometimes refuse food and starve in the midst of plenty. These can be tempted with large live brine shrimp or bloodworms, and once feeding, offered a wide variety of live foods and cut fish, squid, clams, and crab meat. A skate tank should be kept cool for these fish are uncomfortable in temperatures much over 70°.

RETICULATED MORAY
(Muraena retifera)

Range and Habitat: Florida to North Carolina, rarely straying northward to Massachusetts during the warmer months. Morays are widely distributed in the eastern Pacific. This is a deepwater species, though it is sometimes seen near shore in rocky or reef areas. Morays are very territorial and large ones will defend their niche with fin and fang against all comers, including human divers. Approach with care.

Field Marks and Collecting: There's no mistaking a moray. They are not true eels. They are large, heavy-bodied fish lacking pectoral and ventral fins and having a small, circular opening in the side of the head in place of conventional gill covers. The skin is thick, smooth, and leathery. The dorsal, caudal, and anal fins are continuous. Morays respire with the mouth gaping open, lending a threatening appearance even when they are at rest.

Collecting a large moray is best left to the experienced diver and fish collector, for a big moray can be a formidable adversary when molested. It can bite, and will hang on like a bulldog, inflicting very painful lacerations. Very young morays (under 12 inches) can usually be flushed from their hideaways with a pokestick and coaxed into a hand net. Because of their snake-like agility when alarmed, you should quickly flip the net's bag over the rim to hold the fish. Morays will readily enter a baited fish trap, normally eating every other occupant they can catch. This is one reason why a trap set in a productive habitat should be checked frequently.

Aquarium Care: Morays ideally should be kept in their own quarters, though they usually will not molest other fishes if the latter are larger. The size of the tank depends on the size of the moray, but the larger the better. As in nature, the fish will use rock or coral grottoes as hideaways, emerging primarily at night in search of food. Morays will accept smaller live fishes and crustaceans as food and can be trained to take frozen smelt or strips of lean beef heart. This fish is more comfortable under lower light conditions.

INSHORE LIZARDFISH
(Synodus foetens)

Range and Habitat: Brazil north to Cape Cod, but rarer north of the Carolinas. This is an inshore species favoring sand bottoms where it is a burrowing ambush predator. It is prevalent around inlet mouths and is frequently collected in shallow estuaries among eelgrass-sand locations.

Field Marks and Collecting: The lizardfish is an elongate fish that somewhat resembles a freshwater darter in both form and color. It is slender and little compressed in form, and variously checkered or banded in dark reddish-brown over a pale tan ground color. The mouth is prominent, extending beyond the eye, and almost reptilian in appearance, hence the common name. Unlike a darter, the pectoral fins are small rather than large and fanlike.

Most lizardfish are caught in the seine as they will rarely enter a trap and, as burrowers, they cannot be spotted for dip netting. Other collectors say they have caught many with cast nets.

Aquarium Care: The lizardfish will thrive in a well-aerated, open tank with a sand bottom and little or no decor. It will get along fine in a community setup only if provided with the required burrowing substrate. They should not be quartered with fish much smaller than they are, for they are voracious predators that can down prey of surprising dimensions. They spend much of their time buried with only the eyes showing, exploding from the sand at the approach of a prey animal. They will not accept dead or prepared foods; live fish or invertebrates are a must. I have found to my dismay that the lizardfish is a confirmed jumper. Keep the tank covered at all times.

MUMMICHOG
(Fundulus heteroclitus)

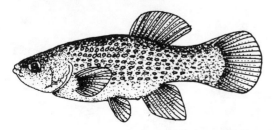

    Range and Habitat: The Gulf of St. Lawrence to the Gulf of Mexico, with three geographical races recognized: *F. h. macrolepidous,* from the Gulf of St. Lawrence to about Virginia; *F. h. heteraclitus,* from Virginia to Florida; and *F. h. grandis,* from the Florida peninsula to Yucatan. The main difference between the races is a tendency for larger size and more brilliant colors in the more southern forms. The California killifish *(F. parvipinnis)* occurs in brackish coastal waters in southern California and Mexico.

This fish, also known as the common killifish, chub, and bullhead minnow, is one of the hardiest and most adaptable of fish. They occupy a wide variety of marine and brackish habitats, often of water qualities that would quickly kill most other fish. These estuarine fishes favor weedy or muddy areas of strong tidal influence. Salt marshes usually abound with them, along with the sheepshead minnow and rainwater fish.

Field Marks and Collecting: A saying often applied to the familiar mallard duck, "It would be beautiful if it weren't so common," could be used in reference to this little fish. Although known primarily as a bait fish, the male mummichog is a very attractive fish at all times, but especially so when breeding. At this time, he becomes a constellation of gold, green, and steel-blue spots, with the edges of the caudal and anal fins and the entire underside taking on a brilliant, saffron yellow hue. The larger female is like the female guppy, a pale olive-brown above fading to white below, accented by various tints of blue and rose and occasionally crossed by faint vertical bands.

This little fish has been caught by virtually every fish-catching device and method known. The two most common are the bait seine and the killie trap. The latter is most effective if baited with bread, fish heads, or a ripe chicken neck and set in an indentation in a weedy shoreline on the rising tide.

Aquarium Care: This is one of the toughest of fishes and can tolerate a lot of abuse before succumbing. But it has a few basic requirements that should be met if it is to thrive in aquariums. First, this fish does better when kept in brackish water. The tank should be well-aerated and filtered to avoid fouling and it should be 20 gallons or more, as these fish are active, grow quickly, and will soon crowd each other. They will accept all foods from live through prepared and, like most killies, will eat floating foods. The mummichog is a peaceful fish, but due to its activity and boundless curiosity, it could prove troublesome to such shy tankmates as seahorses or small flounders.

 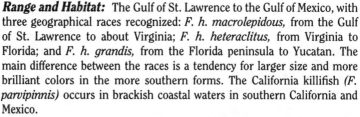

STRIPED KILLIFISH
(Fundulus majalis)

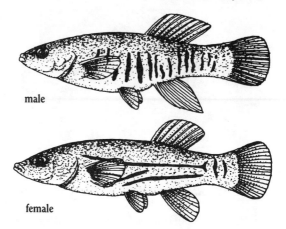

male

female

Range and Habitat: Cape Cod to Florida, more common at the northern extremes of the range. The striped killy likes shallow, sandy areas of bays and estuaries where it occasionally schools with the more common mummichog. It is less apt than the latter to be found in waters of lower salinity or poor quality, or in places where debris and trash are discarded.

Field Marks and Collecting: This is the largest of the North American killifishes, reaching a length of about seven inches at maturity, though five or six inches is more common. This fish is more elongate in form than the mummichog and has a more pointed snout. It is a pale sandy brown or olive above, fading to clear white below. The male displays a series of short vertical bars or stripes, while the female has three or four horizontal lines. Observed from above, the fish closely match the pale color of the sandy substrates they prefer.

The striped killifish is best seined, as it is very agile and usually found in open areas that make collecting with a dip net difficult. It often turns up in seine hauls of mummichogs and silversides. This fish is less tolerant of handling than the mummichog. It should not be crowded in the collection bucket or subjected to stress.

Aquarium Care: The striped killy is less able to tolerate stress or poor aquarium conditions than most of the other species. Clean, well-aerated water is a must, and this fish will suffer in an overcrowded tank. If kept in a tank by themselves or with other killifishes, these fish will retain their striking markings to a considerable degree. They have not yet spawned in captivity. Striped killies, like the mummichog, are quite omnivorous, accepting frozen and live foods as well as grazing on algae in the tank.

SHEEPSHEAD MINNOW
(Cyprinodon varigatus)

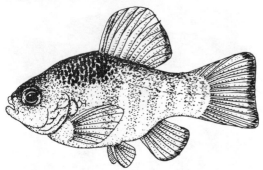

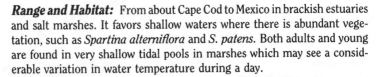

Range and Habitat: From about Cape Cod to Mexico in brackish estuaries and salt marshes. It favors shallow waters where there is abundant vegetation, such as *Spartina alterniflora* and *S. patens*. Both adults and young are found in very shallow tidal pools in marshes which may see a considerable variation in water temperature during a day.

Field Marks and Collecting: The sheepshead is a stocky, robust little killifish with a high-powered temperament and an activity level to match. It is a laterally compressed fish, olive above, silvery on the sides and belly, and crossed by six to eight irregular dark bars. Breeding males are most attractive, with a bright, iridescent blue shoulder patch and yellow or orange on the belly and unpaired fins. Females and young are plain silvery, mottled with dusky or black and usually appear less chunky than the adult male. A large and rather prominent humeral scale is located above the insertion of the pectoral fin. A very large sheepshead measures a bit over three inches. Most average about two inches.

Sheepshead minnows are found in habitats that make collecting them relatively simple—usually. They congregate in the upper reaches of salt marshes in shallow pools and in mosquito control ditches often no wider than a foot or two and about as deep. Although sheepsheads can be seined, they are best collected with a dip net. A baited killie trap, placed in a drainage ditch, will quickly bag all the sheepsheads you can use if the fish are at all abundant.

Aquarium Care: This fish will harass and often kill other fishes kept with it. *C. varigatus* is an extremely pugnacious little brute. Although most of its aggression is directed at others of its own kind, it can be trusted with few other species in an aquarium. Exceptions are hogchokers, pipefishes, and seahorses, which are usually left alone.

The sheepshead eats both animal and vegetable matter. In confinement, it will accept all live and frozen foods as well as flakes and pellets. Either allowing a growth of algae to form in the tank or augmenting the diet with parboiled spinach or lettuce is beneficial. Although the sheepshead is a small fish, a tank housing several should be roomy and provided with plenty of hiding places, for a dominant male will kill weaker rivals if they cannot escape him.

RAINWATER FISH
(Lucania parva)

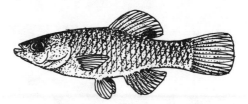

Range and Habitat: Brackish water from Cape Cod to Key West, Florida. This fish is prevalent in heavily vegetated bays, ponds, and tidal creeks where it is most frequently found very near the shoreline.

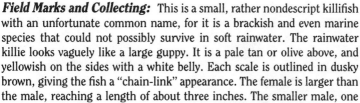

Field Marks and Collecting: This is a small, rather nondescript killifish with an unfortunate common name, for it is a brackish and even marine species that could not possibly survive in soft rainwater. The rainwater killie looks vaguely like a large guppy. It is a pale tan or olive above, and yellowish on the sides with a white belly. Each scale is outlined in dusky brown, giving the fish a "chain-link" appearance. The female is larger than the male, reaching a length of about three inches. The smaller male, one to two inches, usually has a black spot on the dorsal fin. Both sexes often have a pale dusky band extending from the gill cover to the base of the caudal fin. The unpaired fins are often suffused with orange and blue.

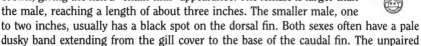

The rainwater killie turns up in seine hauls made through dense eelgrass beds or stands of *Spartina* during higher tide levels. It can also be collected by sweeping a dip net through similar growth, and has been taken in killie traps baited with bread.

Aquarium Care: This fish does well in the brackish aquarium, though it tends to be shy and may be intimidated by larger, more aggressive fish. A dimly lit tank, heavily planted in either plastic or with salt-tolerant plants such as *Saggitaria,* is best for this retiring little fish. Good tankmates are small sticklebacks, hogchokers, pipefish, small blennies, and other inoffensive estuarine fishes. The species is omnivorous, eating small crustaceans and algal growths in nature. In the aquarium, live brine shrimp or bloodworms augmented by vegetable-based prepared foods can be fed. The rainwater fish is short-lived in aquariums, with few surviving their second year.

NEEDLEFISH
(*Scomberesox* species)

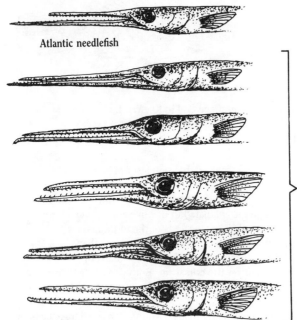

Atlantic needlefish

These figures show some of the variations in the head and jaw structure of some of the other temperate and tropical *Scomberesox* needlefishes.

Range and Habitat: The Atlantic needlefish *(S. saurus)* is typical of the group of some six temperate and subtropical species. Most are very similar in appearance, the chief differences being head structure and the length of the bill. This species occurs from Newfoundland to the Carolinas. It is abundant toward the northern part of the range, above Cape Cod. Needlefish are most often encountered offshore, swimming at the surface where they are preyed upon by a host of larger fish.

Field Marks and Collecting: Often erroneously called gar or pencilfish, the needlefish is an extremely elongate, slender fish with very thin, teeth-lined jaws. It is bluish-green above, silvery below, and usually displays no pattern or banding. From above, it can be very difficult to see, so closely does it match the color of the water.

Needlefish are common inshore fish during the warmer months, when they approach the shoreline in pursuit of silversides and other small forage fish. Although they are extremely agile and can easily elude a dip net, they can be collected with a cast net or larger seine. Needlefishes are among the few fish that will actively attempt to avoid a seine by leaping over it—quite an exciting sight.

Aquarium Care: Needlefishes must be ranked among those fishes best left to either the aquarist with a very large home tank or the public aquarium with unlimited space, for they don't adjust to confinement easily. They are also carnivorous and will accept nothing but living prey, meaning endless feeder guppies, goldfish, or live killies. Needlefish will quickly batter themselves senseless in a tank that is too small or lacks a current, which they must have in order to orient themselves and school up. A minimum 200-gallon tank with strong filtration, with few or no decorations, is recommended. I have found that needlefishes will accept only live fish as food, refusing all other live foods, including sand or clam worms, which they apparently don't recognize as natural prey. They are surface fishes and as such, will quickly find their way out of an improperly covered tank.

STICKLEBACKS
(Gasterosteus, Pygosteus, Culaea, and Apeltes)

Brook

Ninespine

Threespine

Breeding Males

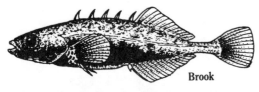

Brook

Ninespine

     Range and Habitat: The threespine stickleback *(Gasterosteus aculeatus)* occurs in northern brackish waters, reaching New Jersey in the western Atlantic. The ninespine stickleback *(Pygosteus pungitius)* is found in both fresh and salt water situations circumpolar, south to New Jersey in the western Atlantic. The fourspine stickleback *(Apeltes quadracus)* ranges from New Brunswick and Nova Scotia south to Virginia, being more common in the north. The brook stickleback *(C. inconstans)* occurs from western Canada to Maine and south to Kansas and Ohio. It has been introduced into New Mexico and California. All sticklebacks are littoral, or shoalwater, species rarely found far from estuaries, salt marshes, and coastal creeks.The ninespine is frequently collected in major rivers and lakes far from the sea. I have also collected the ninespine in tide pools in Maine.

Field Marks and Collecting: Sticklebacks are bony little fishes (three inches or under) with sharply pointed snouts, very slim caudal peduncles, and the anterior dorsal consisting of between two and nine separate spines. In the threespine species, the body is protected by a series of transverse plates running along the sides; the nine- and fourspine species are scaleless. Color varies according to the habitat and time of year. Breeding threespine males show intense black and red coloration, and the male fourspine is a rich, mottled golden-olive and has brilliant red ventral fins in spring and summer.

Sticklebacks can be collected by dip net, seine, or the minnow trap. In estuaries, the fish are extremely secretive, never straying far from the protection of the dense eelgrass or sea lettuce beds. Random dip net sweeps or seine hauls are the best methods of collection there.

Aquarium Care: Most sticklebacks are unable to hold their own in a tank full of larger, aggressive tankmates due to their very small size. Keep them with other smaller estuarine species such as seahorses, pipefishes, and small killies. Sticklebacks are most comfortable in heavily planted, dimly lit quarters. They should be offered smaller live foods such as brine shrimp and bloodworms, though they will sometimes learn to accept flake foods. Filtration and water flow should be gentle, for sticklebacks do not like to be buffeted about. Sticklebacks normally exist with each other in harmony except at spawning time, when the males set up territories and threaten each other. They will not usually bother other species kept with them.

CORNETFISH
(Fistularia tabacaria)

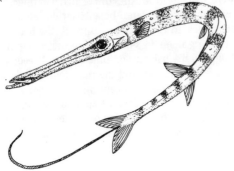

Range and Habitat: The West Indies north to Chesapeake Bay, regularly straggling to Massachusetts in summer. The cornetfish is primarily a reef species found inshore in quieter waters. The young, which are carried north on the Gulf Stream, often appear in estuaries and near wharves and jetties in late summer and early fall.

Field Marks and Collecting: The cornetfish is a bizarre creature, a thin, elongated fish with a long, tubular snout set with a small mouth. The central caudal ray is extended into a wispy filament that is about one-quarter the length of the fish's body, which may be six feet in exceptionally large specimens, though most are between two and three feet in length. Young fish observed in temperate waters in late summer are usually under a foot in length. These can, with some difficulty, be kept in the aquarium. Cornetfish are an olive-greenish above and white below, with from 9 to 11 dark brown vertical bands. Several rows of pale blue spots line the dorsal area, and the long caudal filament is dark blue. The banding pattern is very noticeable as the stick-like fish holds a motionless position against the current.

Cornetfish are fairly easily approached and may be collected either with a hand net or cast net. Although they do not panic when placed in the close quarters of a collecting bucket, they should be given as much room as possible on the trip home and the container covered to reduce capture stress.

Aquarium Care: The cornetfish, its long, streamlined shape nonwithstanding, adapts readily to the confines of an aquarium, though it should be a large one. The main problem appears to be inducing the fish to eat. Give it a tank of its own and offer it live guppies or very small killies. These it will stalk like a pickerel and pluck from the moving water of the filter setup, much as it waits for smaller prey in the wild. Although it will fare best with as few food competitors as possible, it is so unusual and interesting a fish that devoting a large tank to it alone could not be considered a waste of space. Once acclimated, the cornetfish will outgrow its quarters. Thus it should be released as soon as it becomes a problem for its keeper—during the warmer months, of course.

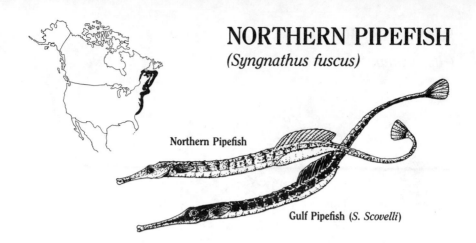

NORTHERN PIPEFISH
(Syngnathus fuscus)

Northern Pipefish

Gulf Pipefish (*S. Scovelli*)

Range and Habitat: Nova Scotia to the Carolinas. The center of its abundance is the Middle Atlantic states. There are many members of this essentially tropical family (the Sygnathidae, which includes seahorses). As
most are similar in appearance, habits, and aquarium requirements, a
discussion of the northern pipefish covers all but the seahorses. Pipefish
are salt marsh and estuarine animals, found in shallow, muddy, or sandy
areas with lush eelgrass and sea lettuce beds or other aquatic vegetation.
The fish match their surroundings so closely that they are almost impossible to see moving about unless the water is very calm.

Field Marks and Collecting: Pipefish are elongated with the body more
or less completely covered with bony plates. They have narrow, tubelike mouths. At
first glance, they appear eel-like, but compared to an eel, the plated body is rigid and
feels rough or hard. Pipefish are often incorrectly called gars or pencilfish, depending
on the locality. The northern pipefish is a rich, olive-green variously mottled and banded
wth dark brown or black. The fish moves smoothly about with rapid vibrations of its
dorsal and anal fins and only resorts to the typical fish swimming motion when alarmed.
   Pipefish can be collected by traps and dip nets, but the best method is a seine hauled
through eelgrass or sea lettuce beds.

Aquarium Care: Pipefish should not be kept with overly active or aggressive fishes
that might harrass them. They must have smaller live or frozen foods that are manageable in the tiny mouth. These fish, like the closely related seahorses, can be difficult
to acclimate in that they will often refuse all but living foods, at least at first. Live
brine shrimp are the ideal starter food and are adequate as a staple, though some variety
should be provided in the form of baby guppies or tubifex worms. Pipefish prefer densely
planted surroundings to provide shelter and support and tanks without turbulent filtration. Given these conditions, they will thrive for several years in the home aquarium.

SEAHORSES
(*Hippocampus* species)

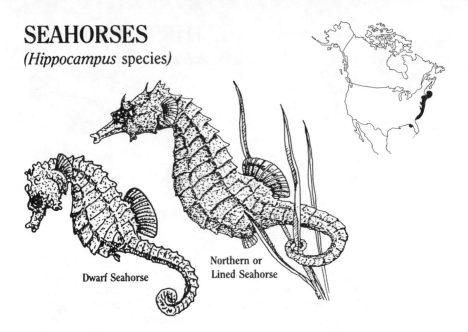

Dwarf Seahorse

Northern or
Lined Seahorse

Range and Habitat: The northern seahorse *(H. erectus,* formerly *H. hudsonius)* occurs from the Carolinas to Cape Cod, but is much more abundant in the southern part of the range. The dwarf seahorse *(H. zosterae)* occurs only in extreme southern Florida, mostly in the area of Pensacola Bay. Seahorses are usually closely associated with eelgrass and other submergent marine vegetation where they move deliberately about using their prehensile tails to secure themselves among the plants. The northern seahorse is extremely variable in abundance from year to year and appears to have declined in the area of New Jersey in recent years.

Field Marks and Collecting: The seahorse is well-known in appearance to almost everyone with even a casual interest in the aquatic environment. It looks like a chess knight with fins, with the body covered with bony plates rather than conventional scales. The northern or lined seahorse varies in color, with brown, gray, red, and yellow individuals reported depending on the habitat. The northern seahorse attains the length of six inches, though most of those collected are about half that. The dwarf seahorse is a mottled brown and tan. The snout is much shorter than in the northern species and the fish seldom exceeds two inches at maturity.

Most seahorses are picked up by recreational seiners working eelgrass flats in summer, although occasional specimens can be spotted moving about and bagged with a dip net. They will often enter minnow traps, and larger specimens have been taken in lobster and eel pots.

Aquarium Care: Volumes have been written on keeping this little fish in the aquarium, for it is very popular with both marine hobbyists and public aquarium visitors. This sedate, gentle creature, like the closely related pipefish, should be kept in quarters that reflect its mild temperament, having subdued lighting, plenty of either live or plastic plants, and no aggressive tankmates. Filtration should be gentle. Given these conditions and offered plenty of live brine shrimp and other small prey, the seahorse will live out its potentially long aquarium life in contentment. The seahorse shares with the pipefish the mode of reproduction in which the female deposits her eggs in the brood pouch of the male by means of an ovipositor where they are fertilized and carried for incubation. Although countless baby seahorses have been born in aquariums of "pregnant" males either purchased or collected in the wild, only a few spawnings in captivity have been reported.

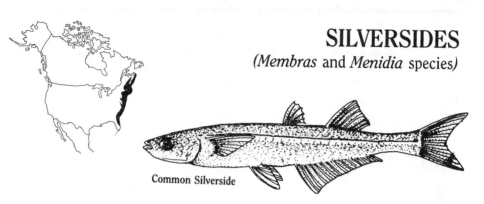

SILVERSIDES
(Membras and *Menidia* species)

Common Silverside

Range and Habitat: There are four Atlantic species of small (six inches), silvery fishes known as silversides or spearing. They are coastal inshore and estuarine fishes occurring from about Nova Scotia to the Gulf of Mexico where they regularly enter brackish and sometimes fresh water. Most are important bait fish and forage for larger game species. Although not normally thought of as food, they are sometimes fried and eaten whole as whitebait. The two most common species are the rough silverside *(Membras vagrans)* and the common silverside *(Menidia menidia).*

Silversides are widespread in most estuaries as well as along the oceanfront very close to the shore. They move about in vast numbers. Their presence is often shown by their frantic leaps en masse to avoid predators, such as bluefish or small striped bass, attacking from below. The various species are common on sand bottoms or among beds of eelgrass, especially when smaller.

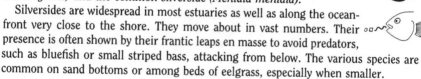

Field Marks and Collecting: Silversides are identified by their elongate, slim form, two distinct dorsal fins, moderately forked tail, and prominent, bright silver lateral stripe, this often bordered above and below by a thin, darker line. The snout is sharply pointed and the eye large in the two commoner species. In short, this is a typical, saltwater "minnow."

These abundant little fish are seined in great numbers by fishermen seeking fluke bait. Seining is the only practical way of collecting them as they are too agile and nearly invisible in the water to be caught in any numbers by any other method. Although silversides are very attractive, their fragility and extremely nervous temperament render them unsuitable for aquariums, except for the very largest tanks. Easily damaged during collecting and handling, a silverside, when injured, will almost certainly contract a fatal fungus before it can be acclimated to confinement.

Aquarium Care: If you're still determined to try your hand at silverside keeping, use extreme tender, loving care every step of the way. The fish should be collected and transported without ever leaving the water. This can be done by leaving the belly of the seine submerged while a third person carefully bails the desired specimens out and into the collecting bucket with a smaller container. During the trip home, the container should be sealed to keep out light in order to calm the fish, and well aerated with a battery-powered air stone to keep oxygen levels high. Silversides have very strong schooling instincts and a single individual will not long survive being kept alone. A school of between 20 and 30 fish should have at least a 50-gallon tank, well aerated and with few decorations. A strong filter current is needed to stimulate schooling behavior. The fish should be offered smaller live or frozen foods that they can pluck from the moving water. They will also accept flakes and other prepared foods that float, though they will usually ignore food that reaches the bottom. Ideally, silversides should be maintained in a single-species tank, with the possible exception of smaller, bottom-dwelling species. Most larger tankmates would either make them even more jittery than they are by nature or simply eat them.

MULLET
(Mugil cephalus)

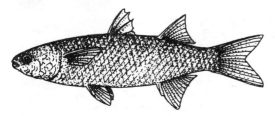

 Range and Habitat: Temperate and subtropical waters in the Atlantic and parts of the Pacific Oceans as well as the Mediterranean. In the western Atlantic, it is found from Brazil to Cape Cod, with stragglers reaching Nova Scotia. The mullet is an inshore species often seen in large schools just outside of the surf zone and in estuaries.

 Field Marks and Collecting: The mullet is a robust but sleek and fusiform fish with a blunt head and rounded snout. The striped mullet is blue-gray to green above and silvery below with the dusky scales on the sides forming a series of longitudinal lines. There is a bluish spot at the base of the pectoral fin. The very similar white mullet *(M. curema)* is dark green above and plain silver below, with a dark bluish-black spot at the base of the pectoral fin. Mullet grow to about three feet in length in the tropics, but specimens collected north of the Carolinas are under six inches long.

Large schools of young mullet (two to six inches) are often seen feeding in summer in the shallows where they are recognized by their habit of grazing food either on the bottom or at the surface of the water. The latter produces a curious rippling, or "dimpled" effect. At this time, they are easily collected with a cast net. They can also be collected with a seine, though if they sense its approach, they can move fast to avoid it or jump over it, a behavior for which they are well known.

Aquarium Care: For an active, schooling, open-water fish, the mullet adapts readily enough to aquariums and does surprisingly well if adequately fed. Although adult mullet are vegetarians, feeding mostly on algae and microscopic plants and animals, and seldom showing interest in a baited hook, the young fish will readily eat brine shrimp and other smaller live foods. Their tank should contain a reasonably healthy growth of algae. Under these conditions, the fish will be observed actively grazing the rocks and the glass itself with a rapid, shimmying movement as they move quickly over the substrate. I have kept mullet for nearly two years in a ten-gallon brackish aquarium. The only problem has been that they eventually outgrow the tank, requiring release back into the natural habitat. The mullet is a confirmed jumper, so its quarters should be kept covered at all times.

SENNET
(Sphyraena borealis)

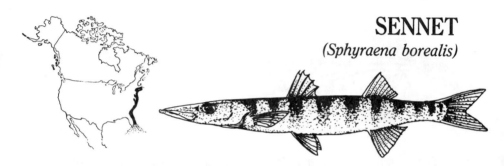

Range and Habitat: The sennet, or northern barracuda, is found from Cape Cod to Florida, and is more common in the southern portion of the range. This reef and inshore species is often found near docks and inlets at the northern extremes of the range, where they stalk silversides and other schooling fishes.

Field Marks and Collecting: The little sennet is a true barracuda and shares the same genus with its legendary big brother, the great barracuda *(S. barracuda).* This fish reaches the length of about 13 inches. The adult is olive or bluish above and silvery below. Smaller specimens are pale olive or brown, regularly banded or blotched with dark brown. They are pike-like in appearance, with an elongate, cylindrical body, and long, pointed snout. Sennet usually travel in small parties of between four and ten individuals, making swift dashes into the milling swarms of silversides and anchovies found in bays in the summer.

I have found the best method for collecting this species is with the cast net, which can rather easily be dropped over a group of them in shallow water. There is, however, the chance that smaller individuals may become gillnetted in the mesh, making for a difficult job of removing them and usually injuring or killing the fish. Sennet are considered a game fish of sorts in the South, providing some sport on ultra-light tackle. I have had smaller fish in New Jersey follow and make repeated passes at spinners intended for snapper bluefish, but they will rarely strike a lure.

Aquarium Care: The sennet presents the usual problems inherent to open water, cruising predators: providing enough room and enough food of the alive-and-kicking kind. This fish should be kept in small groups, say four to six, in a minimum of 30 gallons. The water should be well-aerated and a strong filter current provided by a powerhead to give the fish a flow to orient themselves into. Ideally, they should be maintained by themselves as they are strongly attracted by any movement and may strike at other fishes kept with them, even those too large to eat. Sennet should be fed live killies or silversides, or, if these are unavailable, as in winter, feeder guppies or goldfish purchased from a pet shop. They will not accept dead or prepared foods.

SQUIRRELFISHES
(Holocentrus and *Sargocentron* species)*

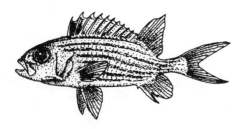

Range and Habitat: The reef squirrelfish *(S. bullisi)* occurs from the West Indies and Florida north to Bermuda, with juveniles straying occasionally to New York on the mainland in the warmer months. The family (Holocentridae) is a large and confusing one, occurring widely in both the tropical Atlantic and Pacific oceans, mostly in coral reefs. Young individuals (under four inches) are often observed near jetties, groins, and dock pilings in the north in late summer.

Field Marks and Collecting: The squirrelfishes, or soldierfishes, have predominately red colors and laterally striped patterns, large, prominent eyes, deeply forked tails, and long, spinous dorsal fins, usually brightly colored and marked in several species with a dark spot. As the large eyes indicate, they are primarily nocturnal, often seen flitting about reefs or jetties at night by divers using lights. Squirrelfish are sometimes spotted during the day, when they can be more easily collected with a slurpgun or hand net as they tend to move about very little in an effort to escape. These fish should be handled carefully. Avoid using a net, if possible. The large eyes are easily damaged by rough treatment and may leave the fish open to fungus infection.

Aquarium Care: Squirrelfishes do well in aquariums and are very popular. Some species grow quite large (9 to 12 inches) and this, coupled with their often aggressive nature, may make them unsuitable for smaller tanks or community setups, and certainly as tankmates of smaller or inoffensive fishes. Squirrels prefer dimly lit quarters with rock or coral hideaways. They will quickly set up a territory and defend it against other fishes. As their prominent mouths would indicate, these fish are predators, eating a wide variety of invertebrates and smaller fishes. In the aquarium they will accept virtually all live foods as well as cut fish or lean beef and prepared marine foods.

NORTHERN GOATFISH
(Mullus auratus)

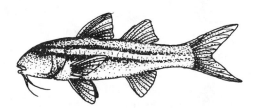

Range and Habitat: Throughout the West Indies north to Florida, with young fish straying north to New Jersey and rarely to Cape Cod during the summer. Many other goatfishes of this genus, as well as *Upeneus*, occur throughout the eastern Pacific and Indo-Pacific. Goatfish are shallow-water, inshore fish that prowl over sand or mud bottoms in search of small crustaceans and other invertebrates. Young fish are often seen in the quieter waters of estuaries and around docks and bulkheads.

Field Marks and Collecting: The goatfish, called that because of the two long, mobile chin barbels, is somewhat reminiscent of a carp, especially when viewed from above. It has an elongate, cylindrical body and rounded head and dorsal profiles. The mouth is on the underside of the snout. There are two distinct dorsal fins, and the tail is strongly forked. The northern goatfish is a brownish-gold or red. A broad, dusky, lateral stripe bordered with lighter gold runs from the gill covers to the base of the caudal fin.

Goatfish are placid bottom-grazers and scavengers that can move quickly when they have to. They can often easily avoid a hand net or slurpgun as they are usually seen in open areas that allow few opportunities for cornering them. In my own limited experience with goatfish, I have found that a cast net skillfully thrown over a school in shallow water is about the surest way to collect them.

Aquarium Care: Goatfish are hardy, adaptable creatures that will do well in the aquarium as long as they are provided with enough to eat. Being effective scavengers, these fish are often kept, like catfish, to clean up after other fish. They should not be expected to survive solely on the leavings of others. Offer them smaller live foods and enough sinking-type prepared foods to allow them to find it on the bottom, which is where they will spend most of their time. The substrate should be of finer gravel or soft sand to accommodate their rooting and grubbing.

GOGGLE-EYE SCAD
(Selar crumenopthalmus)

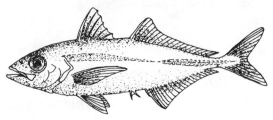

Range and Habitat: Widespread in warmer seas north to Cape Cod. Smaller individuals are often very abundant near inlets and other coastal areas in summer. The scads are well-represented in both the Atlantic and Pacific oceans.

Field Marks and Collecting: The various scads *(Selar, Decapterus,* and *Trachurus* genera) are members of the Carangidae—the jacks—and look like slimmer versions of these familiar game fishes. The goggle-eye is a small (up to ten inches), streamlined fish with a strongly forked tail on a slim caudal peduncle. The tail stem is strengthened with a row of bony, ridged scutes, much like the jacks. The pectoral fins are slender and elongate, and the eye is rather large. This fish is olive or light brown above, fading to silvery on the sides and belly. The pectoral, ventral, and caudal fins usually show a yellowish tint. The fish appears reddish-tan when viewed from above, such as from a dock, a factor which separates it from the small, bluish-green tinker or spike mackerel and adult silversides with which they often associate.

I have collected this species with relative ease using a cast net when they collect in dense schools around marina docks. They are usually large and robust enough to prevent them from being gill-netted in the net's meshes.

Aquarium Care: For active, open water, schooling fishes, scads do surprisingly well in aquariums if given a large enough tank. Several three-inch specimens I caught were given to a friend who placed them in a 30-gallon high tank with a few lookdowns and sea bass. The scads adapted to their confinement readily and accepted both natural and prepared foods at once. A problem eventually arose due to their active, inquisitive nature. They began to chase and harrass the lookdowns, picking at their long fin filaments, and had to be released.

Scads prefer clean, well-aerated water with a moderate to strong current flow. Avoid slower-moving or shy tankmates. Scads are quite undemanding in food requirements and will accept all live foods and some prepared foods, such as marine flakes.

COMMON JACK
(Caranx hippos)

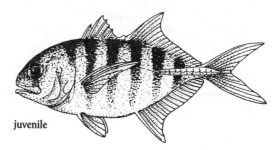

juvenile

Range and Habitat: Tropical and subtropical Atlantic, ranging as far north as Massachusetts in summer. Similar species—the horse-eye, hardtailed, and yellow jacks, and skipjacks—range throughout the West Indies north to Florida and Cape Cod. Many carangid fishes occur in the Pacific Ocean. Jacks are pelagic fishes, though they are usually seen near the coasts. The strikingly patterned young are often observed in shallow estuaries in late summer, especially near eelgrass beds and other submerged vegetation.

Field Marks and Collecting: An adult jack may reach a length of 30 inches and weigh up to 20 pounds, though most average about half that size. Jacks can be recognized by their deep-bodied profiles and blunt, rounded heads. The caudal peduncle is very slender but is strengthened by a rough, hard transverse keel in all species. Young jacks of three inches and under, the only size suitable for the home aquarium, are quite striking and hard to miss when observed. They are a bright silvery-gold crossed by four to six black vertical bands; the body profile is similar to that of the adults.

Young jacks cruise about in shallow water either singly or in small groups of between five and ten. At such times, it is often possible to get a seine around the school and capture them all. Otherwise, you'll have to be content with stray individuals turning up in random seine hauls through eelgrass beds. Once jacks attain the size of, say, four inches, they become too swift and agile to bag easily with a dip net.

Aquarium Care: Jacks are by nature open water, schooling fishes that are on the move almost constantly. It is cruel to crowd them into a small tank that affords them little swimming space. Ideally, four two-inch jacks should have at least 20 gallons of water with a minimum of plants or other decor to impede their travels. The water should be clean and well-filtered, with a moderate current. Jacks accept all of the popular live foods as well as bits of chopped fish or clam. The tank containing young jacks collected in temperate areas in summer should be moderately heated (74°–78°) during the winter.

LOOKDOWN
(Selene vomer)

Range and Habitat: Both coasts in tropical and subtropical waters. On the Atlantic coast it is found from Central America north to Chesapeake Bay, with juveniles straggling to Cape Cod and the Gulf of Maine. In the Pacific the lookdown occurs from British Columbia south to Peru. The lookdown is a coastal species found both inshore and in deeper waters offshore. The young, under four inches, are frequently found in shallow estuaries in late summer.

Field Marks and Collecting: This is one of the more bizarre marine fishes. It is a strongly compressed fish laterally, being wafer-thin when viewed from above, and the body is very deep. The dorsal and anal fins are extended into long filaments, and the eye is set very high on the long face, giving the fish its characteristic "looking down its nose" expression. Juvenile lookdowns have the first dorsal and ventral fins drawn out into very long, wispy black streamers which may be two to five times the length of their owner's body. These are lost as the fish matures. The adult lookdown, which reaches about a foot in length, is bluish-green above and bright silver on the sides and belly. The young are similar, but they have four or so dusky bars on the sides, and individuals also may show a number of large, pale gold spots on the flanks.

Large lookdowns are commonly caught on hook and line as a food fish. The juveniles are usually collected by seining eelgrass and turtle grass beds or shallow, sandy areas in bays and estuaries.

Aquarium Care: The lookdown looks like a fragile, exotic creature when first collected and examined, and to a great extent, it is. It should be handled gently and given plenty of room, both in the collecting bucket and in the aquarium, as its very long fin filaments can easily become tangled. The species should be given ample swimming space (fifty-five gallons or more) in the aquarium and not housed with any active or even slightly aggressive fish, for these will surely be attracted to the trailing fins and attack them. Seahorses, pipefishes, sticklebacks, and other more placid fish are good tankmates. Clean, well-aerated water and live foods are advisable. As the lookdown can be difficult to keep alive in captivity for a long time, it should be observed and enjoyed for several days or weeks and then released.

PERMIT
(Trachinotus falcatus)

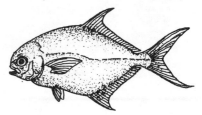

Range and Habitat: Throughout the Caribbean and Florida waters; irregularly straggling north to Cape Cod in summer. The four members of the genus *Trachinotus* (pompanos) are similar in appearance and general range, from Massachusetts to Argentina, with the center of abundance from Florida to the southern Caribbean. They are coastal fishes inhabiting open shoal waters over sand or hard bottoms. Most are important food and game fishes.

Field Marks and Collecting: Pompanos have deep profiles, high, blunt foreheads, and elongate dorsal and anal fins. The tail is strongly forked and the caudal peduncle slender. The mouth and the eye are small in relation to the size of the fish. Pompano are a steel blue or green above, fading to a bright silvery-white ventrally.

The permit, typical of the group, is a ceaselessly active, nervous, schooling fish that can be difficult, if not impossible, to collect in deeper waters. Most specimens taken in temperate waters are young individuals that have strayed north on the Gulf Stream and ended up in estuaries, where they are occasionally seined in eelgrass beds. These are usually about an inch or so in length and thus easier to corral and bag with a seine.

Aquarium Care: The permit adapts well to aquariums, presenting no particular problems except that it must have adequate room in order to accommodate its highly active schooling nature. This is a fish for large, open tanks (100 gallons, minimum, for about six individuals). Anything smaller will crowd the fish as they grow and create chaos among tankmates as the permits sweep nervously and endlessly back and forth. Given enough room, though, a large tank of young permits (or pompanos) is a spectacular sight. The fish, are smart and very expressive, and will react to the presence of their owner, especially to one bearing food. This species should get clean, well-aerated water with a moderately strong filter current and plenty of meaty foods, live foods in particular. Permit will put on weight and size rather quickly and thus should eventually be released back into the wild if at all possible.

BLUEFISH
(Pomatomus saltatrix)

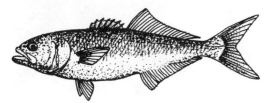

Range and Habitat: Tropical and temperate Atlantic and Indian Oceans, as well as the Mediterranean. The bluefish, the sole member of its family, the Pomatomidae, is essentially a pelagic or open ocean fish that spawns at sea and approaches the coastal zone in early spring and summer. It is a voracious predator of legendary ferocity around which revolves an intensive recreational and commercial fishery.

Field Marks and Collecting: The blue is a powerfully built, streamlined super-predator armed with a heavy, underslung jaw studded with very capable teeth. It is known to reach 46 inches in length and weights of up to 25 pounds, but most average 8 to 15 pounds. The living bluefish is a beautiful sea green above, fading to silvery-white on the sides and belly. The small spinous dorsal has six to eight spines, and there is a blackish spot at the base of the pectoral fin. This latter fieldmark is especially prominent in the young, locally called "snappers." The latter are the only size bluefish that could be even remotely considered for the home marine aquarium.

Little snapper blues—between one and four inches—are often seined in considerable numbers in summer along with the silversides and killies upon which they unceasingly prey. The smallest specimens possible should be retained for aquariums and not crowded in the collecting bucket as they stress quickly due to loss of oxygen. For all their toughness, bluefish injure easily and lose scales if handled carelessly. Damaged specimens should be rejected for aquarium use as they will almost surely contract a fatal fungus.

Aquarium Care: Bluefish of any size seem unlikely candidates for the home aquarium, but they can be kept successfully if a few hard and fast guidelines are followed. First, the species is highly predaceous and considers virtually anything that moves food, thus it is suited only to the single-species setup. If hungry, they will pick at and harrass even tankmates their own size or larger, so there are virtually no other fishes or invertebrates (except for anemones and echinoderms) that can be safely quartered with them. Second, blues require relatively powerful and effective filtration to keep the water clean (they are messy eaters) and provide a current for schooling. They will accept any meaty fare, living or dead, with chopped smelt or clam and small live fish the best options. A bluefish tank requires little decor. The less obstruction to schooling the better, as the fish are shown off to better advantage when engaged in this behavior. Bluefish are capable of spectacular growth if fed adequately, so that a four-inch snapper may more than double that size in one growing season. The bluefish is definitely a "keep for awhile and let it go" species.

SNOWY GROUPER
(Epinephelus niveatus)

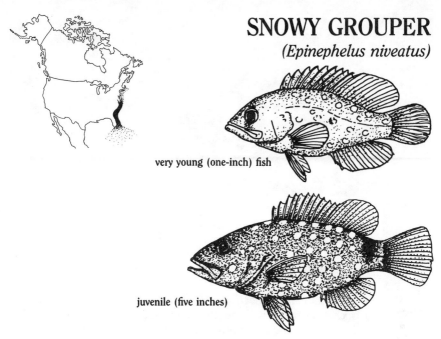

very young (one-inch) fish

juvenile (five inches)

Range and Habitat: Brazil north throughout the West Indies and Florida. Juveniles stray with fair regularity to Massachusetts in summer. It's a deepwater reef species in the tropics. In temperate waters, the young are observed in a variety of habitats, from shallow water estuaries and around docks to inlet mouths and jetties.

Field Marks and Collecting: The juvenile (the only size suitable for aquariums) snowy grouper is a very striking little creature, being a dusky, chocolate brown liberally spotted with bright white dots arranged in vertical rows. The tail is orange or yellow to its base. The bright colors fade and become a rather uniform red or brown as the fish grows.

Most young snowy groupers are collected at night by divers using lights and hand nets or slurpguns, but a number have turned up in seine hauls made in eelgrass beds along the shores of New Jersey and on Long Island, New York.

Aquarium Care: All groupers are large-mouthed, voracious predators. That's fact number one to be remembered by any aquarist contemplating keeping any grouper species. The snowy grouper is no exception to this rule. Since it grows fast and reaches a length of about three feet at maturity, think hard before putting one in a home tank. If you do, keep it in a spacious tank by itself, or, if you must, with other fishes only as large or larger than it is, for everything small enough to be eaten will be eaten. This grouper uses rock and coral shelters as its territory base, and should get the same arrangement in the aquarium. Groupers will accept all meat and fish fare, alive or dead, once acclimated to tank life. As with most fishes with the capacity for eating a lot and attaining large size, the snowy grouper will sooner or later present its owner with the "what to do with it?" problem, for this fish is long-lived if well cared for. Think about that, too, before keeping that attractive little grouper you've just collected.

BLACK SEA BASS
(Centropristes striatus)

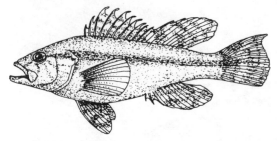

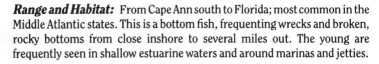

Range and Habitat: From Cape Ann south to Florida; most common in the Middle Atlantic states. This is a bottom fish, frequenting wrecks and broken, rocky bottoms from close inshore to several miles out. The young are frequently seen in shallow estuarine waters and around marinas and jetties.

Field Marks and Collecting: The adult sea bass may reach a length of 17 inches and weights of about three pounds, though eight-pounders have been reported. It is a dark fish, with each scale outlined in black, giving the fish a latticed look. The ground colors are a blackish-blue or purplish, with older males showing a light grayish-blue nape often raised in a fatty hump. The young have a dark, irregular transverse band running along the side from nose to tail and the pupil of the eye usually reflects a bright iridescent green. In nearly all sizes, the tips of the spinous part of the dorsal fins are bright white, which is a very noticeable field mark. The pectoral and ventral fins of both adult and young fish are long and prominent and individuals spend much time propped up on the latter on the substrate.

Young sea bass under three inches are usually seined in estuaries, though they can be hand-netted with relative ease on sand bottoms around docks. The best approach is to slowly position the net just behind a fish resting on the bottom and then spook it into the bag with a stick or hand.

Aquarium Care: Sea bass acclimate well to aquariums, the only problem being their highly predaceous nature, which will be noted with a glance at the large mouth. Young bass like rock hiding places in a tank but they are quite active creatures and will occupy all levels of the water column. They should receive meaty fare such as smaller live fish and chopped clam or fish and not kept with any fishes they can swallow—which they surely will do if given the chance. Smaller specimens can tolerate the warmer water of a tropical setup without ill effects, but bass at four inches or longer should get an unheated tank.

DEEP BIGEYE
(Pseudopriacanthus altus)

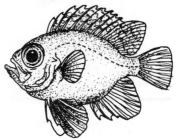

Range and Habitat: West Indies and Brazil to the Carolinas, straying north to Massachusetts in summer. Adult bigeye are primarily deepwater tropical fishes inhabiting rocky or reef areas but the strikingly colored young are often seen in shallow estuaries among eelgrass and around wharves and jetties in late summer. The closely related common bigeye *(Priacanthus arenatus)* frequents essentially the same habitats and range.

Field Marks and Collecting: Once seen, a young bigeye won't soon be forgotten for it is among the most beautiful and yet bizarre of fishes. The fish can be recognized at once by its brilliant carmine red color, accented by dusky or black pelvic fins and the huge eye. The dorsal fin has a delicate, chainlike pattern of red, white, and black vermiculations, and the tail and pectoral fins are transparent. The marvelous eyes pick up and reflect light to such a degree that tiny beams of gold brilliance are emitted when a light is played on the fish. Bigeyes of both species, sometimes called glasseyes or catalufas, reach an adult length of 12 to 14 inches, but most young fish caught and kept in aquariums are between one and four inches.

Although bigeyes often turn up in seine hauls made over eelgrass beds in shallow water, most are collected by hand nets around docks, bulkheads, jetties, and other such locations. They are primarily abroad at night, when they are easily spotted with a strong light and bagged with a hand net or slurpgun. Slow, deliberate swimmers, bigeyes make little effort to avoid capture if approached slowly and guided into a net.

Aquarium Care: The striking bigeye is an attention-getting addition to any marine tank and does very well if given the right environment and care. This fish adjusts to confinement very quickly, being essentially a sedentary creature that establishes a small territory and sticks pretty close to it. Its sedate, almost serene temperament will not make it a threat to any other fish kept with it unless they are small enough to be swallowed. A look at the bigeye's ample mouth will tell you that it is a predator of no meager reputation. Most bigeyes collected in summer are between one and four inches long and these will do very well in tanks of between 20 and 50 gallon capacity. The setup should be amply landscaped with rock or coral hideaways so the fish can establish its territory. Two or more bigeyes kept together may threaten each other but seldom will any border dispute come to blows. Bigeyes will accept nearly all live or frozen foods and can be induced over time to take some of the marine prepared foods. Given good care, a bigeye may live for five to ten years in the aquarium.

GRAY SNAPPER
(Lutjanus griseus)

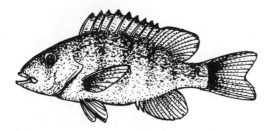

 Range and Habitat: Throughout the western tropical Atlantic, from Brazil and the Caribbean to the Carolinas and casually to Massachusetts in the warmer months (juveniles). The species wanders a great deal, and one individual was caught several miles up the Congo River. The snappers (Lutjanidae) are well-represented throughout the Pacific Ocean.

This is primarily a littoral species, found in shallow estuaries and mangrove swamps, from which it takes its other common name, mangrove snapper. It also frequents coral reefs and in the north may be looked for around jetties, groins, and marinas, where the juveniles prowl about among the dock piling and bulkheads. Other common tropical Atlantic snappers include the mutton snapper *(L. analis)*, the dog snapper *(L. jocu)*, the lane snapper *(L. synagris)*, and the schoolmaster *(L. apodus)*.

Field Marks and Collecting: Snappers look somewhat like elongated freshwater basses but have a longer, more convex head profile and a large mouth armed with a set of very impressive canines. They are not to be confused with juvenile bluefish, also widely called snappers. The gray snapper is a pale grayish-blue, light gray, or brown with a metallic green cast. The dorsal and caudal fins are dark, the anal is white-edged, and the ventrals are white streaked with red. The scales are often individually tipped with reddish brown spots, giving the fish a speckled look. The young are very dark, almost black, with slightly darker bands. They sometimes have bright red ventral fins and iridescent blue streaks on the snout. The gray snapper reaches a length of about 20 inches and weighs between five and eight pounds.

Snappers are eternally hungry and will strike almost any bait, live or cut. Larger specimens may be caught for aquariums this way, but by far the preferred method is to collect the very young ones with a slurpgun, hand net, or seine. They are surprisingly incautious and can usually be approached closely with ease.

Aquarium Care: Snappers can be a problem in that they are aggressive, eat a lot, and grow fast. I collected a beautiful one-inch gray snapper one August and within a year it had grown to nearly six inches long and was the sole inhabitant of what had once been a community tank. They should be given a lot of room and kept only with fishes equally large, combative, and able to take care of themselves. The tank should contain plenty of rock, coral, or driftwood cover and maintained under lower light conditions, for snappers are primarily nocturnal. They will accept virtually all live, cut, or prepared foods and they require a lot of it to stay in fighting trim. An underfed snapper will emaciate and decline in health. Given good care and well fed, a gray (or any other snapper) will quickly become very tame, come to recognize its owner, and will live for years in an aquarium.

PORKFISH
(Anisotremus virginicus)

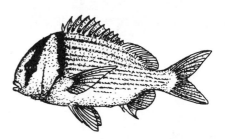

Range and Habitat: Throughout the West Indies and from Brazil north to Florida. It has been introduced into Bermuda waters. The porkfish is a shallow water, reef species and is often seen in large schools near marinas and harbors in Florida.

Field Marks and Collecting: The porkfish is a member of the grunt family (Pomadasyidae) and is readily recognized by its deep-bodied profile, steep forehead, and striking color and pattern. The head is bright yellow and silver with a black bar running from the forehead through the eye. A second bar runs from the origin of the dorsal fin to the base of the pectoral fin. The body is longitudinally striped with pale blue and gold, and all of the fins are a soft yellow. Juveniles are quite different in appearance. The head is yellow and there are two thin black stripes running from the eye to the base of the caudal fin which terminate in a large round spot.

Porkfish can be collected with a cast net, slurpgun, or hand net. They will enter a fish trap baited with crushed crab or shrimp.

Aquarium Care: This species does well in aquariums and is frequently seen in pet shop marine sections. As it is an active, schooling fish, it is happiest when kept in groups of four or more and given a large, roomy tank. The water should be kept clean and well filtered and maintained on the warm side (76° to 80°) with no sharp fluctuations in temperature. This fish is catholic in its food preferences, accepting a wide variety of fare, brine shrimp, chopped shrimp and clam, crab meat, and sea worms. The young are reported to engage in cleaning behavior. That is, they will seek out larger fishes and devour any ectoparasites they can find on them.

PINFISH
(Lagodon rhomboides)

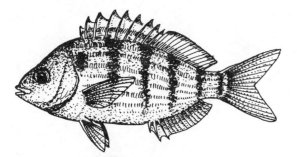

Range and Habitat: The pinfish is a coastal species found from Texas in the Gulf of Mexico north to the Chesapeake Bay and casually to Massachusetts in summer. It is a fish of littoral waters and is often found in estuaries and around inlet jetties. Only juveniles of four inches or under are found north of Maryland.

Field Marks and Collecting: This is a sparid fish closely related to the sheepshead and other porgies. Like them, it is a deep-bodied fish with a high forehead, a continuous dorsal fin, and a moderately forked tail. It is olive-green above and silver below; the sides have a series of blue and yellow longitudinal lines and are crossed vertically by four to six dusky bands. It reaches a length of about 13 inches in the south, where it is a food fish, but most specimens collected in the Middle Atlantic states are one to four inches at most.

Pinfish are most easily collected with a seine in late summer, when the young are found in the protection of eelgrass or sea lettuce beds. I have also collected a few strays around docks and marinas, though here they are much more wary.

Aquarium Care: The pinfish is an omnivorous fish that adapts readily to aquarium life and accepts a wide variety of foods, both natural and prepared. It is relatively inoffensive and will seldom molest tankmates, though, like nearly all fishes, it will eat any other fish small enough to be considered prey. When small, pinfish are quite shy and prefer a tank with abundant plants (plastic or live) or other such shelter. Younger specimens can tolerate a wide range of salinities and can live in a brackish as well as strictly marine environment. Some natural algae should be provided during the warmer months, with small pieces of boiled spinach or vegetable-based pellets being offered in winter.

SPOT
(Leiostomus xanthurus)

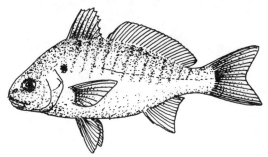

Range and Habitat: From Cape Cod south to the Gulf of Mexico and Texas, becoming more abundant in the southern part of the range. The spot, lafayette, or silver gudgeon is a coastal fish that undergoes periods of cyclic abundance and decline from year to year. It is a popular food fish caught from piers, jetties, and small boats within a mile or so of shore. The young are often extremely abundant in harbors and estuaries in late summer and early fall, where great schools of them can be seen grazing over the bottom in search of small crustaceans, hydroids, and fishes.

Field Marks and Collecting: A very large spot will stretch the tape at about 13 inches and weight 1½ pounds, though most are under a foot and weigh three-quarters of a pound. Both the adults and juveniles are quite attractive; the living fish is blue-gray and rose above and silvery below, crossed by 12 oblique yellow bars. A small, yellowish gray shoulder spot is usually prominent. The species name, *xanthurus,* means yellow tail, but on most specimens it is dusky, not yellow. The spot shows the typical drum and croaker profile—the deep body, rounded forehead, and mouth on the underside of the head. The spinous part of the dorsal fin is rather high and not separated from the soft posterior dorsal.

The spot lends itself to capture with a cast net when it is observed in shallow water for it is relatively slow and its deep body-profile prevents it from becoming gill-netted in the meshes, a problem with many smaller fishes. Otherwise, most spots are collected with a seine, for they do not readily enter traps and they become skittish and simply vanish whenever a diver with a hand net appears.

Aquarium Care: Spots are placid bottom-feeders that do well in aquariums, though their tank should be large as they are restless, ceaselessly roving fish that need room to move around in. They will accept most live and prepared foods and are especially fond of chopped clam or sandworms, the best baits in the recreational fishery. Spots will grow quickly if well fed, and thus should be released when they become too large to be comfortably housed.

KINGFISHES
(*Menticirrhus* species)

Range and Habitat: The two species in this genus are very similar. The northern kingfish *(M. saxatilis)* is found from Massachusetts to Florida but is common only north of Chesapeake Bay. The southern species *(M. americanus)* is known from New Jersey to Texas, being uncommon north of Chesapeake Bay and in the Gulf of Mexico. Kingfishes, members of the croaker family (Sciaenidae), are bottom feeders that favor sandy bottoms near channels fairly close to shore. The young are common in shallow estuaries and salt marshes in late summer.

Field Marks and Collecting: Like most drums and croakers, the kingfish has an inferior mouth set on the underside of the head and a single sensory barbel on the lower jaw. Both species are elongate fishes with a split dorsal fin, the first ray of the spinous section often extended into a long filament. Kingfish are dark grayish green above, fading to silvery-white on the sides and belly. Both species are obliquely barred in black, but in the northern species, the first two bars form a V-shape; the southern form lacks the elongated dorsal filament and, at an adult size of 16 inches, is smaller than the northern kingfish (20 inches). The young closely resemble the adults but their color and pattern is brighter and stronger in contrast.

Young kingfish (between one and six inches) are often collected in seine hauls over sandy or weedy bottoms in sheltered bays and estuaries. Due to their striking color and pattern and their habit of prowling slowly about in open sandy areas in search of food, they can often be spotted and bagged with a dip net or a fine-meshed cast net.

Aquarium Care: Juvenile kingfish are attractive and docile, and with careful acclimation, make good marine aquarium tenants. I stress careful, as, in spite of their voracious, bottom-grubbing habits, I have found them to be somewhat difficult to feed in captivity. Young fish often refuse food and slowly starve in spite of a variety of tempting offerings. Through experimentation I have found that keeping them by themselves in a small quarantine tank with a soft sand bottom and lower light levels will usually induce them to accept live brine shrimp as a starter food. Once acclimated, they will accept a wide variety of fare, with chopped clam being a particular favorite. In the aquarium, smaller kingfish are placid, peaceable creatures that will not trouble tankmates.

HIGH-HAT
(Equetus cubbyu)

High-hat or
*Equetus cubbyu
acuminiatus*

Jackknife Fish *Equetus lanceolata*

Range and Habitat: Throughout the West Indies, straying north to the Florida Keys and to Pensacola on the Gulf side. This is a reef species which tends to stick closely to the shelter and protection of the coral growths than does the similar striped ribbon, or jackknifefish *(E. lanceolata)*, which favors more open, sandy areas.

Field Marks and Collecting: The high-hat, or cubbyu, is a member in good standing of the diverse croaker family (Sciaenidae), but unlike such gargantuan relatives, such as the sea drum *(Pogonius cromis)* which reaches the length of four feet and weights of up to 150 pounds, this creature can be considered large at ten inches. The adults are a uniform brownish gold, but the very beautiful and striking young are very popular with marine tropical hobbyists. The common name stems from the high, pointed dorsal fin, usually carried erect in the healthy fish. The overall color is a clear white or gold. A broad, black curving band runs from the nape across the gill covers to the base of the pectoral fins, and another from the base of the prominent dorsal fin to the base of the caudal fin. This is a highly conspicuous little fish.

Most high-hats are collected with drop nets or baited fish traps, which they will readily enter. These very active fish gather in small schools that quickly hide deep under ledges and coral heads when pursued. They can be bagged rather easily by herding them into a hand net with the hand.

Aquarium Care: Like most drums and croakers, these fish are bottom feeeders that require some area of sand or mud in which to forage for food. Thus a tank with open space and with bleached coral or rocks providing some hideaways will suit them best. Water should be clean and the temperature not allowed to fluctuate greatly. They will accept a wide variety of foods from live and cut natural foods to the prepared foods that sink to the bottom. High-hats and other related fishes are peaceful and will coexist with most other smaller marine species.

BEAUGREGORY (and other damselfishes)
(Stegastes leucostictus)

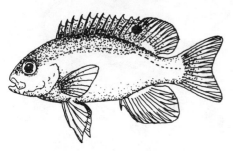

Range and Habitat: In the Caribbean north to Florida and straggling to New England during the warmer months. The beaugregory, as well as other damselfishes, is a reef species common about coral reefs in the tropics and near jetties and docks in temperate waters. It is a highly territorial, aggressive little fish that sets up and defends small territories, from which it rarely strays very far. Damselfishes are very widely distributed in the tropical Atlantic and Pacific, as well as the Red Sea.

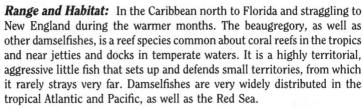

Field Marks and Collecting: Although subject to considerable variation, the beaugregory is a small pomacentrid, bright blue dorsally and gold ventrally. It is a deep-bodied little fish with a strongly forked tail that flits in and out of crevices and grottoes of its environment with amazing speed and agility. For this reason, all damsels can be a challenge to collect, with the best methods being the slurpgun or a hand net and pokestick. I recently collected a bicolor damselfish *(Stegastes partitus)*, a state record for New Jersey, using a pokestick and a gallon mayonnaise jar after all other methods to bag the elusive creature had failed. The glass container approach works well with many smaller reef or jetty species as they can often be easily prodded and maneuvered into it and the jar lifted before the quarry realizes its error.

Aquarium Care: Damselfishes are hardy and adaptable and acclimate well to aquariums. They are highly popular in the aquarium hobby as marine beginner's fish as they readily accept most commercial fish foods and live foods and are not overly sensitive to water chemistry problems. If there is a drawback to the group, it would be their temperment, for most damsels are rather territorial and aggressive and thus often squabble among themselves. Normally, however, they will exist peaceably enough with other fishes of like size, and their sprightly personality always makes them a pleasing addition to any tank.

SERGEANT MAJOR
(Abudefduf saxatilis)

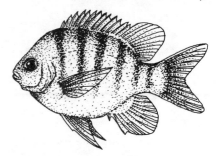

Range and Habitat: Circumtropical; in the western Atlantic it occurs from Uruguay to Florida and regularly north to about Rhode Island during the warmer months. This is an abundant reef fish throughout its range. In the north it is usually seen near jetties, among dock pilings, and near floating debris. I have seen very small individuals (about one inch) hiding under moored boats, from which they make quick sorties to pluck food from the water column.

Field Marks and Collecting: This is a typical damselfish. It is a deep-bodied fish, dusky to olive above, yellowish to silvery on the sides, with five broad, black vertical bars. A faint sixth bar may be present posteriorly on the caudal peduncle, and there is a black spot at the insertion of the pectoral fin. The species attains the length of about seven inches, though most are between four and five inches. In the wild, the male guards the eggs, which appear as a dark red or purple patch on rocks or pilings.

The sergeant major can be a challenge to collect for it is a highly active, alert little fish that isn't cornered easily and puts some distance between itself and an approaching diver. They often feed in aggregations well above the bottom, only to disappear into the coral or rocks at the slightest sign of danger. Young specimens are less wary than the adults and can be slurpgunned from crevices. A drop net placed over a coral head or rockpile will usually yield a few.

Aquarium Care: This is a very hardy little fish and, like all damselfishes, makes a good fish for the beginning marine aquarist. Its only drawback is its temperament; it is aggressive and may prove troublesome, as a fin-nipper, or worse, to slower-moving fishes. In addition, it is highly territorial, and males will scrap vigorously. But, other than that, the sergeant major is a delightful aquarium fish that makes itself right at home and will eat a wide variety of foods. In nature, it consumes everything from algae through zooplankton, copepods, nudibranchs, and small fish, and as long as that catholic diet is matched in captivity, the fish will be fine. All damsels should be housed in roomy tanks with plenty of hideaways to allow them to set up individual territories.

CUNNER
(Tautogolabrus adspersus)

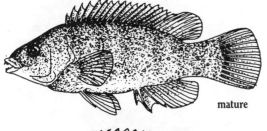

mature

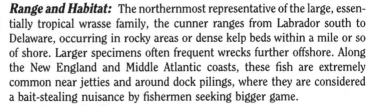

young

Range and Habitat: The northernmost representative of the large, essentially tropical wrasse family, the cunner ranges from Labrador south to Delaware, occurring in rocky areas or dense kelp beds within a mile or so of shore. Larger specimens often frequent wrecks further offshore. Along the New England and Middle Atlantic coasts, these fish are extremely common near jetties and around dock pilings, where they are considered a bait-stealing nuisance by fishermen seeking bigger game.

Field Marks and Collecting: This interesting fish, known under a number of aliases, including choggie, chogset, sea perch, and bergall, occurs in two distinct color phases with many intergrades, depending on the habitat. Jetty-bred cunners are a brownish-green finely speckled with reds, while those living among kelp tend toward a brick red with fine red and blue spotting. All color variations display the whitish lower jaw, or chin, characteristic of the species. Most young cunners display six to eight irregular vertical bars of darkish brown, but those collected among *Ulva*, or sea lettuce, are usually a bright grass-green, sometimes showing a small but dark postdorsal spot. Others may be mottled with varying shades of green, bronze, and gold—quite attractive overall. In general, the cunner is a chunky perchlike fish with a long, spinous dorsal fin and a squared-off tail. A very large specimen may be 15 inches long and weigh close to three pounds, but most average half that size.

Most cunners are caught with hook and line. Although this is not the recommended method of capture for aquariums, small ones caught this way can be acclimated successfully if handled carefully. Juvenile fish, by far the best suited to the aquarium, can be seined in shallow bays and estuaries where they are most commonly found in eelgrass and sea lettuce beds. The greatest challenge will be in separating the greenish-gold little fish from the mass of weeds of exactly the same color in the net. Cunners transport well, but they are highly stressed by exposed situations. They should be given a few pieces of sea lettuce to hide under in the collecting bucket.

Aquarium Care: The cunner adapts readily to confinement as long as it is provided with plenty of hiding places in the tank and not subjected to overly warm water or bright illumination. Individuals will select a rock grotto or plant thicket and use it as a home base, making frequent forays throughout the tank in search of food. Although they are not overly aggressive, individuals will defend their small territories against other cunners if necessary. In the wild, cunners form loose schooling aggregations. These are based less on a liking for each other's company than on the presence of favorable feeding habitats. In captivity as in nature, these fish will accept a wide variety of foods, with live or frozen brine shrimp, bloodworms, or tubifex and chopped fish and clam being favored. Cunners normally ignore prepared flake and pellet foods. These wrasses should be kept in the aquarium only until they grow too large for their quarters and then released back into the natural habitat. They should be kept in a cool tank (68° to 75°) in order to maintain health and vitality.

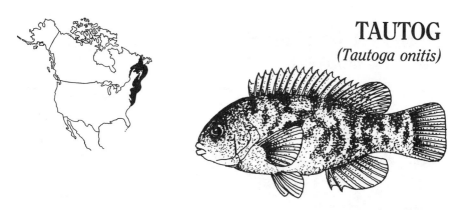

TAUTOG
(Tautoga onitis)

Range and Habitat: The tautog, blackfish, or oysterfish is another northern wrasse similar in many respects to the cunner, with which it shares much of its range, along the coast from the Chesapeake Bay north to New Brunswick. It differs from the cunner on two points: the tautog grows to a much larger size and it is somewhat less catholic in its tastes in foods. It prefers rocky habitats offering plenty of cover and an abundant supply of mussels, barnacles, and crustaceans. Unlike the cunner, this fish is only infrequently found near docks and wharves, preferring either natural rocky coasts or man-made jetties and groins. The young, however, are often found in estuaries and salt marshes during the early stages of growth.

Field Marks and Collecting: A fully adult tautog is a big fish, reaching a length of nearly three feet and weights of up to about 30 pounds, though most caught on hook and line average six to ten pounds. It can be told from the closely related cunner by its more stocky profile, darker color, and thicker lips. The ground color is a brownish-purple, crossed by several, irregular dark vertical bars. Like the cunner, this species displays a pure white lower jaw, lending it its other nickname, "whitechin." The young are very striking, attractive little fish, strongly barred in black against a silver-gold ground color. They are always chunkier in profile than young cunners, with which they commonly associate. When about three inches in length, they gravitate to the rocky areas favored by their elders, where divers can collect them with hand nets or slurpguns. Young tautogs appear to be less tame than cunners and thus more skill is required to approach and bag them in a net.

Aquarium Care: The tautog does best under the same conditions as given for the cunner—plenty of shelter and lower light and temperature levels, with the exceptions that they are less tolerant of poor water conditions and are usually slower to begin feeding in captivity. Being more selective feeders (principally mollusks and crustaceans), newly caught tautogs should be offered live brine shrimp or wild-collected mysid shrimp to get them started. They also relish minced clam or mussel when acclimated, and larger fish will eagerly pick apart a crushed green or mole crab. Once acclimated and feeding well, a tautog will grow relatively quickly so that within a year the fish may be aggressive toward tankmates and should be released at the site of capture.

BLUE PARROTFISH
(Scarus caerulens)

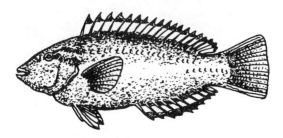

Range and Habitat: Widely distributed throughout the West Indies and Florida shore, with juveniles straying north to New York and occasionally to Massachusetts during the warmer months. Many *Scarus* parrotfish occur in the eastern and Indo-Pacific. This parrotfish is always found near reefs in the wild, or, in the case of northern strays, around jetties and marinas.

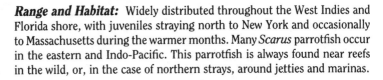
Field Marks and Collecting: Parrotfishes as a group are robust, often very large fish recognized by their heavy, fused, platelike teeth giving the impression of a parrot's beak. They are large-scaled fishes and have either a squared-off or moderately forked tail. The blue parrotfish is primarily a bright, cerulean blue, variously marked with red and orange on the head and gill covers.

The young under five inches are the only size really suited to the home aquarium. They are usually collected by chasing them down until they seek refuge in a crevice or hole and then placing a net over the opening and using a pokestick to flush them out. They also readily enter a trap baited with crushed crab or sea urchin. All larger parrotfish should be handled with care as they can deliver a powerful bite.

Aquarium Care: Parrotfishes are hardy and adaptable creatures and will thrive in aquariums under good care. They are very popular with marine tropical hobbyists.

When small, they are relatively peaceful, but larger individuals can be aggressive. Virtually all will attack sea urchins, crustaceans, live coral, and many other invertebrates that might be kept with them. For this reason, the tank holding parrotfish should be decorated with bleached coral and other inanimate objects and the fish offered live brine and chopped shrimp or clams, crab meat, and some algae or mustard greens. They will usually accept most prepared marine foods. The parrotfish tank should be large and well-aerated as this group has high oxygen requirements and will often succumb if kept too long in an unaerated transport container.

SPADEFISH
(Chaetodipterus faber)

Range and Habitat: From Brazil to Cape Cod, but uncommon north of Chesapeake Bay. Juveniles are sometimes reported in some abundance in the New York/New Jersey area in late summer. This species is common over rocky bottoms and near reefs and wrecks. Very small individuals often turn up in estuaries and around jetties in more northern waters.

Field Marks and Collecting: The spadefish is a close relative of the tropical butterflyfishes and has their general form, though it grows to a much larger size, up to three feet. The adult spadefish is grayish, greenish, or yellowish overall and has four to six often indistinct dark vertical bars. These are faded or absent in larger specimens and quite dark and intense in the young, hence the other common name, angelfish. The forehead is strongly rounded in large individuals, and the mouth and eye are small.

The spadefish is frequently caught on hook and line in the tropics, where it is regarded as a good food fish. In the north, young specimens can be collected with a hand net, slurpgun, or, in shallow waters, a seine.

Aquarium Care: Most captive spadefish are seen in large, public aquariums where they make impressive display animals as they move sedately about in large schools. Small ones can be kept in the home aquarium, where they will generally coexist well enough with other peaceful species. Like the butterflyfishes, they prey upon a variety of invertebrate and plant life and thus should be offered smaller live foods and some algae growth. The tank should be as large as possible, for these fish are restless schoolers and thus need room to move about freely.

COMMON BUTTERFLYFISH
(Chaetodon ocellatus)

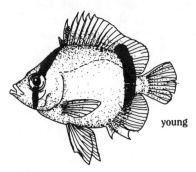

young

Range and Habitat: From Brazil north to Massachusetts, to the latter as a summer transient. Most abundant in the Caribbean and in Florida waters. The butterflyfishes (Chaetodontidae) are a large, diverse group found in both the Atlantic and Pacific Oceans. A reef species, this fish prefers jetties, groins, and docks for both the food and the shelter they provide. It is almost always found in such locations in the northeast, although occasionally individuals are seined in eelgrass beds. They are particularly common near bulkheads lining boat channels and marinas in the Middle Atlantic states, where they can be best collected at night.

Field Marks and Collecting: Although the species reaches a length of eight inches in the tropics, most butterflyfish seen in temperate coastal waters are juveniles under two inches in length. This is a laterally compressed fish of pearl-white body color with a black vertical line through the eye and a second near the tail. As the fish matures, the caudal band fades until it remains as a prominent black spot on the dorsal fin, lending the species its other common name, spotfin butterflyfish. The ventral, caudal, and dorsal fins are usually tinted with a beautiful saffron yellow.

These fish are most effectively collected with a dip net at lower tides during the night. They can be rather easily spotted with a bright light and normally make little attempt to evade capture. Larger specimens may be caught around jetty rocks by divers using slurpguns or hand nets. Collecting is much easier at night, however, as the fish are far less active. Observed from above, the thin, white body and fanlike ventral fins are diagnostic field marks.

Aquarium Care: Careful acclimation is a must for this species. It should be housed in the water the fish was collected in until accustomed to captivity and eating satisfactorily, and not kept with aggressive species that may harass it. Provide adequate cover and clean, well-aerated water. Offer it live foods (brine shrimp) to induce feeding, or better yet, place chunks of marine growth in the tank to encourage the fish to begin picking at recognizable food. When thoroughly acclimated, however, it will accept most frozen and freeze-dried aquarium foods. Ideally, the butterflyfish should be kept by itself or with other butterflies, at least until it is over three inches.

BANDED BUTTERFLYFISH
(Chaetodon striatus)

Range and Habitat: Throughout the Caribbean and eastern Gulf of Mexico, straying north to New Jersey and south to Brazil. A typical western Atlantic butterflyfish, this species favors coral reefs and rocky habitats. At the northern extreme of the range, the young are usually seen near jetties and around wharves and dock pilings.

Field Marks and Collecting: This fish has a deep-bodied, laterally compressed butterflyfish shape. The body is a pearl white, crossed mid-dorsally by two broad black bars, with a narrower band through the eye, and a fourth running from the base of the soft dorsal through the caudal peduncle and into the anal fin. It reaches a length of six inches, though specimens collected in the north are usually one- to two-inch juveniles.

This species is third in frequency of occurrence north of the Carolinas—after the spotfin and foureye butterflies—and is usually seen near sheltered bulkheads and among dock pilings in late summer. Collecting methods are the same as for the spotfin—hand net, slurpgun, or, in rare instances, seining through eelgrass beds.

Aquarium Care: As with all wild-caught butterflyfishes, the banded butterfly should be acclimated in as large a tank as possible and with few (or no) fish that might harrass it. Like the others, it may be shy at first about eating, thus chunks of marine growth placed in the tank temporarily may get it started, as will the smallest live brine shrimp available at pet shops. This is a peaceful fish, though larger ones may be territorial and show aggression toward others of their own kind.

FOUR-EYED BUTTERFLYFISH
(Chaetodon capistratus)

Range and Habitat: Throughout the West Indies to Florida and casually north to Massachusetts during the summer. Like most butterflies, this species is primarily a reef-dweller. When the young are carried north to the Middle Atlantic states and New England by the Gulf Stream, they are usually seen near jetties and around dock pilings in sheltered inlets.

Field Marks and Collecting: In both the adult and juvenile stages, this species can be identified by the prominent, round eyespot, or ocellatus, adorning the base of the caudal peduncle. It is present even in specimens one-half inch in length. The eyespot is thought to be a diversion to predators, who aim at the tail when striking at the fish instead of at the vulnerable head. Very young fish have three broad, dark vertical bands and a second dark ocellatus at the posterior edge of the dorsal fin.

Four-eye butterflies occupy the same type habitat as the spotfin and are collected by essentially the same methods. In my own experience, the juveniles are not as jumpy as the young spotfins and are rather easily maneuvered (slowly, of course) into an aquarium net. Green nets seem the best as they somewhat approximate the colors of the surrounding marine algal growths.

Aquarium Care: The four-eye, like most butterflyfish, can be a challenge to induce to begin feeding in captivity. I've found that, as with the spotfin, collecting hunks of marine growth and placing them in the tank with the fish facilitates this crucial step greatly. The fish will usually pick at what it recognizes as a natural source of food and can then be gradually weaned over to more standard aquarium fare.

REEF BUTTERFLYFISH
(Chaetodon sedentarius)

Range and Habitat: Resident throughout the Caribbean, regularly straying north to the Carolinas and uncommonly to New York during the summer. Like the spotfin, this butterflyfish is a reef dweller, frequenting warm, shallow waters of constant clarity and salinity. In the north, it occurs most frequently near jetties and inlet mouths.

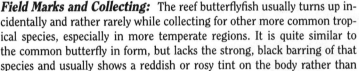

Field Marks and Collecting: The reef butterflyfish usually turns up incidentally and rather rarely while collecting for other more common tropical species, especially in more temperate regions. It is quite similar to the common butterfly in form, but lacks the strong, black barring of that species and usually shows a reddish or rosy tint on the body rather than the yellow of the spotfin. Small specimens display a black band through the eye and a dark spot and pale brownish band anteriorly on the dorsal fin. Most of those collected in the north are dime-sized or smaller and thus are most often caught by use of a dip net or quarter-inch mesh seine.

Aquarium Care: Essentials of care are the same as for the preceding species.

GRAY ANGELFISH
(Pomacanthus arcuatus)

Gray Angelfish

juvenile Gray Angelfish

juvenile French Angelfish

Range and Habitat: From the West Indies and Brazil north to Florida, and to New York as a stray in summer. This is a reef species, found inshore and near inlets and estuaries. In the north, the young are found in marinas and around bulkheads, areas that are much like the natural habitat in the tropics. The passer angelfish (*Holacanthus passer*) occurs in the eastern Pacific from southern California to Mexico. It is very popular in the marine aquarium hobby.

Field Marks and Collecting: The gray angel is a large (up to 23 inches), robust, and impressive creature when adult. It is a pale blue-gray with each scale tipped with a dusky spot, giving the fish a speckled look. The area of the mouth is often whitish and a pale band runs from the nape to the lower edge of the gill cover.

The closely related French angelfish (*P. paru*) is much darker, almost black, with each scale edged in yellow. There is a yellow patch at the base of the pectoral fin and often a yellow eye ring. The French is a smaller fish, reaching a length of about 16 inches.

The young of both species are quite different in appearance from the adults and can be difficult to tell apart. Both are velvety black with four bright yellow bands encircling the body. In the gray angel juvenile, the black tail spot takes the form of a vertical bar; in the French it is circular. The forehead band of the French angel ends at the base of the upper lip, while in the gray it extends down into the chin area.

Larger angelfishes are usually collected by diving with a hand net. Juveniles can be taken with a slurpgun or hand net. They will sometimes enter a killie trap strategically placed among rocks or near a bulkhead.

Aquarium Care: This species, like most marine angelfishes, gets along well with other species but it will not tolerate others of its own kind, especially when young. Unless a very large tank with ample coral or rock hideaways is provided, there will be constant warfare between two individuals, with the loser being injured or even killed. Thus only one should be kept in a tank. The gray angelfish is omnivorous, feeding on a multitude of invertebrates and on marine vegetation. In the aquarium this diet can be duplicated by offering live foods along with vegetable-based prepared marine foods and naturally collected algae. Boiled spinach, mustard greens, or lettuce will serve in a pinch as a substitute for algae, which should be allowed to grow in angelfish quarters. Given good care, this large angelfish will live for years in the aquarium.

BLUE ANGELFISH
(Holacanthus isabelita)

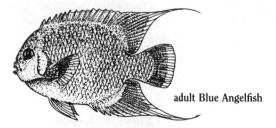

adult Blue Angelfish

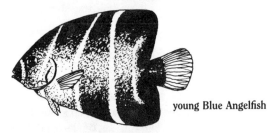

young Blue Angelfish

young Queen Angelfish

Range and Habitat: Bermuda, southern Florida, parts of the Gulf of Mexico, and the Bahamas. The young stray regularly as far north as New York in summer. This is an inshore reef species often found about marinas and inlets. The small juveniles (two inches and under) are sometimes seen around docks and jetties where their bright blue color contrasts sharply with the somber northern environment.

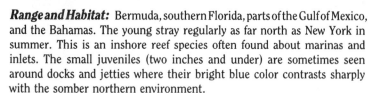

Field Marks and Collecting: The adult blue angel (16 to 18 inches) is a pale bluish-gray or tan with bright yellow, blue-edged dorsal and anal fins. The unpaired fins are extended in rather elongated filaments in the typical angelfish profile. The mouth is small for the size of the fish. The closely related queen angelfish is similar, but has a conspicuous dark blue ocellus on the nape. The highly colored juveniles are dark aquamarine blue crossed by a series of white vertical lines. The mouth and tail are bright yellow. In the young blue angel, the second pale bar is straight while in the queen, it is curved. The two species hybridize freely and have produced intergrades at one time recognized as a valid species (*H. townsendi*).

Angelfish can be collected by any one of several methods, the most common being diving with hand net or slurpgun. The juveniles are much less wary and can be approached quite closely when found in temperate waters in late summer. The blue angel is more cautious and less likely to enter a trap than are butterflyfish, which can be collected in that manner.

Aquarium Care: Smaller specimens do well in the open, brightly lit community tank provided they are given ample room, as they can show some aggression toward other fishes. One rule that many an aquarist/collector has learned to his dismay and too late is not to quarter two blue angels together in the same tank, no matter how large it is, for the dominant fish will pursue, harrass, and kill the other if it can. Otherwise, the blue and queen angels are relatively undemanding provided they are offered a varied diet and temperature fluctuations are avoided.

BLUE TANG
(Acanthurus caeruleus)

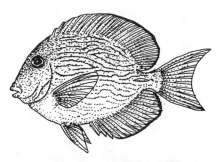

Range and Habitat: Widespread throughout the West Indies and north to Florida, with juveniles straying to New York in the summer. Tangs, or surgeonfish, are widespread throughout the tropical Atlantic and Pacific. This is a reef species common in coastal habitats, including jetties, bulkheads, and marinas. The young are frequently seen in the north, usually in late summer and early fall.

Field Marks and Collecting: The blue tang, or surgeonfish, is a deep-bodied, laterally compressed fish that changes color as it grows. Juveniles up to about four inches are bright yellow with blue eyes and edging to the dorsal and anal fins. As they grow, the yellow fades and becomes a grayish blue. This color intensifies until in the adult it is a bright aquamarine blue horizontally crossed by many fine wavy lines or reticulations. Vestiges of the juvenile yellow color often remain in the tail and pectoral fins of larger specimens. Like all surgeonfish, the blue tang is armed with a sharp, retractable spine on the caudal peduncle with which it can inflict nasty damage to any unwary collector and to other fishes.

Aquarium Care: Tangs are hardy fishes that require little more than roomy quarters and a diet combining both animal and vegetable matter. They are relatively peaceful creatures that form loose schools and thus are best kept in groups of between four and ten. Tangs will actively graze any coral or living rock in their tank.

QUEEN TRIGGERFISH
(Balistes vetula)

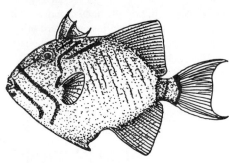

Range and Habitat: In the Caribbean, the Bahamas, and Florida, straying north to Massachusetts during the summer. This is a coastal or littoral species, common on coral reefs and other such habitats offering mixed open water and shelter. In the north, the juveniles are found near docks, bulkheads, and jetties offering a base for the abundant algal and invertebrate (*aufwuchs*) growth upon which this species grazes. The triggerfish family is abundant throughout the eastern Pacific and Indo-Pacific.

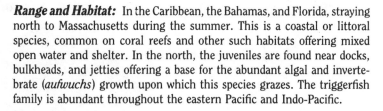

Field Marks and Collecting: The queen trigger, locally called the old wife or old wench, is one of the larger triggerfishes, reaching a length of about 16 inches. It is a striking creature, being a rich, warm brown or olive with a network of dark brown lines radiating from the eye and diagonally crossing the flanks. There are two intense blue lines running from the nape and the mouth to the base of the pectoral fin. The dorsal, caudal, and anal fins are banded or outlined with blue. The tail is squared off with the upper and lower rays extended into long filaments. The prominent first dorsal spine is modified into the locking defense device typical of all triggers.

Larger triggers are commonly caught on hook and line throughout the range, using chunks of conch or clam as bait. The young are best collected by checking empty conch or whelk shells, in which they frequently hide. They can also be seined on grass flats in the more northerly parts of the range. Smaller ones will readily enter a fish trap baited with crushed crab or sea urchin.

Aquarium Care: This species, and most triggerfishes, cannot be trusted with other fishes and invertebrates. The larger ones can be quite aggressive. A roomy tank of 20 to 30 gallons for a single fish allows it the space to grow. Triggers will accept a wide variety of foods from live brine or chopped shrimp to mussel and clam meat. They require some algae in the diet. This can be supplied by collecting it in the warmer months, or by algae-based marine foods or fresh-frozen mustard greens weighted and placed in the tank. They will graze any coral, so live rock would be a waste of money, except as food for the triggerfish. The water should be clean, well-aerated, and kept from 76° to 83°.

PLANEHEAD FILEFISH
(Monacanthus hispidus)

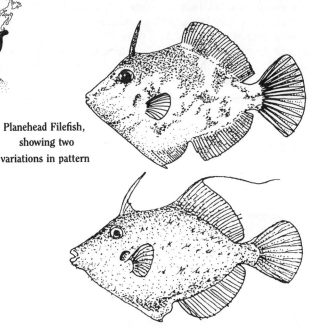

Planehead Filefish,
showing two
variations in pattern

Range and Habitat: From the Caribbean to the Gulf of Maine during the warmer months. A closely related filefish with similar range and habits is the fringed filefish (*M. ciliatus*). Filefish are usually closely associated with reefs and other habitats providing plenty of shelter. They are not strong swimmers, thus in temperate waters, the young are often observed in quieter waters around dock and marina pilings or in eelgrass beds in shallow estuaries.

Field Marks and Collecting: Filefish are laterally flattened fishes with triangular heads and very small mouths. Most have an erect first dorsal spine that usually has a hooked barb at the tip. The pectoral fins are small and are the main source of the fish's propulsion. They glide slowly and rather stiffly through the water unless alarmed, when they dart off for a short distance. The planehead filefish is normally a grayish-brown, sometimes accented with pale mottlings or light-colored filaments. The young can be highly variable. I have seen them a rich chocolate brown to bright emerald green, depending on the habitat.

Filefishes are easy to collect. Their tame, confiding nature allows a close approach with a hand net. Even when alarmed, the fish seldom flees very far before seeking cover, so that with patience it can be followed and nudged into the net. Some will turn up in seine hauls. These fishes should be looked for closely hugging the shelter of reefs, pilings, or bulkheads thick with marine growths.

Aquarium Care: Filefishes require no special care beyond that of providing live or frozen foods small enough so they can be handled by the fishes' small mouths. Live or frozen brine shrimp is a good staple. Bloodworms, tubifex, or any of the commercially prepared marine fish foods are perfectly acceptable alternates. These fish are most at home in well-planted tanks with a moderate filter current. They will graze on any algae or other marine growths, and it's often a good idea to collect chunks of natural marine growth during the summer to give them something to pick over for food. Files are peaceable, but, like the closely related triggerfish, larger specimens may become aggressive fin nippers. Thus they should not be kept with such placid, slow-moving fishes as seahorses.

ORANGE FILEFISH
(Aluterus schoepfi)

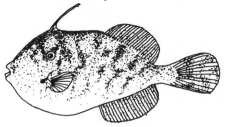

Range and Habitat: Maine to Texas, primarily in coastal areas with plenty of reef or rock habitats and abundant algal growth. This fish is common around dock pilings and bulkheads, especially in temperate waters, where it grazes on sedentary plants and animals. By using a bright light, it can be spotted at night in such places, where it is conspicuous because of its pale color and slow movements.

Field Marks and Collecting: Reaching a length of two feet, this is one of the largest filefishes. Once seen, it won't soon be forgotten for it is a most bizarre creature. It looks like a floating pork chop, with its flat, oblong body variously blotched and marbled in shades of orange, white, and brown. The fish is extremely lethargic and tame, often rolling awkwardly about and even standing on its head in the water. Its demeanor has earned it the widespread nickname, foolfish. Young orange filefish of four inches and under are varied in color and pattern, being blotched or streaked with dusky brown and spotted with yellow or white. As with all filefishes, the small eye is set high on the head, the mouth is small, and the first dorsal ray is modified into a separate, erectile spine.

Orange files are easily maneuvered into a hand net, but their normal lethargic swimming behavior can be deceptive. The fish can move fast when it has to, as when it sees a net approaching. I've found them to be easiest to collect at night, when they may be spotted with a strong light as they bumble about pilings and bulkheads, and can be bagged with a quick sweep of a dip net. The fish may often be seen drifting about in shallow water during the day, sometimes in groups of between two and ten. Under such circumstances, the skillfully thrown cast net is without a doubt the most effective way to collect them.

Aquarium Care: Like most filefish, the orange file is strongly omnivorous and consumes a good deal of vegetable matter in the natural diet. A moderate algal growth should be encouraged in the tank, and the fish should be fed commercial marine aquarium foods with some vegetable content. Being rather weak swimmers, the fish should not be subjected to powerful filtration currents. They should be maintained in a single-species tank as they may be harrassed by more active, curious tankmates. Kept by themselves, they are fascinating, entertaining creatures to watch in action, and will live for years under good care.

NORTHERN PUFFER
(Sphaeroides maculatus)

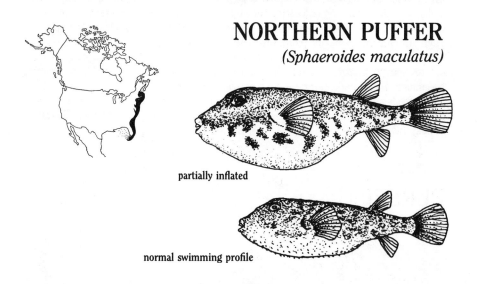

partially inflated

normal swimming profile

Range and Habitat: Widespread from Florida to New York as a breeder; strays regularly north to Maine. The species is, like most puffers, a coastal fish favoring sandy or muddy bottoms in which it pokes and roots about in search of food. The young are common in estuaries in late summer, where they are prevalent in eelgrass beds. Half-grown fish are frequently caught around inlet mouths and from marina docks. The puffers are distributed throughout the warmer parts of the Atlantic and Pacific oceans.

Field Marks and Collecting: All puffers, variously called blowfish, swellfish, or puffing toads, are short-bodied, stocky fishes that have the ability to inflate themselves with air or water when molested. The northern puffer is brownish-olive above, fading to a clear white below, variously mottled with black or brown. Seen from above, the fish has a rather squat teardrop shape. The rotund body sharply tapers into the short tail. The mouth is small and set with flat, beaklike teeth used in the grazing of plants and animals from firm objects or the substrate. Puffers lack conventional gill covers; a small slit just forward of the pectoral fins serves the purpose. The dorsal and anal fins, which are small and set far back on the body, are the principle means of locomotion. Observed in profile, a puffer at ease and uninflated is not a round little fish, but rather shows a flat belly and elongated profile.

Juvenile puffers, under four inches, frequently turn up in seine hauls made through eelgrass beds in late summer as they are quite slow-moving and less able than most fishes to avoid the net. Others can be collected rather easily by snorkeling over sandy or weedy areas or around docks. The fish are very tame and can usually be coaxed into a hand net with little trouble.

Aquarium Care: The northern puffer is typical of nearly all the members of the family worldwide in that while it can be a most engaging and interesting aquarium animal, its habits and sometimes belligerent temperament can spell trouble at times. Puffers in the wild state have been observed engaging in cooperative assaults on large blue crabs, successfully killing and eating the pugnacious crustaceans, whereas a lone puffer wouldn't stand a chance against such a dangerous adversary and obviously knows it. Such "intelligent" behavior, combined with the fish's active curiosity and hearty appetite, can make puffers dangerous to other fishes sharing their tank. They can be determined fin nippers and may attack a tankmate if hungry enough. Only smaller specimens should be kept, and a vigilant eye kept on these. Puffers relish all live and frozen foods and will readily eat chopped clam or small pieces of fish. If more than two or three are kept together, give them plenty of room as they can be argumentative among themselves.

BURRFISH
(Chilomycterus schoepfi)

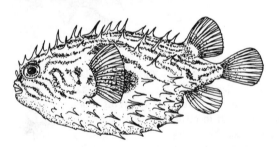

Range and Habitat: From the West Indies to New York and occasionally to Cape Cod. This is an inshore reef and sand-bottom species that occasionally turns up in estuaries in the northern part of the wide range. Most of the specimens collected north of Florida are smaller juveniles.

Field Marks and Collecting: The striped burrfish, also called the spiny boxfish, is a combination of the puffer and the porcupine fish. It is a rotund, inflatable fish that has spines, but these are much shorter and fewer in number than those of the porcupine fish. The burrfish is whitish-gray with irregular, wavy black or dusky horizontal stripes on the dorsal surface. Like the related puffers, it is stout, with a short caudal peduncle. The dorsal and anal fins, the principal means of propulsion, are set far back on the body. Adults reach 10 to 12 inches, but most collected in the north are between three and six inches. The teeth are plate-like, giving the fish a comical, bucktoothed appearance.

Burrfish are nowhere very common and most are caught on hook and line with clam or squid bait intended for food species. Very young specimens infrequently turn up in seine hauls and are sometimes caught with hand nets near jetties and other shelter.

Aquarium Care: The burrfish perfectly illustrates the "wolf in sheep's clothing" syndrome among aquarium fishes. The seemingly inoffensive creature is in reality a troublemaker. I found this out with the only burrfish I collected years ago in Long Island's Peconic Bay. Introduced into a community setup, it at once selected a wrasse as a potential victim and determinedly and doggedly followed it about the tank, taking bites out of its fins at every opportunity. The burrfish also quickly assassinated every crab in the tank and was starting to work on a sea urchin when I moved it to its own quarters. Like the related puffers and porcupine fishes, the burrfish is a slow-moving but relentless predator that cannot be housed with anything else. It is primarily a crustacean eater, and will often gobble down hermit crabs, shell and all.

In captivity, the burrfish will accept clam and crab meat and usually will not refuse squid, though it will ordinarily ignore (or spit out) chopped fish. With its buck-toothed, round mouth and wide-eyed expression, the burrfish makes a fascinating pet.

COPPER ROCKFISH
(Sebastes caurinus)

PAINTED GREENLING
(Oxylebius pictus)

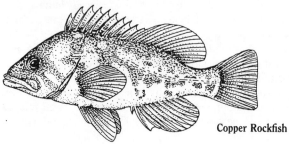

Copper Rockfish

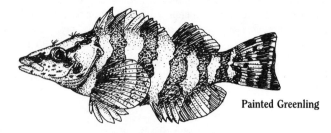

Painted Greenling

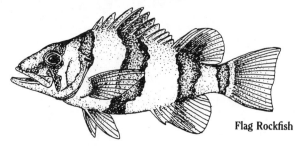

Flag Rockfish

Range and Habitat: Both species found from the Gulf of Alaska to central Baja California. They are coastal fishes that occupy the zone near the rocky substrate, though they may often be seen resting among kelp fronds and other marine vegetation.

Field Marks and Collecting: There are over 100 species in the genus *Sebastes* and many are important commercial and food fish. They are somewhat bass-like in form, with large heads and mouths and broad, fanlike pectoral fins. The copper rockfish is silvery-gold, crossed by irregular reddish or brown bars. It is cryptically colored and patterned and can be difficult to spot among the multicolored benthic debris and marine growth it frequents.

182 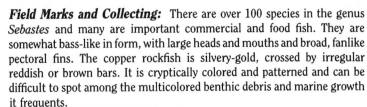 **Our Native Fishes**

Greenlings (family Hexagrammidae) are cool-water fishes closely associated with the rock substrate. The painted greenling is quite striking with its pattern of irregular deep red or pink bars against a tan or gray background. The color varies considerably according to the substrate. Some individuals may be dark green liberally speckled with white. In all color phases the bars are evident. This fish is also called the convict fish. This greenling has the habit of hanging motionless in a vertical crevice or against a rock face.

Both rockfish and greenlings are important food fishes and readily take a hook baited with clam or abalone. Small specimens can sometimes be collected for aquariums this way, but it's best to seek the juvenile fish in tide pools, where they may be dip netted from weed beds or found under rocks.

Aquarium Care: These are cool-water fishes and their quarters should be unheated and well aerated. Both species are highly territorial and will defend their niches with vigor, so they should not be crowded with other tankmates. They can be fed larger live foods such as feeder guppies, goldfish, or bait minnows, and they can be trained to accept cut fish, clams, or lean beef.

LITTLE SCULPIN
(Myoxocephalus aeneus)

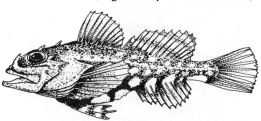

Range and Habitat: Newfoundland to New Jersey, being more abundant at the southern end of the range. This big-headed, spiny little fish, also called the brassy sculpin, or grubby, is found in shoal waters from the tide line to depths of about 100 feet. It favors rocky situations and is also found among wharf pilings and near jetties and bulkheads, where it prowls about, even up and down vertical surfaces, in search of invertebrates and small fish.

Field Marks and Collecting: This large-headed and -mouthed, cryptically patterned fish is nearly impossible to spot until it moves. The highly variable and varigated color matches the prevailing habitat, but is usually a rusty brown or dark olive-green above, irregularly blotched and mottled with black and white on the flanks. The abdomen is a clear white or pale gray. The double dorsal fin is usually carried erect, and the broad, fanlike pectoral fins are characteristic of the family. It reaches a length of about eight inches. When caught and handled, the grubby invariably opens its capacious mouth and spreads its gill covers as a defense mechanism.

Although the grubby can move fast when it has to, it is usually a simple matter to nudge one into a hand net as the fish swims with short, quick jerks when alarmed. It is often collected by running a net through dense marine growths on seawalls and pilings and it not infrequently turns up in killie traps set in such locations. Marine sculpins can be difficult to maintain in aquariums, and for reasons that will soon be apparent, only the smallest (under two inches) individuals should be kept or the species passed up entirely unless you're prepared to meet its specific requirements.

Aquarium Care: Most sculpins are cold-water fishes with high oxygen requirements. They will stress very quickly and die in a warm tank. It may be possible to maintain it successfully if plenty of areation is supplied, but there is no guarantee of success if the temperature is above 70°. The best course, for the aquarist seriously interested in working with the group, is to invest in a commercial aqua-chiller and set it to maintain the water temperature at a maximum of about 65°. Young individuals are far better able to adapt to confinement than larger adults, and thus should be selected whenever possible.

Once adjusted, the grubby will accept nearly all live foods as well as chopped clam or small pieces of squid. It will make a meal of any tankmates small enough to swallow. That includes members of its own species.

GRUNT SCULPIN
(Rhamphocottus richardsoni)

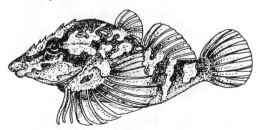

Range and Habitat: Throughout the western and eastern Pacific in cold and temperate waters; in North America, from Alaska to southern California. The grunt sculpin is common in littoral situations and is found both in rocky tide pools and more open sandy areas from near the beach to depths of about 150 feet.

Field Marks and Collecting: Once seen, the little (up to six inches) grunt sculpin is not a fish soon forgotten. It is a robust, squat creature with a high dorsal profile and the snout drawn out into a long tube-like affair. The pectoral fins are large and fanlike, and the lower three or four rays are modified into mobile organs like searobins. The grunt sculpin is a pale tan or pearl white, variously scrawled and blotched with rich browns, reds, gold, and black. The common name comes from the fish's ability to produce sounds when handled.

This fish is not a strong swimmer, moving about in a head-high position and more often seen moving over the substrate in a series of short hops. For this reason, it is usually easy to collect with a hand net. Smaller specimens are often found in tide pools where they may be caught easily by hand.

Aquarium Care: This fish does well in aquariums, living several years under good care. It should be quartered in a tank containing plenty of rock hiding places and maintained at lower temperature levels, 60° to 70°. Juvenile grunt sculpins feed heavily on copepods and other small crustaceans as well as fish larvae in the wild state. The captive diet should duplicate this as closely as possible and the food provided in abundant supply.

NORTHERN SEAROBIN
(Prionites carolinensis)

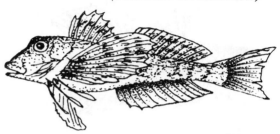

Range and Habitat: This oddly attractive creature occurs from Cape Cod to the Carolinas, frequenting habitats ranging from offshore ledges to shallow, inshore sandy areas. It is a common summer fish in the Middle Atlantic states where, in spite of the fact that the flesh is excellent eating, it is considered a nuisance by most recreational fishermen. Young searobins are most engaging little creatures, with their odd, expressive faces and winglike pectoral fins. Small specimens are common in estuaries in late summer, particularly in eelgrass beds.

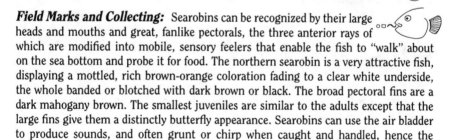

Field Marks and Collecting: Searobins can be recognized by their large heads and mouths and great, fanlike pectorals, the three anterior rays of which are modified into mobile, sensory feelers that enable the fish to "walk" about on the sea bottom and probe it for food. The northern searobin is a very attractive fish, displaying a mottled, rich brown-orange coloration fading to a clear white underside, the whole banded or blotched with dark brown or black. The broad pectoral fins are a dark mahogany brown. The smallest juveniles are similar to the adults except that the large fins give them a distinctly butterfly appearance. Searobins can use the air bladder to produce sounds, and often grunt or chirp when caught and handled, hence the common name.

Most aquarium specimens are collected by seining, although smaller ones can be spotted and rather easily bagged in shallow water with a dip net.

Aquarium Care: Searobins acclimate well to aquariums, but they must have clean, well-aerated water if they are to begin feeding and thriving. They are constant prowlers and rooters, and should get small but frequent feedings of live or frozen foods if they are to maintain adequate weight and energy levels. If not offered enough food, these fish gradually become emaciated and die. Searobins are most content in a brightly lit, open tank with a sandy bottom that affords them plenty of swimming and grubbing room. The sand should be soft and fine-grained, as coarse gravel will prevent the fish from burrowing and may injure their delicate feelers. Slow-moving and inoffensive to fishes of similar size, searobins should not be housed with aggressive species that might nip at the flowing pectoral fins or otherwise harrass them.

NAKED GOBY
(Gobiosoma bosci)

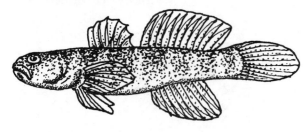

Range and Habitat: From Massachusetts to Florida, in shallow water and estuaries. The closely related *G. ginsburgi* occupies a smaller range, from New York to Virginia, in similar situations except that while *G. bosci* is restricted to shoal water, *G. ginsburgi* is often found at depths of 150 feet or more. Both species favor eelgrass beds and freely use empty cans and bottles tossed into the water by thoughtless beachgoers.

Field Marks and Collecting: The naked goby is a tiny fish, reaching a maximum length of 2½ inches. It has a double dorsal fin, rather broad, fanlike pectorals, and a large head with small eyes. The skin is smooth and scaleless, hence the common name. It is greenish-olive or brown above, paler below, and the sides are vertically banded with about seven broad, dark crossbars. Spring males are quite dark, almost black.

This little fish is abundant in shallow bays and estuaries where there is a heavy growth of eelgrass or other marine vegetation. They can be seined or dip netted from grass beds, or better yet, any submerged cans or bottles can be emptied through a dip net and the gobies bagged on the way out.

Aquarium Care: Coastal gobies are hardy and undemanding fishes. They cannot be kept with any fish large enough to attack or eat them. Gobies are best suited to the brackish aquarium provided with abundant plant growth or rock hideaways and maintained under low-light conditions. Although they can be trained to accept prepared foods, they do best on smaller live foods such as brine shrimp, bloodworms, or very small fish fry. The best goby tankmates are those species that share the natural habitat with them—pipefish, sticklebacks, seahorses, rainwater fish, and the like. Avoid the sheepshead minnow, for it is very aggressive and will harass the goby and keep it in perpetual hiding and away from food.

CATALINA GOBY
(Lythrypnus dalli)

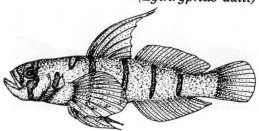

Range and Habitat: This fish has a limited range, from Morrow Bay, California, to the Gulf of California. It is found both offshore and inshore during the winter, but retires to depths greater than 50 to 60 feet during the summer. This goby, like most species of the Gobiidae, prefers broken, rocky substrates that provide plenty of cover and hideaways for territories.

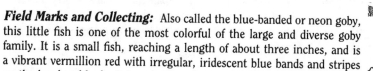

Field Marks and Collecting: Also called the blue-banded or neon goby, this little fish is one of the most colorful of the large and diverse goby family. It is a small fish, reaching a length of about three inches, and is a vibrant vermillion red with irregular, iridescent blue bands and stripes on the head and body. It is a slender, elongated, bigheaded little creature with large eyes. Until the invention of scuba gear, this was thought to be a very rare fish, but deep-divers found it quite common at greater depths.

Catalina gobies can be collected in shallow tide pools during the cooler months by turning over rocks or sweeping a dip net through dense marine growth. At greater depths they are taken mostly with a slurpgun as they quickly duck into their rock grotto on the approach of a diver.

Aquarium Care: Gobies do well in the reef tank, one with an abundance of bleached coral or rock hideways. They may be kept with most other smaller littoral species, though they can be aggressive toward others of their own kind. Thus, if more than one is kept, the tank should be roomy to give them avoidance room. In spite of its brilliant colors, this is not a tropical fish and thus it should be maintained in unheated, well-aerated water and kept under low illumination for the best display of the fish's rich hues. It will accept most commercially available live foods. Even under the best of conditions, this goby is shortlived in captivity.

NORTHERN STARGAZER
(Astroscopus guttatus)

 Range and Habitat: From New York to Virginia in estuaries and other shallow-water areas. The very similar southern stargazer is found from about Cape Hatteras to the West Indies. Both like soft sandy bottoms in which they burrow with only eyes, the top of the head, and the prominent mouth exposed. These fish are sedentary, often remaining buried in the substrate for long periods while they await the passage of prey animals. Because of this, they are more numerous than is generally believed, as they are rarely seen and not often collected by either researchers or aquarists.

Field Marks and Collecting: Unearthed, the stargazer looks somewhat like a huge (up to about 15 inches) tadpole with upward-facing eyes and a capacious, fringe-lined mouth. The color is highly variable, but, in general, it is an olive-brown or reddish fish with a black head and back spotted with white. Some may be irregularly banded in dusky browns. The dorsal, caudal, and large, fanlike pectoral fins are usually a rusty brown with dark brown or black bands extending outward from the body pattern. The eyes are on the top of the head. The fish has two electrical organs that appear as squarish plates just behind the orbs. Specimens as small as four or five inches are capable of delivering a perceptible though harmless shock if picked up by the head.

Stargazers are secretive burrowers and thus not often collected by the usual net methods. They are sometimes flushed by the approach of a seine and swept into the bag. Medium-sized specimens (four to six inches) are sometimes taken by hook and line, but handling and hook removal can be ticklish. Such specimens should not be retained for aquariums if they are injured. One effective tool is the basket rake used by fishermen in search of calico crabs for striped bass bait. This rake is dragged through sand, and any crabs (or bottom-dwelling fishes) are unearthed and swept into the wire mesh basket attached to the back of the tool.

Aquarium Care: Stargazers are ambush predators, so only smaller specimens should be kept with other fishes unless the latter are intended as food. The fish prefers a substrate soft enough to burrow into. The main drawback to keeping one will be that you won't see much of it once it settles into tank life. Stargazers require living, moving prey and this usually means small feeder guppies or goldfish. They will also accept earthworms and mealworms, and with patience can be coaxed to take strips of fish or lean meat held in forceps.

OYSTER TOADFISH
(Opsanus tau)

Range and Habitat: From Maine to Cuba, though most abundant from Cape Cod to about Cape Hatteras. The toadfish is a shallow-water species rarely found far from the littoral zone, where it occupies a wide variety of habitats but favors hiding places. The toadfish has benefitted from man's abuse of the marine environment. They seem to be much more common in areas where trash is discarded, showing a preference for empty cans, bottles, or other containers as homesites over the traditional clam and oyster shells.

Field Marks and Collecting: The toadfish looks like a mottled brownish-gold tadpole with a big head and a mouth to match, armed with very capable teeth. The fish is quite aggressive and may bite when handled. Large ones (up to 14 inches long and weighing about a pound) can deliver a bite to be remembered. It readily nips the ankles of seiners or waders who get too close to its nest, which is usually inside an empty can or clam shell and is vigorously defended by the male. Specimens suitable for aquariums, from one to four inches, can be seined in eelgrass beds in shallow bays. A more effective way of collecting them is to empty submerged cans or bottles through a hand net, intercepting the resident toadfish (or blenny or goby) on its way out. In suitable habitats, virtually every empty container will harbor an occupant, so that some marine collectors regularly visit shoreside drinking spots to tap this offensive but highly productive "habitat."

Aquarium Care: The toadfish looks tough enough to eat nails but can be tricky to acclimate. The problem is providing food, lots of it, for if the toadfish doesn't get enough, it will quickly slim down and die. It's best to keep only a single toadfish in a community marine tank to limit the competition with others of its own kind for available food and occasionally to offer it larger chunks of fish or clam held in forceps to make sure it gets enough. This fish ambushes its prey in the wild and if it doesn't get enough small live fish or if nothing reaches the bottom in a tank full of active feeders, the creature will starve. Otherwise, a toadfish will thrive in most marine setups as long as it is provided with plenty of cover and cooler water. Such a voracious predator should be released when it becomes large enough to pose a threat to its tankmates.

BANDED BLENNY
(Chasmodes bosquianus)

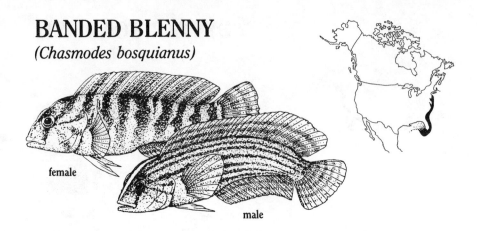

female

male

Range and Habitat: From New York to Florida, most common south of Maryland. This is a fish of the littoral zone, only rarely being found in depths over 50 feet. It is most common in protected bays and estuaries where there is an abundant growth of eelgrass and other marine vegetation. It is frequently found in empty bivalve shells, much in the manner of toadfish and gobies. This fish, like the toadfish, has appropriated the discarded artifacts of mankind and often makes its home in empty cans, bottles, and other trash thrown into coastal waters by thoughtless people.

Field Marks and Collecting: This is a strongly laterally compressed little fish, reaching the length of about four inches at maturity. It is a warm brownish-gold. The male is laterally striped in dark brown or black, while the female is banded vertically. Both sexes show a narrow gold band running down the forehead from the nape to the mouth. The forehead is steep and the eye is placed high on the head. The pectorals are large and fanlike, and the dorsal and anal fins appear continuous with the caudal.

This species can be seined throughout its shallow water habitats, but the most productive method of collection is to investigate individual hiding places. In areas where oyster shells or trash abounds, this is done by emptying a shell, can, or bottle through a hand net, bagging the resident blenny (or goby) on the way out. In favorable locations, a fish will be found in virtually every container checked. The banded blenny is a small fish, but it can and will bite when handled. The bite is no more than a slight pinch, but be prepared for a nip. The fish curls itself in a defense posture when handled and when it grabs hold of a finger, it hangs on for dear life.

Aquarium Care: This fish, and most coastal blennies, acclimate well and do best in a brackish tank with an abundance of rock or coral hideaways. They are highly territorial and will secure and defend a small personal space, making regular forays away from it in search of food. Adult blennies can be aggressive toward smaller tankmates, though as they normally stick to the substrate, they will usually not cause trouble for active fishes moving about higher in the water column. Blennies will accept all live foods as well as bits of fish, clam, or lean beef.

SUMMER FLOUNDER
(Paralichthys dentatus)

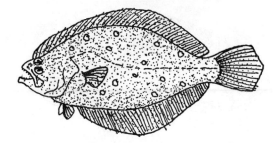

Range and Habitat: From Cape Cod to South Carolina, casually north to central Maine and south to northern Florida. This is the coveted fluke of the Middle Atlantic states, where it is primarily a sand-bottom fish found in the littoral zone from the surf to about two miles offshore during the warmer months. The young are often extremely common in estuaries from late June through October.

Field Marks and Collecting: The fluke is one of the "left-eyed" flatfishes; the fish lies on its right side with the eyed, or upper side, on the left. It can be told from the smaller winter flounder by its large mouth armed with prominent teeth and by its paler color. It is a warm grayish-brown spotted with from six to eight round eye spots or occelatum. The fluke grows to a much larger size than the biggest flounder could ever hope to. "Doormats" may reach a length of 45 inches and weights of up to 25 pounds, though most average much smaller, four to eight pounds. This is due, no doubt, to the intensive recreational and commercial fishery for them.

Juvenile fluke are often among the most abundant fish in the estuarine environment in good years, and many one- to five-inch specimens turn up in seine hauls in late summer. Hauling a ten-foot minnow seine over sandy or weedy substrates is probably the best method for collecting this species.

Aquarium Care: Fluke are hardy creatures that transport well and normally acclimate with ease to aquarium life. They, and all flatfishes, have very specific requirements that must be met if they are to thrive in confinement. First, the fluke is a benthic, or bottom, fish, and likes flat expanses of soft sand or mud in which to burrow and await prey. If they are kept in a tank equipped with coarse gravel and jungles of coral or other decor, they will be unable to burrow and hide and will quickly become stressed. In addition, turbulent filtration and bright lights will also make them quite unhappy, as will boisterous, aggressive tankmates that may harass them by picking at their protuberant eyes. Most flatfishes prefer their food alive and kicking, but they will accept most frozen foods in time. They will usually ignore prepared pellet or flake foods.

SUNDIAL
(Scophthalmus aquosus)

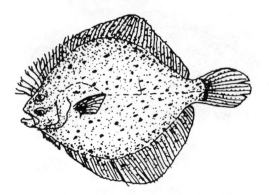

Range and Habitat: From South Carolina to Cape Cod, occasionally to the Gulf of St. Lawrence. The sundial, sand dab, or windowpane flounder prefers hard, sandy bottoms from the low tide mark out to about the 40-fathom depth. It is a summer fish, appearing in shallower waters within its range in late May or early June.

Field Marks and Collecting: The adult sundial reaches a length of about 16 inches, but, as the name windowpane suggests, it is a rather thin-bodied flatfish, reaching a weight of about 1½ pounds in the largest specimens. It is nearly round in outline. Most individuals are a pale sandy-brown, liberally speckled with black and white spots. In some areas this species may be heavily infested with skin parasites on the blind side, giving it a grayish, speckled appearance. The first eight to ten rays of the dorsal fin are extended and modified into filaments. The eyes are on the left side.

Sundials are found on clean, sandy bottoms, though junveniles are occasionally encountered in eelgrass beds. The most efficient method of collecting them is using the beach seine because their cryptic coloration renders them virtually invisible to the dip net collector hunting by sight.

Aquarium Care: As with all flatfishes, the sundial should be provided with plenty of soft sand for hiding. Experience has shown that this species is particularly sensitive to harassment by aggressive fish and thus should either be kept alone or with more passive tankmates such as seahorses, sticklebacks, hogchokers, and the like. Avoid crabs of any kind in the tank just to be on the safe side. Live foods are definitely preferred, with brine shrimp the old standby.

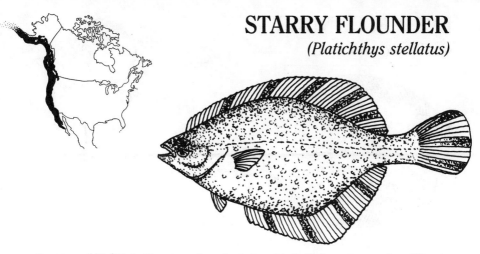

STARRY FLOUNDER
(Platichthys stellatus)

Range and Habitat: The starry flounder is found in both the eastern and western Pacific, from Japan north throughout boreal waters and south on the North American coast to northern Mexico. It is a shallow water species that is common in bays and estuaries and often enters coastal rivers where it may be found in nearly fresh water.

Field Marks and Collecting: This is one of the more attractive Pacific flatfishes, being a rich, warm brown on the eyed side, with numerous darker spots. The dorsal and anal fins are orange or amber, with black streaks radiating out from the body, giving the fish its common name. Although the starry flounder is one of the left-eyed flatfishes, some are occasionally reported with the eyes on the right side. Although a popular food fish, this is not a large flatfish, reaching the adult length of about 18 inches.

Many starry flounders under six inches in length are caught on hook and line by pier and small-boat anglers. These can be acclimated to aquariums if handled with care. These are not the ideal candidates for tank life, however, and the aquarist should seek juveniles in shallow bays. These are best collected with a seine hauled over sandy or weedy areas near the mouths of rivers.

Aquarium Care: Aquarium conditions for the starry flounder are the same as those recommended for other flatfishes—plenty of open, sandy substrate for hiding and burrowing and no larger tankmates that might pick at its prominent eyes or otherwise harass it. This flatfish prefers small live foods such as live brine shrimp, bloodworms, and small killies, but can be trained to accept cut fish or clam.

EYED FLOUNDER
(Bothus ocellatus)

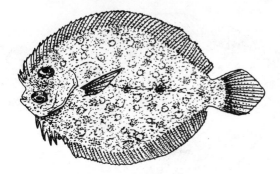

Range and Habitat: Western Atlantic, from Bermuda and New York to about Rio de Janeiro. This species, as well as other bothid flounders, is a shoal-water fish common about shallow reefs and sandy areas. In the north, smaller juveniles are sometimes encountered in bays and estuaries, particularly in the sandy areas between eelgrass beds.

Field Marks and Collecting: This is a left-eyed flatfish readily recognized by the prominent, widely spaced eyes, the dorsal fin extending forward to the snout, and three large, dark spots along the lateral line; the latter arches sharply just above the pectoral fin. The fish is pale tan to light gray with irregular pale rings or rosettes, some of which are dark-edged. The closely related but more colorful peacock flounder (*B. lunatus*) is similar in form but darker in color, with numerous circles and curved spots of light blue on the body and fins. The fins and tail are also speckled with small bright blue dots. Both species are about a foot long.

These flatfish, like most members of the family occurring in shallow waters, can be seined off sandy or weedy bottoms or caught with a hand net in the sandy clearings among coral heads.

Aquarium Care: These small, attractive flatfish will thrive in a spacious, well-filtered tank with broad, open, sandy areas for hiding, lower light conditions, and plenty of live foods. Adult eyed and peacock flounders are primarily piscivorous and will eat any smaller fish kept with them, so any tankmates should be considered with size firmly in mind. The young will accept virtually any smaller live foods and can usually be coaxed into accepting bits or strips of shrimp, clam, or sea worm.

HOGCHOKER
(Trinectes maculatus)

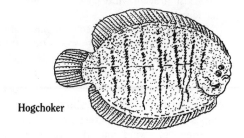

Hogchoker

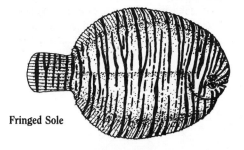

Fringed Sole

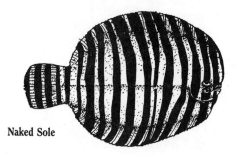

Naked Sole

Range and Habitat: From Cape Ann, Massachusetts, to the Gulf of Mexico. A similar species, the striped sole (*Achirus lineatus*), is found throughout the Caribbean north to southern Florida. Two other more colorful sole species, the fringed sole (*Gymnachirus texae*) and the naked sole (*G. melas*) are commonly encountered from the Carolinas south into the Gulf of Mexico. This delightful little fish is found on sandy or muddy bottoms in the shallow water of estuaries, though it may ascend rivers into fresh water, especially when young. Hogchokers collected in such habitats occasionally turn up in pet shops under the label "freshwater flounder."

Field Marks and Collecting: The hogchocker, or sole, is a small, right-eyed flatfish rarely exceeding six inches in length. It is nearly circular in outline, has tiny eyes and mouth, and lacks pectoral fins. It is unique among temperate flatfishes in that both sides of the body are often pigmented. The eyed side is a rich chestnut brown crossed by five or six transverse dark lines. The blind side may be a solid brown or blackish gray, or white covered round dark spots, with considerable variation among individuals.

Most hogchokers are collected incidentally during seine hauls over shallow, muddy areas. They can be difficult to see in the net unless they betray themselves by moving. Like animated suction cups, they often adhere tightly to the walls of the collecting bucket and can be a challenge to dislodge.

Aquarium Care: This appealing little flatfish does well in aquariums, thriving in the brackish, rather than strictly marine setup. The substrate should be as soft as practical to permit burrowing, and the fish should be offered live foods as much as possible, though they will accept most frozen foods. Once acclimated, they become quite active, often adhering to the sides of the tank where they provide endless interest for visitors. Keep the light level low and quarter them with such gentler estuarine tankmates as seahorses, pipefish, and gobies, and the sole will be content.

SURFPERCHES
(Embiotocidae)

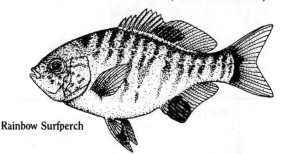

Rainbow Surfperch

Range and Habitat: There are about 24 species of surfperches, most of them occurring from Alaska to Baja California. Two species occur in the western Pacific. With the exception of the tule perch, alll surfperches are marine. As indicated by the common name, most surfperches are inshore fishes found in or near the food-rich surf zone along both rocky and sandy shores. They are often found in kelp beds and in tide pools. Some surfperches are popular with sport fishermen and are caught near rocky areas and around dock pilings.

Field Marks and Collecting: Surfperches are robust, elliptical, laterally compressed fishes with a continuous dorsal fin. They are reminiscent of the freshwater perch or temperate basses in overall appearance. Most are olive or bluish above and silvery below with rose or goldish tints and variable barrings of dusky brown. The tail is moderately forked. Most species attain a length of about a foot at maturity. The family name, Embiotocidae, means "living and bringing forth," and all surfperch are livebearers that give birth to anywhere between 20 and 100 large (one to two inches) young after a gestation period of about five months. It is reported that the young males may be ready to breed shortly after birth.

Most surfperch are caught by sport and food fishermen using light tackle. These can be acclimated to aquariums if handled with much TLC. Small specimens can often be collected by prowling rock or kelp beds at low tide with a dip net, especially at night when the fish are easier to spot and approach.

Aquarium Care: Surfperch are not overly popular due to their need for cooler water, but many have been successfully kept at room temperature, especially if the tank is well aerated and the water kept clean. Provide plenty of rock or plastic plants for shelter and feed smaller live foods such as brine shrimp, bloodworms, or small live fish such as feeder guppies.

BATFISHES
(Ogcocephalidae)

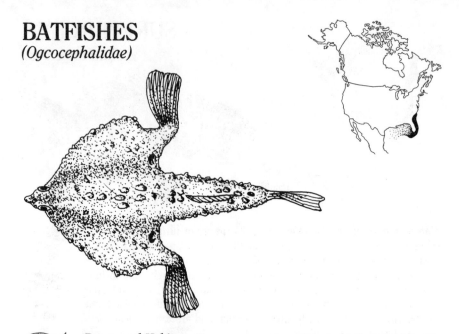

Range and Habitat: There are a number of tropical Atlantic and Pacific species. Atlantic forms are found throughout the Caribbean north to Florida and the Gulf of Mexico, casually north to the Carolinas. These are strictly benthic, or bottom-dwelling, fishes that swim only infrequently and then in a rather awkward manner. They are reef and littoral zone fishes usually found on soft sand or mud bottoms, where they "walk" about on their specialized pectoral fins.

Field Marks and Collecting: Batfishes (not to be confused with the true batfishes, the Platacidae) are recognized by their dorsally flattened, rough-textured bodies and arm-like pectoral fins that give the fish a rather frog-like look when viewed from above. The fish progresses along with a series of hopping or walking motions and can bury itself in the sand when alarmed or when lying in wait for prey. Batfishes are variously colored in tones of red, gold, or browns and the pectoral fins are often strikingly banded or spotted. The snout in most species is elongated and fleshy and is modified to serve as a fishing lure. Fleshy tabs or fringes often extend laterally from the body.

Some smaller batfish are caught on hook and line with clam, shrimp, or squid baits, but aquarium specimens are best collected with a seine or a dip net if they are seen in very shallow water.

Aquarium Care: Batfishes must be given quarters uncluttered with a lot of decor for they need open sandy areas to both maneuver about and burrow. They will accept most live foods, from brine shrimp to small fishes, but like most ambush predators that react to the movement of prey, they will usually ignore dead or prepared foods. Avoid overly bright illumination. These odd fish are quite placid and will not normally bother tankmates of similar size. They will, of course, quickly devour any smaller fishes or invertebrates introduced into their quarters.

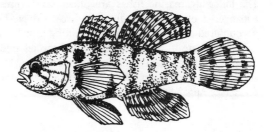

FAT SLEEPER
(Dormitator maculatus)

Range and Habitat: Brackish and coastal waters from North Carolina to Brazil, occasionally straying north to New Jersey. Sleepers occupy a wide variety of habitats, from coastal estuaries and bays to mildly brackish coastal streams. They are normally found in shallow waters with abundant plant growth or near oyster beds or other such habitats offering cover where they lie in wait for passing prey.

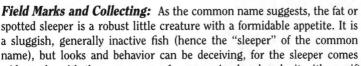

Field Marks and Collecting: As the common name suggests, the fat or spotted sleeper is a robust little creature with a formidable appetite. It is a sluggish, generally inactive fish (hence the "sleeper" of the common name), but looks and behavior can be deceiving, for the sleeper comes

wide awake with the appearance of a prey animal and grabs it with a swift dash, much in the manner of another ambush predator, the pickerel. The fat sleeper reaches a length of about a foot at maturity. It is a brownish-gold, variously mottled and barred with dark brown. A bright blue spot is on the shoulder just above the pectoral fin. The double dorsal fin as well as the caudal and anal fins are banded in black. Sleepers are secretive bottom fishes that are seldom seen until they are in the net. Most are collected with a seine, though they can be caught with a dip net by sweeping through dense eelgrass or other such marine growth.

Aquarium Care: Sleepers can be kept with most other estuarine fishes their own size or larger. They will, of course, summarily devour any other creature small enough to attract their attention and make a meal. This fish prefers a thickly planted tank for hiding, which it does most of the time. The tank should be dimly lit and filtration should be gentle. The sleeper can tolerate a wide range of salinities, from marine to near-fresh water. The species will do well in water with about a tablespoon of artificial seawater mix per gallon of water. Although they do best when offered live foods, they will accept meaty fare such as chopped clam, fish, lean beef, and shrimp.

Sleepers have spawned in captivity, doing this much in the manner of tropical cichlids. The male and female prepare a nest site by carefully cleaning off a rock or other solid object to which the adhesive eggs are attached. The fry emerge in about twenty-four hours at 76°. As soon as the fry become free swimming, the adults should be removed, as parental devotion will be cast aside and appetite will take over. The tiny young may be fed infusoria or newly hatched brine shrimp.

Endangered or Threatened Marine Species

The following marine fishes are under severe pressure, and most are classified as endangered or threatened in some areas. They should be left alone or released if encountered or caught during a collecting expedition. Their pictures and range maps are shown here to help collectors avoid species under pressure. A sighting of an endangered or threatened species should be reported to a local conservation organization, such as the state chapter of the Audubon Society, and to the state or provincial fisheries office (see Appendix III).

GARIBALDI
(Hypsypops rubicundus)

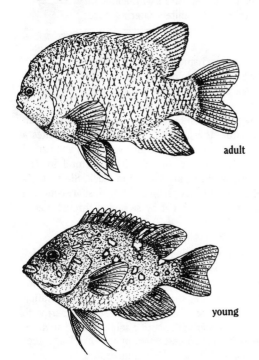

adult

young

Fully protected in California.

CALIFORNIA SHEEPHEAD
(Semicossyphus pulcher)

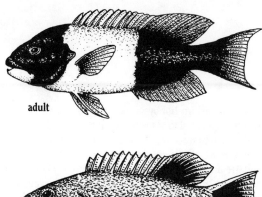

adult

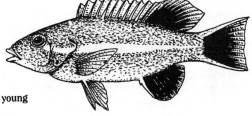

young

Under heavy angling and spearfishing pressure—avoid collecting.

TOMCOD
(Microgadus tomcod)

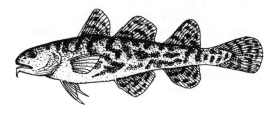

Listed as Endangered in New Jersey; rare throughout its range.

Other Aquatic Creatures

The aquarium hobby is, naturally enough, centered on fishes, but its pursuit is by no means limited to creatures with fins. A wide variety of other animals—both vertebrate and invertebrate—as well as aquatic plants will inevitably come to hand as the hobbyist grows more proficient in observation and collecting techniques. Many of the other aquatic animals collected during the course of a field trip can be kept safely in the aquarium with most fishes, but there are exceptions. Baby turtles, for example, are quite appealing when hatchling size, but they will quickly prove a threat to life and fin as they grow and their appetites begin to include their tankmates. Likewise, common pond snails are a most effective algae control agent in the aquarium, but in the absence of snail predators, their population will reach epic proportions in a surprisingly short time. Some native aquatic plants will thrive in the confines of the aquarium, while others decline and disintegrate in accordance with their natural cycles. This chapter describes a selection of the more common animals and plants which the native fish collector is likely to encounter, with comments on the pros and cons of each.

MARINE ALGAE

Some of the many and varied and often quite beautiful marine macro algae can be used as decor in the saltwater tank, much as living plants are in the freshwater setup.

Marine algae, unlike freshwater aquatic vascular plants, take no nourishment from the substrate to which they are attached but rather photosynthesize it directly from sunlight. The temperate species require a lot of sunlight and meeting this requirement with artificial light in the aquarium can be difficult. There's also the considerable problem of providing adequate circulation and exchange of water to alleviate toxic buildup if the plants begin to decline. For these reasons, most of the red and brown algae can be maintained in the aquarium only for a week or so before they begin to disintegrate and present a fouling problem. Given cooler water and powerful and effective filtration, some species of filamentous red algae can be maintained in some health for considerably longer periods, but still cannot be considered permanent floral additions to the tank as can *Vallisneria, Anubias,* or *Cabomba* in a freshwater aquarium. When collecting red or brown algae for aquarium use, remove the substrate as well, if possible, in order to avoid destroying the plant's holdfast.

Filamentous green alga and the bright green, cellophane-like *Ulva,* or sea lettuce, can be added to the tank in moderate quantities during the warmer months. Many fishes and invertebrates will eat these plants and thus these algae will often not get the chance to fall apart and foul the tank. However, many algae, *Ulva* in particular, may release spores in quantity in summer and the result could well be a fouling problem of considerable magnitude. In all cases, temperate or cool-water algae should be added to the tank as a decor item sparingly and watched carefully for signs of deterioration; the plants should be removed at once if such signs appear.

One species of marine algae common in subtropical and tropical shallow marine environments that has long been popular with aquarists is *Caulerpa prolifera*. *Caulerpa* is a very attractive green alga (*Chlorophyta*) that occurs throughout the world's tropical marine waters. There are some ten species in the Caribbean and Florida environs alone. The plant often forms dense mats and thus can be collected easily for aquarium use. It is sometimes available at most well-stocked aquarium shops featuring marine fishes.

Many *Caulerpa* species have delicate, leaf-like structures that bear some resemblance to terrestrial ferns, while the leaves of *C. prolifera* are generally blade-like and "rippled" in appearance.

Caulerpa prolifera does quite well in the conventional marine tank. It does not need sophisticated metal halide or actinic lighting to survive but will thrive under fluorescent or the typical plant-growth type lights commonly sold for tank hoods at pet shops and garden supply stores.

The plant proliferates through fragmentation. A piece placed near a rock, shell, or the gravel itself quickly sends out fine, hair-like rootlets called rhizoids, which gain purchase. Once attached, growth is very rapid if conditions (warmth and plenty of light) are to *Caulerpa's* liking. Your main problem may turn out to be controlling it. *Caulerpa* is undemanding and will survive in salinity densities of between 20 to 32 parts per thousand and at temperatures ranging from 65° to 84°. Though it is a hardy alga, *Caulerpa* should not be roughly handled. Damaged leaves lose their color, become almost transparent, and then disintegrate.

As with any alga, *Caulerpa* serves as fine fare for vegetable-eating fish and invertebrates, thus tangs, triggerfishes, or other fishes with vegetarian leanings should be excluded if a lush, attractive growth is desired.

Common cold-water and temperate marine algae. From left: rockweed (Fucus); red algae (Cystoclonium); sea lettuce (Ulua); filamentus (green) algae (Cladophora).

SEA ANEMONES

The multitude of sea anemone species found worldwide in both the temperate and tropical marine environment offers the marine aquarist entry into another fascinating world entirely separate from that of keeping fish. Many fine books are offered on the subject of these animals and other marine invertebrates as objects of interest and study in the home aquarium.

The temperate anemone species *Metridium* is a common and widespread animal along the Atlantic seaboard from northern seas south to about the Carolinas and will serve as an example of the group.

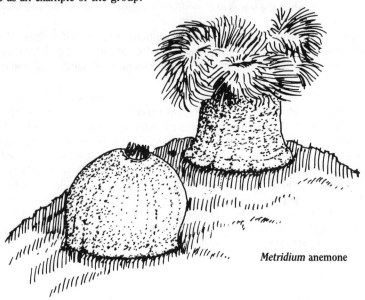

Metridium anemone

These anemones are extremely numerous on dock pilings, floating docks, and rock jetties and groins throughout their range. They grow to about seven inches in height and three or four inches in diameter, and they vary from a light brown to a rich brick-red with fine, pale yellow or white tentacles.

Being stationary creatures anchored to the substrate, anemones would appear to be easy to collect, and they are, but not without considerable care. The ideal method is to remove some of the substrate the anemone is attached to, place it in the collecting bucket, and let the anemone "walk" off it and onto the wall of the container. Then it can be carefully removed later with a blunt plastic spatula or other thin, flat utensil.

Anemones are often attached to mussels and other removable objects, and thus can easily be transferred, base and all, to the collecting pail. A sharp knife used in an on-site attempt to scrape the creature off its base may lacerate the foot, an injury from which the anemone may not recover, hardy creature though it may be.

I once inadvertently snagged a large anemone on a fish hook, hooking it solidly through the body column. After carefully removing the hapless creature, I took it home and placed it in a small, fishless tank for recovery. The anemone remained shrunken and motionless for about two days, then slowly began to expand and finally attached itself to a rock. It is still alive today, four years later.

Striped anemone

Anemones can be offered any of the marine invertebrate foods available today or tweezer-fed bits of clam, fish, or meat, depending on the animal's size. Some aquarists prefer using a meat baster to inject liquid or semi-liquid foods directly into the animal's buccal opening. If you collect natural seawater for water changes, myriad micro and macroscopic food items will be introduced to the tank with each change and most smaller anemone species will thrive.

STARFISHES

Although officially known as sea stars to the scientific community, most of us stick to old habits and refer to these familiar echinoderms as starfish even though, obviously,

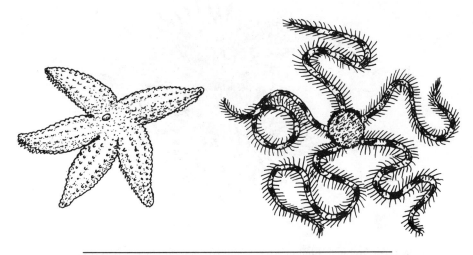

Left: the common starfish, or seastar, Asterias forbesi, *a common and hardy echinoderm that adapts readily to the cool-water marine tank. Right: The brittlestar,* Ophiothrix. *These bizarre seastars are as fragile as they look, and most temperate species will not thrive in aquariums except under expert care.*

fish they are not. Starfish are benthic animals that are found in a wide variety of habitats from the littoral zone to the darkest depths of the open sea. They are seldom if ever found in areas of lower salinity such as shallow estuaries or salt marshes. Most temperate species favor rocky areas or bulkheads and dock pilings, though they may often be seen prowling slowly about over sand or mud bottoms.

The common sea star (*Asterias forbesi*) is easily collected and can be kept for some time in the cooler, well-aerated marine tank. It is primarily an eater of bivalves and will thus attack and eat any clams, mussels, or scallops kept with it in addition to scavenging any dead animals. At most, one or two smaller (up to five inches across the arms) starfish should be kept in a setup as their constant rovings and continual appetite for living prey can be difficult for the average hobbyist to satisfy.

SEA URCHINS

Urchins are easily observed and collected and will do well in the marine aquarium if there is an abundant growth of algae. Most of the commoner temperate and subtropical species will scavenge dead animals as well. Sea urchins are abundant in the littoral and inshore zone where there is a solid substrate, such as a coral reef, rock jetty, or dock piling, and can be collected by hand.

The common purple sea urchin (*Arbacia punctulata*) occurs from the boreal Atlantic coast south to the Middle Atlantic states. It makes a good aquarium tenant as long as

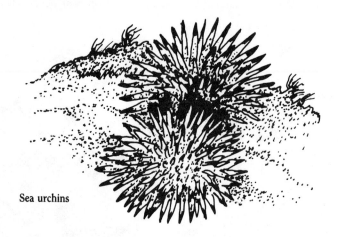

Sea urchins

it (or any other urchins) is not quartered with larger triggerfish, puffers, or parrot fish, which will attack and devour it. This urchin, as well as the common Pacific species (*Strongylocentrus franciscanus*) requires very little care and feeding if enough algae is present, and will thrive for years in aquariums. I have five that are approaching their sixth year in my marine tank with no apparent signs of advanced age or ill health.

In the overly clean tank, the sea urchin diet can be supplemented with bits of fish offered with forceps or small bunches of romaine lettuce or mustard greens placed where the urchins can find them.

One commoner tropical Atlantic sea urchin, the long-spined black sea urchin (*Daidema*) should generally be avoided as it will attack and devour coral and has long, sharp spines that can deliver a mild but very painful dose of venom to the careless aquarist.

AQUATIC INSECTS

Aquatic insects and fish don't mix. Insects are either avidly eaten by fish, or, as in the case of larger, predatory insect larvae, smaller fish will be avidly attacked and eaten by them. The more familiar aquatic insects include dragonfly and damselfly nymphs (Odonata); dobsonfly nymphs (Corydalis), the hellgrammite of trout and bass bait fame; predaceous diving beetles (Dystiscidae); whirligig beetles (Gyrinidae); caddis flies (Trichoptera); backswimmers (Notonecta); water boatmen (Corixidae), and water striders (Gerridae).

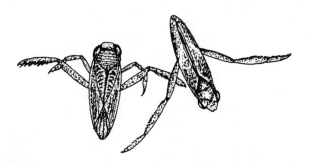

Most aquatic insects will coexist with fishes of a size and habit that walk that fine line between being too small to eat them and too large to be attacked and devoured by the insect. I have found that larvae such as the dragonfly nymph will usually mind its own business in a tank of smaller fish, but the fish themselves may pick at it out of simple curiosity as it clambers clumsily about the aquatic foliage. Whirligig beetles and water striders, intriguing as they may appear in the natural environment, do not, in my experience, adapt gracefully to confinement, no matter how roomy the tank. They are surface-cruising animals that require a lot of room and they soon resent the narrow confines of an aquarium and seek a way out. It's also wise to remember that these insects, as well as water boatmen, backswimmers, and predaceous diving beetles are air-breathing creatures fully capable of flight. Enough said.

Aquatic larvae can be kept easily in an "insect aquarium." The best quarters are a one- to five-gallon tank heavily planted and equipped with very gentle filtration. A small, inside box filter will do nicely. Most larvae will accept the same larger live foods offered fish, and some aquatic insects, such as the water boatmen, will feed on organic detritus and plant material. Dragonfly nymphs will often accept bits of lean beef or fish if you're squeamish about offering them baby fish. Remove any uneaten food promptly to prevent fouling. Keep tank containing aquatic insects or their larvae tightly covered to prevent escapes. A final word of warning: the backswimmer, hellgrammite, and whirligig beetle can deliver harmless but quite painful bites if handled carelessly. I speak from experience.

CEPHALOPODS

The two more common groups of these animals encountered by the marine collector and hobbyist are the squids and octopuses. Both are difficult to keep alive in the home aquarium, though the latter are much easier and thus can be realistically considered. Squids, at least the adults, are not practical, though a colleague and I collected several tiny (½-inch) larvae (Loligo) we spotted swimming at the surface in open water and kept them alive for some time in a five-gallon tank. The water was well-aerated, changed every three days, and the animals were offered live baby brine shrimp, which they chased down and devoured with apparent relish. After about a month, they were released where they were collected—among the docks of a marina, of all places.

Octopuses can be kept with relative ease as long as their water is maintained at a high level of purity, temperature fluctuations are avoided, and the tank is KEPT SECURELY AND TIGHTLY COVERED for these creatures can effect an escape through an astoundingly small space! The common octopus (*Octopus vulgaris*) ranges from about

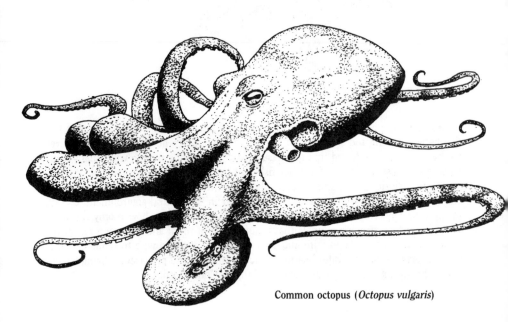

Common octopus (*Octopus vulgaris*)

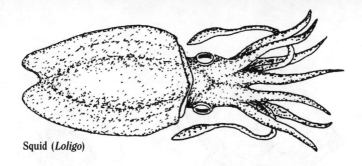

Squid (*Loligo*)

New Jersey (uncommon) south throughout the West Indies and the Gulf of Mexico. Smaller specimens, usually caught by hand in rocky areas, can be offered live crabs or shrimp. They will catch and eat fishes if they can get them, particularly at night, thus an octopus is not an animal for the average community tank. The small, very colorful blue-ringed octopus of the Pacific (*Hapalochlaena maculosa*) is somewhat popular in the marine tropical hobby in spite of the fact that it is highly venomous and fatalities have been recorded. All octopuses can deliver a painful bite (with the parrot-like beak) and thus should be handled very carefully and as little as possible. Octopuses will discharge the famous ink when molested or disturbed and if this occurs in the aquarium, the water must be changed as soon as possible as the ink is mildly toxic to both fishes and the octopus itself.

SNAILS

Freshwater snails can be considered a welcome and viable addition to the aquarium's fauna, but with a few reservations and cautions kept in mind. Most temperate snails avidly eat plants, the desirable, decorative kinds right along with the less desirable algae. As they also possess an astounding capacity for reproducing themselves under favorable conditions, a few small snails in a tank may quickly multiply into an army, with all of the attendant problems. Most of the snail species sold through pet shops, such as the attractive red ramshorn and the trapdoor or mystery snails, normally will not present the aquarist with a burgeoning population problem, but native pond snails, which usually gain access to the aquarium via collected or purchased plants or wood, can quickly become a visual, if not environmental, plague.

In limited numbers, pond snails perform the useful services of algae control and the scavenging of organic detritus. In large numbers, they will ravage plants and clutter the decor and glass. Snail hordes are not usually a problem in tanks containing centrarchids, for nearly all sunfishes and bass (with the exception of the *Enneacanthus* and *Elassoma genera*) will avidly eat them. Many catfishes will destroy them as well, but most other fishes either cannot handle the hard shells or simply do not recognize a snail as food and ignore them.

My own approach to the snail question is simple: if they are present in reasonable numbers or do no noticeable damage to plants, I ignore them. If they must be controlled, I prefer to avoid commercial snailicides, which may harm fish if used heavy-handedly, and instead introduce one or two small sunfish or even a tropical gourami species, which will also seek out and eat snails. If you've got the stomach for it, adult snails can be crushed against the glass of the aquarium, thereby making the meat accessible to fishes which will then avidly devour them.

A few of the more common species of snails encountered by the native fish collector: top left: the livebearing, or apple, snail (Ampullaria); bottom left: two pond snail species (Physia and Elimia); top right: the introduced red ramshorn snail (Planorbis).

Both native and tropical snails can be offered parboiled leaves of romaine lettuce or swiss chard to keep them from gobbling your aquatic plants.

Many species of marine snails can be successfully maintained in aquariums. The majority, including the whelks and moon snails, are carnivorous, eating bivalves and other benthic animals. Some, such as the temperate periwinkles and mud snails, are vegetarian and will thrive in an aquarium if a good crop of algae is allowed to exist. Lacking an algal bloom, marine snails will often accept romaine lettuce or mustard greens as a reasonable if something less than ideal substitute.

Few, if any, of the marine gastropods have been known to reproduce themselves in an aquarium so the marine hobbyist keeping snails will not have to deal with an overpopulation problem. What he or she may have to keep an eye on is the matter of escapees.

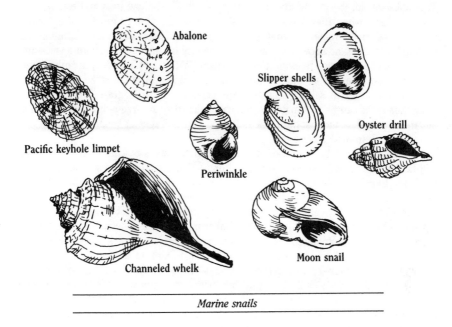

Marine snails

HORSESHOE CRAB

The crab that is not a crab, *Limulus polyphemus* is a still relatively common but declining creature throughout its wide range, which extends from New York to Brazil. The horseshoe crab is an arthropod much more closely related to terrestrial scorpions and spiders than to true crabs.

In spite of its background and rather formidible appearance, it is a gentle, totally

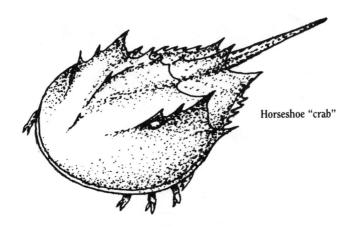

Horseshoe "crab"

harmless creature that feeds on benthic organic debris, plants, and small invertebrates. The tank-like, lumbering adults are familiar sights in shallow bays and estuaries in May and June, when they approach the shore to spawn. One or more of the smaller males attend each female, clasping her with specialized appendages and riding on her back up onto the sand above the wave line. The tiny larvae hatch in about a week and are somewhat pelagic and freeswimming in nature. Within a month, they are miniatures of their elders at about an inch in total length, including the tail spike. At this time they may turn up in seine hauls through eelgrass or turtle grass beds. Although horseshoe crabs can be acclimated to aquarium life (they are frequently sold at marine aquarium shops), it takes some work as they are fairly fragile at smaller sizes and can be quite picky in food preferences.

Horseshoes should be housed in a tank with broad areas of sand or gravel as they will become hung up in complicated coral or rock decor. Filtration should be on the moderate to gentle side. Large fishes, which might well annoy them or worse, should be excluded. Good horseshoe tankmates would be such smaller estuarine fishes as sticklebacks, pipefish, seahorses, rainwater fish, and the like. Probably the best way to get young horseshoes feeding is to place smaller mats of wild-collected algae and other marine growth in the tank temporarily and allow the animals to pick it over for edibles. They will also accept frozen brine shrimp allowed to sink to the bottom. Vegetable-based cichlid pellets make an acceptable last-resort food in the absence of natural fare.

I have found horseshoes decline gradually over time, even with the best of care, so I've always opted to keep them in captivity only temporarily, releasing them at the end of the summer and before the natural environment chills down too far. Adult specimens, however, are often maintained successfully at public aquariums with apparent ease.

LOBSTER

The American lobster (*Homarus americanus*) can, contrary to popular belief, be maintained in a room temperature marine tank. I kept one for nearly seven years back in the 1970s when I lived about 60 miles from the sea in central New Hampshire. The

American lobster

collecting and possession of lobsters is strictly regulated by law and in order to catch and keep one legally, permission must be obtained from fish and game authorities. No very small lobsters can be bought or sold legally anywhere.

My long-lived lobster (whom I named "Homer," after the genus name) was collected on the New Hampshire coast in late spring. He was about two inches in length and grew to a body length of about ten inches in that seven-year period. He was kept in a 30-gallon wall tank that contained a few heavy rocks, no plants, and no tankmates, except for those destined for Homer's stomach. The tank had an outside power filter and was heavily aerated with two large air stones and kept under low light. I made one-third water changes each month, all of artificial seawater mix, and the lobster was fed primarily whole frozen smelt, available in most supermarkets, varied with chunks of crabmeat, shrimp, and an occasional piece of uncooked hotdog (which he loved). Homer was released at the point of collection after he became too large and was clearly being confined in circumstances unfair to the lobster.

Lobsters are stronger and more active and voracious predators than crayfish, and, of course, they will grow to a much larger size if adequately fed. Although I maintained my lobster for an impressive seven years in captivity, these animals are reported to reach much greater ages, both in the wild and in public aquariums. The would-be lobster keeper should either prepare for the long haul in lobster care or, better yet, release the animal where it was collected as soon as it becomes either a problem to care for or a bore to have around the house.

The water in a lobster's quarters should be as cool as possible, but once a smaller individual becomes acclimated to temperatures of 65° to 75°, they will thrive and grow as long as aeration is very brisk.

CANCER AND OTHER CRABS

The swimming and rock crabs are among the most popular of marine aquarium invertebrates, due primarily to their often colorful variety, high degree of activity, and seemingly intelligent behavior. Crabs exhibit a high level of awareness of the world around them, and the nature of that awareness, of a distinctly predatory nature, is at the root of the major drawback to their inclusion in the marine aquarium. Most swimming crabs, such as the blue crab (*Callinectes sapidus*) of culinary fame, are quick, efficient predators and scavengers of lightning-fast reflexes, as many a careless crabber has found to his dismay. This talent carries over into the artificial confines of the aquarium, making a blue crab of any but the very smallest size a dangerous animal to quarter with any fish. I have placed specimens only a half-inch across in a mixed tank as scavengers, only to have them more than double that size within a month and begin thinning the fish population. Their growth rate is truly astounding and their appetite boundless, so most swimming crabs should either be avoided as tank tenants or kept only for a short time and then released.

The best of the temperate crabs for aquariums are the mud (*Neopanopeus*) and rock (*Cancer*) crabs, and the bizarre, slow-moving spider crabs *Libinia*. These animals, although they will certainly eat any fish they can catch and overpower, are generally sedentary enough so that at least in smaller sizes they will pose little threat to larger, more active fish. When contemplating combining any animals of questionable compatibility, common sense must prevail. In other words, you don't want to put an active,

Top: the spider crab (Libinia emarginata); *bottom left: the blue crab* (Callinectes sapidus); *bottom right: the green* (Carcinides maenas), *or rock, crab* (Cancer *species).*

aggressive crab of any species in the same tank with placid, slow-moving fish like seahorses unless your object is to provide the crab with a seahorse diet.

The rule of thumb regarding any of the more active swimming and Cancer crab species is: Few and far between. In other words, crabs certainly can be included in the marine setup as scavengers and animals of special interest, but their number should be limited to no more than three or four small ones in a 55-gallon tank.

GRASS (OR GLASS) SHRIMPS

Few marine animals are found in greater abundance in the summer littoral environment than the grass shrimps of the genus *Palaemonetes*. These small, nearly transparent crustaceans can be seen flitting about like mere shadows against the sand or mud bottoms, and usually turn up in vast numbers in every seine haul made over eelgrass or sea lettuce beds throughout the warmer months.

Two species, *P. pugio* and *P. intermedius,* are common in tidal estuaries and creeks during the spring and summer, moving into water as deep as eight or ten fathoms if the water temperatures exceed their high and low tolerances. They often follow the tides in and out of the estuary or bury themselves in the mud. The average length at adulthood is about an inch, and the lifespan in the wild ranges from 6 to 14 months.

Grass shrimp are excellent animals for the marine invertebrate aquarium, but as they are an important food item in the diet of many fishes, they cannot be kept with any but the smallest or most inoffensive marine fishes. Most larger marine fishes will avidly eat them. Thus they make an excellent starter food for reluctant feeders as well as a continuing food as long as they are available. They can be collected live and frozen for later use.

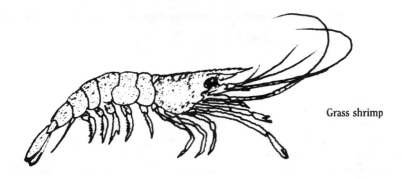

Grass shrimp

Grass shrimp are opportunistic feeders that are essentially detritivores, that is, they eat a wide variety of organisms found in the bottom debris and are important agents in the breaking down of decaying organic material, both in the wild and in the aquarium. They are valuable scavengers that will quickly locate and devour any dead animals as well as uneaten prepared foods. Grass shrimp can be fed any of the foods offered to fishes and become rather tame once they are fully acclimated to aquarium life and have come to associate their keeper with food. I have seen them swim eagerly to the surface to be fed like any pool goldfish or koi. The shrimps' only real requirements are some plant and rock cover, enough plant and animal foods to sustain them, and the absence of larger predators that would quickly make a meal of them.

HERMIT CRABS

The many species of hermit crabs are common and highly visible animals of the summer shallows. As they can be picked up by hand, many find their way into the collecting buckets of the casual and serious beach and bay explorer. The northern or long-clawed hermit crab (*Pagurus longicarpus*) is typical of the family and a discussion of this species will serve for most of the littoral species.

There are two points to consider about hermit crabs before including them in your marine setup: First, although they are active and appealing little critters, they are predators and quite carnivorous and will eat any small animal they can overpower and kill. Second, as crustaceans, they are food for many fishes, among them tautogs, cunners, and snappers (Lutjanidae), and will be attacked and eaten in tanks containing these fishes. The best aquarium community for hermits is one containing smaller,

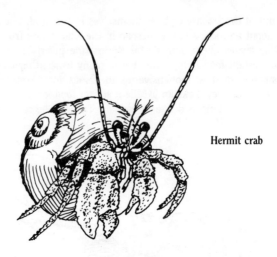

Hermit crab

active non-predatory fish that occupy higher levels of the water column. This would preclude such slowmovers as seahorses or pipefish and certainly any smaller flatfish, which, being bottom dwellers, would be endlessly pestered by the hermits.

Hermit crabs can be considered omnivores in that they will accept a wide variety of meat and fish fare and consume a fair amount of marine algae and other plant growth. They can tolerate a moderate amount of pollution but should be maintained in clean, well-filtered water and provided with an open area of sand for roaming about.

Hermit crabs are pugnacious toward each other, and if too many are kept in the same tank, violent squabbles may result, especially if an individual that has outgrown its snail shell home tries to oust a tankmate from its own desired shell. When keeping several hermits together, it's a wise idea to provide extra, empty snail shells so the animals may exchange them as they grow without warfare. Given good care and not overcrowded, smaller hermit crab species may live as long as three or four years in captivity.

CRAYFISH

Crayfish, or crawfish if you prefer, are a surprisingly popular aquarium animal in the ornamental fishkeeping hobby. They can be kept with fishes without too much trouble if a few simple precautions are taken.

The crayfish species most often seen in petshops are *Procambarus alleni* and *P. clarkii,* and the various color forms thereof. In addition to the mottled brownish wild form, white, blue, and red strains are available. They will coexist with fish if the crayfish are small and if enough room and cover are given the animals. Crayfish are quite territorial and there will assuredly be conflict if two or more are kept in an undersized tank. Ideally, two, or at the most three, small crayfish should be kept together in a tank no smaller than 20 gallons. Their quarters should contain plenty of rock hideaways so that the animals can set up territories and avoid each other, as they are not sociable creatures except at breeding time. Crayfish will scavenge any animal and some plant matter they can find, particularly at night when they are most active. They will accept

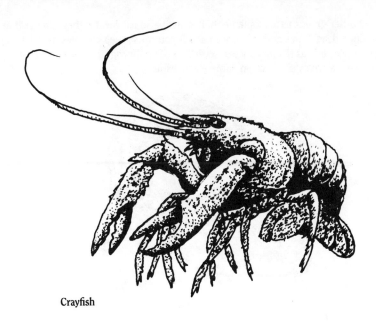

Crayfish

all of the meat and fish foods offered to predatory fishes and will graze living plants. Keep that in mind if you want an attractively planted tank.

Very small (under an inch) crayfish can be kept with most fishes without incident. Surprisingly, very large individuals (five or six inches) are often so lethargic if they're well-fed that they will usually not actively pursue tankmates. The two- or three-inch individuals may be the most dangerous and thus they should be offered ample food and the fish inspected carefully for fin or body damage inflicted at night. If any injuries are noted, remove the crayfish.

TADPOLES

Nearly all aquarium hobbyists have, at one time or another, kept a tadpole in their tank, usually with no unpleasant consequences. Tadpoles very frequently turn up in the net during the late spring and summer and may range in size from the tiny, half-inch black polliwogs of the common toad to the six-inch behemoth that will one day metamorphose into a bullfrog. Although carnivorous and even cannibalistic tadpoles do exist (as in the bizarre South American horned frogs), all North American species are vegetarian and thus, like snails, will pose a threat only to the plants in your tank. Also, these "unfinished frogs" possess none of the alertness and grace of their elders but instead dash and blunder blindly about a tank bumping into things (including the fish), and you have few good reasons to keep one except for short-term observation. Keep in mind also that tadpoles do change into frogs and toads, with the attendant problems of both feeding and confining them.

Tadpoles will graze algal growth on the glass and substrate and can be offered romaine lettuce and other greens as a supplement. They will also eat meat if they can get it and often scavenge dead fishes and other animals. If you must keep tadpoles, restrict their number to one or two as the presence of several larger polliwogs darting and blundering about can have a stressful effect on some shyer fishes.

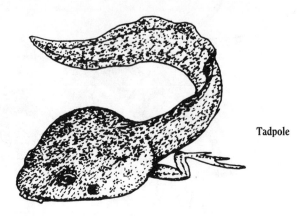

Tadpole

AQUATIC SALAMANDERS

The adult, aquatic phase of the eastern newt (*Notophthalmus viridescens*) and the strictly aquatic mudpuppy (*Necturus maculosus*) are two commonly collected amphibians, and both will thrive in the aquarium if conditions are to their liking. The newt attains the length of four inches at maturity and is recognized by its olive-green color fading to pale gold or yellow below, and the row of six to eight scarlet, black-bordered dots along the sides dorsally. They are normally found in boggy woodland ponds or swamps, usually in heavier aquatic vegetation. The mudpuppy, or waterdog, is a uniformly dull olivaceous or brown, with weakly developed legs and prominent red, bushy external gill filaments. It attains the length of about a foot, but most are about half that size or smaller.

Both these animals are predators, but both the newt and its preferred prey—insects and their larvae and very small fish fry—are too small to pose a threat to any but the smallest of potential aquarium tenants. The miniscule least killifish (*Heterandria formosa*) might be such a species, but few others would find themselves in danger. A larger mudpuppy would be another matter, however, and no specimen larger than about five inches should be kept in a tank containing smaller to medium-sized fishes.

Both the eastern newt and the mudpuppy appreciate dense plant growth to clamber about in, though the latter is much more closely associated with the substrate than the former and prefers some degree of shelter in the form of rock caves and grottoes. The newt is an air breather and must be able to reach the surface, while the mudpuppy is a truly aquatic creature that takes oxygen directly from the water, as do fishes. Both can be offered strips of lean beef or fish and will do quite well on small earthworms. As with any slower, more deliberate feeders, newts and mudpuppies kept with active fishes should at times be offered food with forceps to ensure that they receive adequate nutrition.

Top: the mudpuppy, Necturnus maculosus. This animal may attain a
size that will make it a threat to smaller fishes kept with it. Bottom:
the eastern newt, Notophthalmus viridescens. The land form of this
common salamander is a beautiful coral-red; the aquatic form retains
its original hue only in the bright red spots on its back.

TURTLES

Larger aquatic turtles don't belong in an aquarium containing fishes. Even hatchling
musk, mud, and snapping turtles are enthusiastically carnivorous right from birth;
only the very smallest can be safely maintained with fish, and even then not for very
long. Those three species, plus the young of the eastern painted, red-bellied, and the
map turtles or cooters, are those chelonians that usually turn up in the seine or dip
net: the temptation to take the appealing little creature home is almost always irre-
sistable.

Most of my own experience with turtles in fish aquariums has been with hatchling
musk turtles, which are about the size of a nickle at birth, extremely cute, and very
hard to spot in the net as they look like a tiny lump of mud or other debris unless
they move. They are very hardy and adaptable little creatures, quickly becoming tame
and accepting virtually all meat and fish fare such as chopped lean beef and smelt. I
have found that once the turtle's shell reaches the size of a quarter, it's time to remove
it from the community tank or at least to begin keeping a close eye on it, for it will
soon begin to stalk and attack fish, especially at night. The young painted and red-
bellied turtles are strongly vegetarian and will eat plants as well as animal matter.
These species, unlike the musk and snapping turtles, require either a mat of plants or

a solid floating object for basking and should be maintained in a warm environment with plenty of light for optimum health. But even these, when they begin to grow, become piscivorous and will begin to follow your fishes about with something other than idle curiosity in mind. In general, young snappers of any size constitute a risk in a tank containing fish, for when hungry (which is most of the time) they will strike at any nearby moving object even when very small. If you must keep a snapper as a pet, give it a small tank of its own and release it the following year or as soon as you begin to tire of what is essentially a rather unattractive creature, whichever occurs first.

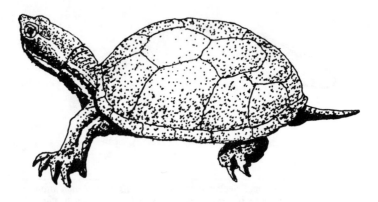

The eastern musk turtle, or stinkpot (Sternotherus odoratus), *often turns up in seine hauls and, if collected very small, makes an interesting aquarium inhabitant. This turtle, like most strictly aquatic turtles, is almost entirely carnivorous, and when it attains a larger size, it will begin to attack fishes kept with it.*

Appendix I

A FISH COLLECTOR'S CODE OF CONDUCT

It should come as no surprise that not everybody who utilizes the outdoors as a place of recreation today is a Mark Trail in behavior and attitude. The growing litter problem is an apt illustration that that old nemeses, *Swinus americanus* or *canadensis*, is still alive and well and very much with us. Add to this the problem of accelerating development in many parts of the United States and Canada, with more and more collecting habitats either disappearing or falling into private hands (with the attendant No Trespassing signs), and you have a real problem of accessibility to productive angling or fish collecting spots. I'm assuming that the readers of this book are with me in the matter of outdoor conscience, and I hope you'll appreciate the code of conduct that's served me well over more than four decades of tromping, sloshing, and paddling about through all sorts of terrain in search of our many-splendored native fishes.

• Pack out what you pack in. This is the first commandment of the outdoorsman. Although it's often said that there's nothing wrong with burying your trash—a debatable piece of advice these days—the average fish collector won't be carrying so much potential garbage that he or she can't cart it back home with little inconvenience.

• Make an effort to get permission to use private land. It beats constantly looking over your shoulder. If you can't and you're confronted by a landowner, be courteous, explain your mission, and display the catch. Most people, even those who are initially hostile, are really quite fascinated by the subject once they know what you're doing and why.

• If you're collecting on state or federal land, make sure your permits are in order and in your possession. It's best to check in at park or refuge headquarters to say you're there, just so you don't have to go through your spiel with every ranger or park employee who passes by.

• Be aware of other anglers in the vicinity and don't intrude on them. It's poor outdoors etiquette to drag a seine across fishing lines or to shuffle rocks or splash about just upstream from a fly fisherman.

• If you're live trapping, check your traps at least once a day during the most productive season, and resist the temptation to inspect another person's killie trap if you happen across it. It is irritating to find that your carefully placed trap has been pulled up, looked over, and carelessly tossed back in the water again.

• Be alert for and stay away from diving flags, as you would expect boaters and others to do when you're down there. Avoid commercial fishing gear, such as lobster traps or eel pots. Unauthorized fooling around with these may earn you a charge of buckshot.

• Don't needlessly destroy aquatic or streamside vegetation. Replace all rocks overturned in tidepools or used in the construction of stream fish traps.

• Resist the temptation to bag a parent fish guarding a nest. This is an understandable urge because this is when the animal is both vulnerable and usually the most colorful. Keep in mind the consequences to the helpless eggs or fry.

• If you're using a motorboat to reach collecting locations, observe the no-wake rule near shore to avoid undue disturbance or erosion of the shoreline.

• If you see people breaking this code, talk to them in a civil manner. Most violators of outdoors ethics are acting through ignorance and not with deliberate malice aforethought. Talk to them with that assumption in mind.

Appendix II

ADDITIONAL INFORMATION SOURCES

National, State, and Provincial Fisheries Offices

The following are the government offices you should contact for information on collecting permits and regulations and on species designated threatened or endangered in specific regions. Normally, sightings of endangered species should be reported to the appropriate state or provincial office, as well as to the local branch of a conservation organization such as the Audubon Society.

U.S.A.
Office of Endangered Species, U.S. Fish and Wildlife Service, Washington, D.C. 20240 Phone: (202) 343-3245

Alabama
Program Coordinator, Nongame Wildlife, Dept. of Conservation and Natural Resources, 64 N. Union St., Montgomery, AL 36130 Phone: (205) 262-3469

Alaska
Director, Division of Sport Fish, Dept. of Fish and Game, P.O. Box 3-2000, Juneau, AK 99802 Phone: (907) 465-4180

Arizona
Office of the Nongame Habitat Specialist, Game and Fish Dept., 2222 W. Greenway Rd., Phoenix, AZ 85023 Phone: (602) 942-3000 Ext. 366

Arkansas
Natural Heritage Commission, Suite 200, 225 E. Markham, Little Rock, AR 72201 Phone: (501) 371-1706

California
Dept. of Fish and Game, Inland Fisheries Division, 1701 Nimbus Rd., Suite C, Rancho Cordova, CA 95670 Phone: (916) 355-0842

Colorado
Office of the Nongame Aquatic Program Specialist, Division of Wildlife, Dept. of Natural Resources, 6060 Broadway, Denver, CO 80216 Phone: (303) 291-7273

Connecticut
Director, Bureau of Fisheries, Dept. of Environmental Protection, 165 Capitol Ave., Hartford, CT 06106 Phone: (203) 566-2287

Delaware
Manager, Wildlife Section, Division of Fish and Wildlife, Dept. of Natural Resources and Environmental Control, P.O. Box 1401, Dover, DE 19903 Phone: (302) 736-5297

Florida
Blackwater Fisheries Research and Development Center, Rt. 1, Box 79F, Holt, FL 32564 Phone: (904) 957-4172

Georgia
Chief of Fisheries, Game and Fish Division, Dept. of Natural Resources, 205 Butler St., Atlanta, GA 30334 Phone: (404) 656-3530

Hawaii
Aquatic Resources Information Specialist, Dept. of Land and Natural Resources, 1151 Punchbowl St., Honolulu, HI 96813 Phone: (808) 548-5899

Idaho
Resident Fisheries Manager, Dept. of Fish and Game, 600 S. Walnut, Box 25, Boise, ID 83707 Phone: (208) 334-3700

Illinois
Endangered Species Project Manager, Endangered Species Protection Board, 524 S. Second St., Springfield, IL 62701 Phone: (217) 785-8687

Indiana
Environmental Unit Supervisor, Division of Fish and Wildlife, 607 State Office Bldg., Indianapolis, IN 46204 Phone: (317) 232-4080

Iowa
Bureau Chief, Preserves and Ecological Services, Dept. of Natural Resources, Wallace State Office Bldg., Des Moines, IA 50319 Phone: (515) 281-8524

Kansas
Supervisor, Environmental Services Section, Dept. of Wildlife and Parks, RR 2, Box 54A, Pratt, KS 67124 Phone: (316) 672-5911

Kentucky
Environmental Section Chief, Dept. of Fish and Wildlife Resources, Arnold L. Mitchell Bldg., #1 Game Farm Rd., Frankfort, KY 40601 Phone: (502) 564-5448

Louisiana
Coordinator, Natural Heritage Program, Dept. of Wildlife and Fisheries, P.O. Box 98000, Baton Rouge, LA 70895-9000 Phone: (504) 765-2821

Maine
Office of the Fishery Research Biologist, Inland Fisheries and Wildlife, P.O. Box 1298, Bangor, ME 04401 Phone: (207) 289-3371

Maryland
Office of the Natural Resource Planner, Natural Heritage Program, Dept. of Natural Resources, Forest, Park and Wildlife Service, Tawes State Office Bldg., B-2, Annapolis, MD 21401 Phone: (301) 974-2870

Massachusetts
Nongame Fish Liasion Office, Division of Fisheries and Wildlife, Field Headquarters, Westboro, MA 01581 Phone: (617) 366-4470

Michigan
Recreational Fisheries Program Manager, Fisheries Division, Dept. Natural Resources, Box 30028, Lansing, MI 48909 Phone: (517) 373-1280

Minnesota
Nongame Program, Box 7, Dept. of Natural Resources, 500 Lafayette Rd., St. Paul, MN 55146 Phone: (612) 297-2276

Mississippi
Director, Bureau of Fisheries and Wildlife, Dept. of Wildlife Conservation, Southport Mall, P.O. Box 451, Jackson, MS 39205 Phone: (601) 961-5300

Missouri
Dept. of Conservation, Fish and Wildlife Research Center, 1110 College Ave., Columbia, MO 65201 Phone: (314) 449-3761

Montana
Bureau Chief, Research/Special Projects, Fisheries Division, Dept. of Fish, Wildlife, and Parks, 1420 E. Sixth, Helena, MT 59620 Phone: (406) 444-3183

Nebraska
Office of the Coordinator Zoologist, Natural Heritage Program, Game and Parks Commission, 2200 N. 33rd St., P.O. Box 30370, Lincoln, NE 68503 Phone: (402) 464-0641

Nevada
Office of the Endemic Fish Biologist, Dept. of Wildlife, Region III, State Mailroom Complex, Las Vegas, NV 89158 Phone: (702) 486-5127

New Hampshire
Endangered Species Program Coordinator, Fish and Game Dept., 2 Hazen Dr., Concord, NH 03301 Phone: (603) 271-2744

New Jersey
Manager, Endangered and Nongame Species Program, Division of Fish, Game, and Wildlife, CN 400, Trenton, NJ 08625 Phone: (609) 292-9101

New Mexico
Endangered Species Biologist, Dept. of Game and Fish, Villagra Bldg., Santa Fe, NM 87503 Phone: (505) 827-7899

New York
Endangered Species Unit, Delmar Wildlife Resources Center, Game Farm Rd., Delmar, NY 12054 Phone: (518) 439-7635

North Carolina
Nongame and Endangered Wildlife Program, Wildlife Resources Commission, Route 4, Box 518, Pittsboro, NC 27312 Phone: (919) 542-5331

North Dakota
Office of the Natural Resource Zoologist, Game and Fish Dept., 100 North Bismark Expressway, Bismark, ND 58501 Phone: (701) 221-6300

Ohio
Fish Management and Research Group, Dept. of Natural Resources, Fountain Square, Columbus, OH 43224 Phone: (614) 265-6344

Oklahoma
Office of the Nongame Wildlife Biologist, Dept. of Wildlife Conservation, 1801 N. Lincoln, P.O. Box 53465, Oklahoma City, OK 73152 Phone: (405) 521-3851

Oregon
Office of the Staff Fish Biologist, Dept. of Fish and Wildlife, 506 SW Mill St., P.O. Box 59, Portland, OR 97207 Phone: (503) 229-5551

Pennsylvania
Herpetology and Endangered Species Coordinator, Division of Fisheries Management, Fish Commission, 450 Robinson Lane, Bellefonte, PA 17105 Phone: (814) 359-5113

Rhode Island
Division of Fish and Wildlife, Dept. of Environmental Management, Box 218, West Kingston, RI 02892 Phone: (401) 789-3094

South Carolina
Nongame and Heritage Trust Section, Wildlife and Marine Resources Dept., P.O. Box 167, Columbia, SC 29202 Phone: (803) 734-3916

South Dakota
Nongame/Endangered Species Coordinator, Game, Fish, and Parks Department, 445 E. Capitol, Pierre, SD 57501 Phone: (605) 773-4229

Tennessee
Coordinator, Nongame/Endangered Species, Wildlife Resources Agency, Ellington Agricultural Center, P.O. Box 40747, Nashville, TN 37204 Phone: (615) 781-6579

Texas
Program Director, Nongame and Endangered Species, Parks and Wildlife Dept., 4200 Smith School Rd., Austin, TX 78744 Phone: (512) 389-4979

Utah
Program Coordinator, Nongame Fish, Amphibians, and Reptiles, Division of Wildlife Resources, Dept. of Natural Resources, 1596 West North Temple, Salt Lake City, UT 84116-3195 Phone: (801) 530-1209

Vermont
Nongame and Endangered Species Coordinator, Fish and Wildlife Dept., 103 S. Main St., 10 South, Waterbury, VT 05676 Phone: (802) 244-7331

Virginia
Fisheries Management Coordinator, Fish Division, Commission of Game and Inland Fisheries, 4010 W. Broad St., Box 11104, Richmond, VA 23230 Phone: (804) 367-1000

Washington
Office of the Wildlife Research Analyst, Dept. of Game, 600 N. Capitol Way, GJ-11, Olympia, WA 98504-0091 Phone: (206) 753-5700

West Virginia
Office of the Fishery Biologist and Curator of Fishes, Wildlife Resources Division, Dept. of Natural Resources, Operations Center, P.O. Box 67, Elkins, WV 26241 Phone: (304) 636-1767

Wisconsin
Natural Heritage Inventory Section, Bureau of Endangered Resources, Dept. of Natural Resources, Box 7921, Madison, WI 53707 Phone: (608) 266-0394

Wyoming
Ecological Services, Game and Fish Dept., 5400 Bishop Blvd., Cheyenne, WY 82002 Phone: (307) 777-7686

CANADA
Chairman, COSEWIC Fish and Marine Mammal Subcommittee, Dept. of Fisheries and Oceans, Resource Research Branch, 200 Kent St., Ottawa, Ontario K1A 0E6 Phone: (613) 993-0600

Coordinator, Threatened Species and Transboundary Wildlife, Wildlife Research and Interpretation Branch, Canadian Wildlife Service, Environment Canada, Ottawa, Ontario K1A 0H3 Phone: (819) 953-1411

Alberta
Salmonid Management Coordinator, Fish and Wildlife Division, Dept. of Energy and Natural Resources, Main Floor, North Tower, Petroleum Plaza, 9945-108 St., Edmonton, Alberta T5K 2C9 Phone: (403) 427-6730

British Columbia
Inland Fisheries Coordinator, Fisheries Branch, Ministry of Environment, Parliament Bldg., Victoria, BC V8V 1X5 Phone: (604) 387-9507

Manitoba
Fisheries Branch, Dept. of Natural Resources, Box 40, 1495 St. James St., Winnipeg, Manitoba R3H 0W9 Phone: (204) 945-3730

New Brunswick
Chief Fishery Biologist, Fish and Wildlife Branch, Dept. of Natural Resources and Energy, P.O. Box 6000, Fredericton, NB E3B 5H1 Phone: (506) 453-2440

Newfoundland
Director, Wildlife Division, Dept. of Culture, Recreation, and Youth, Bldg. 810, Pleasantville, P.O. Box 4750, NF A1C 5T7 Phone: (709) 576-2817

Northwest Territories
Director, Wildlife Division, Dept. of Renewable Resources, Yellowknife, NT X1A 2L9 Phone: (403) 873-7411

Nova Scotia
Director, Estuarine and Inland Fisheries, P.O. Box 700, Pictou, NS B0K 1H0 Phone: (902) 424-5935

Ontario
Office of the Zoologist/Information Manager, Conservation Data Centre, 794A Broadview Ave., Toronto, Ontario M4K 2P7 Phone: (416) 469-1701

Prince Edward Island
Director, Fish and Wildlife Division, Dept. of Community and Cultural Affairs, P.O. Box 2000, Charlottetown, P.E.I. C1A 7N8 Phone: (902) 892-0311 Ext. 268

Quebec
Quebec Natural Heritage Data Centre, 3900 rue Marly, 5e etage, Ste-Foy, Quebec, G1X 4E4 Phone: (418) 644-6107

Saskatchewan
Research Supervisor, Biological Services, Dept. of Parks, Recreation and Culture, 15 Innovation Blvd., Saskatoon, Saskatchewan S7N 2X8 Phone: (306) 933-5776

Yukon Territory
Director, Fish and Wildlife, Dept. of Renewable Resources, Box 2703, Whitehorse, Y.T. Y1A 2C6 Phone: (403) 667-5715

MEXICO
Dr. Jack E. Williams, Chair, Endangered Species Committee, American Fisheries Society, Division of Wildlife and Fisheries, Bureau of Land Management, 18th and C St. NW, Washington, D.C. 20240 Phone: (202) 653-9202

Private Organizations

American Fisheries Society
5410 Grosvenor Lane
Bethesda, MD 20814

The American Littoral Society
Sandy Hook, Highlands, NJ 07732

Bureau of Marine Fisheries
Nacote Creek Research Station
P.O. Box 418
Port Republic, NJ 08241

Center for Environmental Education
624 9th St., NW
Washington, DC 20001

Coastal Conservation Association
4801 Wood Way & 220 West
Houston, TX 77056-1805

Cousteau Society
930 West 21st St.
Norfolk, VA 10017

Desert Fishes Council
407 West Line St.
Bishop, CA 93514

The Fish and Wildlife Foundation
18th & C Streets, NW, Room 2556
Washington, DC 20240

Greenpeace USA, Inc.
1611 Connecticut Ave., NW
Washington, DC 20009

International Game Fish Association
3000 East Los Olas Blvd.
Fort Lauderdale, FL 33316

International Marinelife Alliance—Canada
2883 Otterson Dr.
Ottawa, Ontario, K1V 7B2
Canada

International Marinelife Alliance—USA
94 Station St., Suite 645
Hingham, MA 02043

National Institute of Urban Wildlife
10921 Trotting Ridge Way
Columbia, MD 21044

Native American Fish and Wildlife
Society
750 Burbank St.
Broomfield, CO 80020

Nature Conservancy
1800 North Kent St.
Arlington, VA 22209

North American Native Fishes
Association
123 W. Mount Airy Ave.
Philadelphia, PA 19119

Wilderness Society
1400 I St., NW
Washington, DC 20005

Appendix III

PUBLIC AQUARIUMS

Belle Isle Zoo & Aquarium
c/o Detroit Zoo
Box 39
Royal Oak, MI 48068
(313) 267-7160

Dallas Aquarium
Box 26193
Dallas, TX 75226
(214) 670-8441

Marine World Africa USA
Marine World Parkway
Vallejo, CA 94589
(707) 644-4000

Monterey Bay Aquarium
886 Cannery Row
Monterey, CA 93940
(408) 649-6466

Mystic Marinelife Aquarium
Coogan Boulevard
Mystic, CT 06355
(203) 536-9631

National Aquarium in Baltimore
Pier 3, 501 E. Pratt St.
Baltimore, MD 21202
(301) 576-3800

New England Aquarium
Central Wharf
Boston, MA 02110
(617) 973-5200

New York Aquarium
W. 8th St. & Surf Ave.
Brooklyn, NY 11224
(718) 265-3400

Sea Life Park
Makapuu Point
Waimanalo, HI 96795
(808) 259-7933

Sea World of California
1720 S. Shores Rd.
San Diego, CA 92109
(619) 222-6363

Sea World of Florida
7007 Sea World Drive
Orlando, FL 32821
(305) 351-3600

Sea World of Ohio
1100 Sea World Drive
Aurora, OH 44202
(216) 562-8101

The Seattle Aquarium
Pier 59, Waterfront Park
Seattle, WA 98101
(206) 625-4358

John G. Shedd Aquarium
1200 S. Lake Shore Dr.
Chicago, IL 60605
(312) 939-2426

Vancouver Public Aquarium
Box 3232, Vancouver
B.C., CANADA V6B 3X8
(604) 685-3364

Waikiki Aquarium
2777 Kalakaua Avenue
Honolulu, HI 96815
(808) 923-5335

Steinhart Aquarium
Golden Gate Park
San Francisco, CA
(415) 221-5100

GLOSSARY

Abdominal. Pertaining to the belly of the fish.

Adipose fin. Small, fleshy, rayless fin on the back between the dorsal and caudal fins.

Aggregation. A small, dense group of fish.

Air bladder (swim bladder). A membranous, gas-filled sac in the upper body cavity.

Anadromous. Migrating up freshwater rivers from the sea to spawn.

Anal fin. A ventral, unpaired fin located posterior to the anus.

Barbel. A fleshy, flexible protuberance of the mouth, snout, and chin areas.

Brackish. Water containing varying amounts of both fresh and salt water.

Breast. Ventral surface of fish anterior to the insertion of the pelvic fins.

Brine shrimp (*Artemia*). A tiny brackish water crustacean widely used as a live food for aquarium fish.

Catadromous. Migrating from freshwater to the sea to spawn.

Caudal fin. The tail fin.

Caudal peduncle. The tail stalk; the part of the fish's body between the anal fin and the base of the caudal fin.

Compressed (laterally). Thin from side to side; deeper than broad.

Ctenoid. Scales that bear tiny spines on the exposed surface.

Cycloid. Scales that are flat and smooth.

Daphnia. Tiny freshwater crustacean, often called the water flea.

Depressed. Horizontally compressed; wider than high.

Detritus. Disintegrated organic material, debris.

Dorsal fin. A median, unpaired single or double fin on the fish's back.

Drainage. A river system or river systems that are interconnected and drain into the sea.

Elongate. Stretched out, lengthened.

Endemic. Found only in, or limited to, a particular geographic area.

Estuarine. Found in or limited to the mouth or lower course of a river in which the river's current meets the sea's tide.

Exotic. A non-native fish; one imported from outside the region.

Fin ray. The supporting structures of the fin membranes.

Fry. Newly hatched fish.

Gill. An organ of numerous vascular filaments which functions in the breathing of fishes.

Gonopodium. The modified anal fin of male poecilid (livebearing) fishes used in the transfer of sperm to the genital pore of the female.

Ground color. The basic body color over which are spots, stripes, etc.

Habitat. The specific type of environment in which an animal lives.

Headwater. The source of a river.

Head length. The distance from the tip of the snout to posterior margin of the opercular membrane.

Hyoid teeth. Teeth on the tongue of fish.

Indo-Pacific. The western Pacific, comprising the environs of the Philippines, the Malay Archipelago, and the Pacific islands—up to and including Hawaii. This region is the source of most of the fishes collected for the tropical fish hobby.

Indigenous. Originating in and characterizing a particular river or drainage system.

Interorbital. The space between the eyes.

Invertebrate. An animal without a backbone.

Lateral line. A series of tiny sensory pores usually associated with a horizontal series of scales running along a fish's side.

Lateral stripe. A swath of color running along a fish's side.

Living rock. Chunks of live coral or other marine life commonly sold in pet shops.

Middorsal stripe. A line running along the median ridge of the back.

Nape. The dorsal part of the body from the eye to the origin of the dorsal fin.

Native. A species that is natural to a given range or environment—not introduced by man.

Nocturnal. Active at night.

Ocellus. An eye-like spot, usually round with a light or dark border.

Operculum. The bony flap covering the gills of fishes.

Paired fins. The pectoral and pelvic fins.

Pectoral fins. The anterior or uppermost of the paired fins—one on each side of the breast behind the head.

Pelagic. Frequenting open waters.

Pelvic fins. The paired ventral fins lying below the pectoral fins or between them and the anal fin.

Piscivorous. Fish-eating.

Plankton. Plant and animal microorganisms that live suspended in water.

Predorsal stripe. A line lying along the median ridge between the eye and the origin of the dorsal fin.

Redd. A fish nest, particularly that of stream fishes such as dace and salmon.

Reticulate. Marked with a network of lines.

Serrate. Notched or toothed on the edge.

Sexual maturity. The time at which an animal becomes capable of reproducing.

Snout. Part of the head anterior to the eye but not including the lower jaw.

Soft dorsal. Posterior part of the dorsal fin when composed of soft rays.

Spawning. The act of mating and, more generally, reproduction.

Spinous dorsal. Anterior part of the dorsal fin when composed of spiny rays.

Standard length. The length of a fish from the tip of the snout to the base of the caudal fin.

Substrate. The bottom of a body of water (sand, mud, rocks, etc.).

Total length. The length of a fish from the tip of the snout to the end of the caudal fin when its rays are squeezed together.

Striated. Marked by narrow lines which are usually parallel.

Synonomy. Properly described scientific names for the fish.

Teleosts. The bony fishes.

Tesselated. Marked in a squared or checkered pattern.

Truncate. Terminating abruptly; cut squarely off.

Tubercle. A small lump.

Turbid. Water that is cloudy, roiled.

Ventril fins. Small pair of fins located on the belly of the fish, also referred to as pelvic fins.

Vermiculations. Wavy, fine lines.

Vertebrate. An animal with a backbone.

Water column. The depth from the substrate to the surface in any body of water.

Watershed. An interconnected system of bodies of water or streams.

Year class. All those individuals of a fish species that are born in one year; used primarily in reference to food or game fishes.

Bibliography

Axelrod, Dr. Herbert R. *Starting Your Tropical Aquarium*. Neptune City, N.J.: T.F.H. Publications, Inc., 1986.

Axelrod, Dr. Herbert R., et al. *Dr. Axelrod's Atlas of Freshwater Aquarium Fishes*. Neptune City, N.J.: T.F.H. Publications, Inc., 1988.

———. *Exotic Tropical Fishes*. Neptune City, N.J.: T.F.H. Publications, Inc., 1973.

Axelrod, Dr. Herbert R., and Dr. Cliff W. Emmens. *Exotic Marine Fishes*. Neptune City, N.J.: T.F.H. Publications, Inc., 1973.

Baugh, Thomas. *A Netful of Natives*. Sierra Madre, Calif.: RCM Publications, 1980.

Bigelow, Henry B., and William C. Schroeder. *Fishes of the Gulf of Maine*. Washington, D.C.: U.S. Department of the Interior, 1953.

Breder, C. M., Jr. *Field Book of Marine Fishes of the Atlantic Coast*. Reprint. New York: G. P. Putnam's Sons, 1929.

Burgess, Dr. Warren E. *An Atlas of Freshwater and Marine Catfishes*. Neptune City, N.J.: T.F.H. Publications, Inc., 1989.

———. *Marine Aquaria*. Neptune City, N.J.: T.F.H. Publications, Inc., 1980.

———. *Fishes of California and Western Mexico*. (Pacific Marine Fishes, Vol. #8.) Neptune City, N.J.: T.F.H. Publications, Inc., 1984.

Burgess, Dr. Warren E., et al., *Dr. Burgess's Atlas of Marine Aquarium Fishes*. Neptune City, N.J.: T.F.H. Publications, Inc., 1988.

Eddy, Samuel. *How to Know the Freshwater Fishes*. Reprint. Dubuque, Ia.: William C. Brown, 1957.

Eddy, Samuel, and James C. Underhill. *Northern Fishes*. St. Paul, Minn.: North Central Publishing Co., 1974.

Ghadially, Feroze N. *Advanced Aquarist Guide*. London: Pet Library, Ltd., 1969.

Gregg, William H., and Capt. John Gardner. *Where, When, and How to Catch Fish on the East Coast of Florida*. New York: The Matthews-Northrup Works, 1902.

Hildebrand, S. F., and W. C. Schroeder. *Fishes of Chesapeake Bay, Bulletin, U.S. Bureau of Fisheries*. Washington, D.C.: Smithsonian Institution Press, 1928.

Hubbs, C. L., and K. F. Lagler. *Fishes of the Great Lakes Region, Cranbrook Inst. Science Bulletin #26*. Bloomfield Hills, Mich., 1947.

Innes, William T. *Goldfish Varieties and Tropical Aquarium Fishes.* Philadelphia: Innes Publishing Co., 1931.

Jordan, D. S., and B. W. Evermann. *Fishes of North and Middle America.* Bull. U.S. Nat. Mus., #47. Washington, D.C.: Smithsonian Institution Press, 1896–1900.

Kelly, Jim. *Aquarium Guide.* London: Pet Library, Ltd., 1969.

———. *A Complete Introduction to Setting Up an Aquarium.* Neptune City, N.J.: T.F.H. Publications, Inc., 1987.

LaMonte, Francesca. *Marine Game Fishes of the World.* Garden City, N.Y.: Doubleday & Co., 1952.

Lee, David S. et al. *Atlas of North American Freshwater Fishes.* Raleigh, N.C.: North Carolina State Museum of Natural History, 1980.

McLane, A. J., editor. *McClane's Standard Fishing Encyclopedia.* New York: Holt, Rinehart and Winston, 1965.

Melzak, Maurice. *The Marine Aquarium Manual.* New York: Arco Publishing, Inc., 1984.

Miller, D. J., and R. N. Lea. *Guide to the Coastal Marine Fishes of California.* Calif. Fish and Game Dept., Fisheries Bull. #157, 1972.

Mills, Dick. *You & Your Aquarium.* New York: Alfred A. Knopf, Inc., 1986.

Moe, Martin. *Marine Aquarium Handbook.* Marathon, Fla.: Norns Publishing Co., 1982.

Morgan, Ann Haven. *Field Book of Ponds and Streams.* New York: G. P. Putnam's Sons, 1930.

Page, Dr. Lawrence M., *Handbook of Darters.* Neptune City, N.J.: T.F.H. Publications, Inc., 1983.

Perlmutter, Alfred. *Guide to Marine Fishes.* New York: New York University Press, 1961.

Roberts, Mervin F. *The Tidemarsh Guide to Fishes.* Old Saybrook, Conn.: The Saybrook Press, 1985.

Schultz, Dr. Leonard P. *The Ways of Fishes.* Neptune City, N.J.: T.F.H. Publications, Inc., 1971.

Sterba, Dr. Gunther. *Dr. Sterba's Aquarium Handbook.* London: Pet Library, Ltd., 1973.

Straughan, Robert P. L. *The Marine Collector's Guide.* Cranbury, N.J.: A. S. Barnes & Co., Inc., 1973.

Thompson, Peter. *Thompson's Guide to Freshwater Fishes.* Boston: Houghton Mifflin Co., 1985.

Walden, Howard T. *Familiar Freshwater Fishes of America.* New York: Harper & Row Publishers, 1964.

Walls, Jerry G. *Fishes of the Northern Gulf of Mexico.* Neptune City, N.J.: T.F.H. Publications, Inc., 1983.

Periodicals

American Currents. North American Native Fishes Association, 123 West Mt. Airy Ave., Philadelphia, PA 19119.

Aquarium Fish Magazine. P.O. Box 484, Mt. Morris, IL 61054.

Freshwater and Marine Aquarium Magazine. 120 West Sierra Madre Boulevard, Sierra Madre, CA 91024.

Marine Fish Monthly.

Tropical Fish Hobbyist. One TFH Plaza, Neptune City, NJ 07753.

Underwater Naturalist. The American Littoral Society, Sandy Hook, Highlands, NJ 07732.

Index

Books from The Countryman Press

From pond construction to trout streams, The Countryman Press offers a range of practical and readable manuals on nature, fishing, and rural and urban living.

Nature and How-to

Backyard Bird Habitat—Create Your Own Thriving Bird Sanctuary, by Will and Jane Curtis, $9.95

Backyard Livestock—Raising Good Natural Food for Your Family, by Steven Thomas and George P. Looby, DVM, $14.95

Backyard Sugarin', by Rink Mann, $5.95

Designing Your Own Landscape, by Gordon Hayward, $14.95

Earth Ponds—The Country Pond Maker's Guide, by Tim Matson, $14.95

Stalking the Blue-Eyed Scallop, by Euell Gibbons, $14.95

Stalking the Healthful Herbs, by Euell Gibbons, $14.95

Stalking the Wild Asparagus, by Euell Gibbons, $14.95

Fishing

The Fisherman's Companion, by Frank Holan, $8.95

Getting the Most from Your Game and Fish, by Robert Candy, $16.95

Pennsylvania Trout Streams and Their Hatches, by Charles Meck, $14.95

Taking Freshwater Game Fish—A Treasury of Expert Advice, edited by Todd Swainbank and Eric Seidler, $14.95

Universal Fly Tying Guide, by Dick Stewart, $9.95

Fly Tying Tips, edited by Dick Stewart, $9.95

The Countryman Press offers many more books on country living and outdoor recreation—including hiking, walking, bicycling, canoeing, and cross-country skiing.

Our titles are available in bookstores, or they may be ordered directly from the publisher. Please add $2.50 per order for shipping and handling. To place an order or obtain a complete catalog, please write The Countryman Press, P.O. Box 175, Woodstock, Vermont 05091.

2683